*Study Guide
and Activities for*

D S HAFFER'S
EVELOPMENTAL
PSYCHOLOGY

Childhood and Adolescence
Third Edition

MARCIA Z. LIPPMAN
Western Washington University

Brooks/Cole Publishing Company
Pacific Grove, California

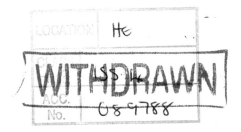
Brooks/Cole Publishing Company
A Division of Wadsworth, Inc.

Printed in the United States of America
10 9 8 7 6 5 4 3 2 1

ISBN 0-534-16993-7

Sponsoring Editor: Vicki Knight
Marketing Representativer: Karen Buttles
Editorial Associate: Heather Graeve
Production Coordinator: Dorothy Bell
Cover Design: Vernon T. Boes and Sharon L. Kinghan
Cover Photo: Ed Bock/The Stock Market
Printing and Binding: Malloy Lithographing, Inc.

CONTENTS

ABOUT YOUR STUDY GUIDE

IMPORTANT: READ BEFORE GOING ON

This study guide was developed to accompany David Shaffer's DEVELOPMENTAL PSYCHOLOGY text. It presents several ways to help you master the material that other students have found enhanced their learning. In addition, the guide presents a series of activities that are designed to either help master the material, to personalize it, or to allow for first-hand observation of children.

Each chapter of the study guide contains the following:

STUDY CHECKLIST: A checklist of study activities is provided at the beginning of each chapter to help you organize for study and to keep track of your progress. It suggests that you read each chapter outline and summary both before and after you read the text material. Doing so can help learning by building your awareness of the structure of the chapter and the main points that the author is attempting to cover. Be sure to allow time to review the text, study questions, vocabulary, and lecture notes.

CHAPTER OUTLINE AND SUMMARY: The chapter summary from the text has been integrated with an outline (based on chapter headings) to provide you an overview before reading the text chapter and to provide you with a summary after reading the chapter. You should find that after reading the chapter, the outline will trigger associations that it did not before. If a heading fails to elicit any associations, take it as a cue to re-read that section.

VOCABULARY FILL-INS: The text author provides a running glossary in the text margins of each chapter. The vocabulary fill-in exercise for each chapter is based on those margin definitions (definitions in the exercise are presented in the order of appearance in the text margin). The exercise provides you with an opportunity to test your grasp of the terms used within each chapter by matching each definition to the appropriate vocabulary word or phrase. After filling in the vocabulary, you may further test yourself by covering your answers and saying the correct vocabulary item to yourself.

STUDY QUESTIONS: Study questions are provided for each chapter. Each can be considered a learning objective, one that tells you what you should know about a particular section of material (minimally). They are designed to help you be more actively engaged with the material, rather than passively absorbing it as you read. It is well-established that active processing facilitates learning.

Many students find it useful to plan time to go over any study questions that were troublesome for them with a fellow student. The discussion that occurs while coming to an agreement on the answer is a form of active learning that fosters cognitive growth since each student is forced to justify his or her response. Keep in mind, however, that it is important to also allow time for independent review and study of the the study questions and your answers, the text, vocabulary, and lecture notes. Group study sessions should be used to supplement/complement rather than replace individual study time. (Note-- Answers to study questions may be checked against those presented at the end of each chapter.)

ACTIVITIES: The study guide also includes one or more activities for each chapter that your instructor may choose to assign and have you complete. The activities are of five types: (a) exercises to facilitate mastery of some part of the material presented in a chapter; (b) self-report activities designed to personalize the material, thereby making it more meaningful and memorable to you; (c) activities that give you the opportunity to work with a child; (d) activities using the media; and (e) activities that involve interviewing other college students or describing other people. Each activity is listed by type in the forward.

Note on activities involving children: Most students find that it is possible to find access to one or more children if they are assigned a project that involves working with a child. Possibilies include a niece or nephew, someone you babysit, the child of a friend or neighbor, a child at the campus day care, etc. You may need to plan to complete the project when you are home on a week-end if your hometown is where you have access to children. **For any activity involving a child you must obtain parental permission before working with the child and follow the guidelines for ethical research described in Chapter 1 of your text.**

ACTIVITIES
(listed by type)

ACTIVITIES TO HELP MASTERY

SELF-REPORT ACTIVITIES THAT PERSONALIZE THE MATERIAL

16-1   Television aggression

INTERVIEWS OR DESCRIPTIONS OF OTHER PEOPLE

14-1a   Family variables associated with aggression: One case

14-1b   Family variables associated with nonaggression: One case

15-1   The impact of divorce from the child's perspective

16-2   Teenage employment during the school year

CHAPTER 1

INTRODUCTION

STUDY CHECKLIST

_____ Read Chapter Outline and Summary (Study guide)

_____ Read Chapter (Text)

_____ Completed Vocabulary Fill-Ins (Study guide)

_____ Re-Read Outline and Summary (Study guide)

_____ Reviewed Lecture Notes and Integrated with Text

_____ Reviewed Vocabulary, Study Questions, and Text Chapter

CHAPTER 1 OUTLINE AND SUMMARY

I. **The concept of development**
    A.   The study of human development is a purposeful enterprise
    B.   Human development is a continual and cumulative process
    C.   Human development is a holistic process

II. **Human development in historical perspective**
    A.   Childhood in premodern times
    B.   Origins of modern-day views on childhood
        1.   Early philosophical perspectives on childhood
        2.   Children as subjects: The baby biographies
    C.   Emergence of a psychology of childhood (and adolescence)

    Developmental psychology is the largest of several disciplines that seek to explain development--that is, the systematic changes in the individual that occur between conception and death. Developmentalists are particularly concerned with describing significant changes in physical growth, mental abilities, emotional expression, and social behavior, with explaining why these changes occur, and with intervening to optimize such development whenever possible. Although we will focus mainly on the development of childhood and adolescence in this book, it is important to recognize that human development continues throughout life and is holistic--meaning that changes in one aspect of development often have implications for other, seemingly unrelated, aspects.

    Children who lived in medieval times (and earlier) were often treated rather harshly by their elders and were afforded few of the rights, privileges, and protections of today's youth. The viewpoints of important social philosophers of the 17th and 18th centuries contributed to a more humane outlook on children and child rearing; shortly thereafter, people began to observe their sons and daughters and to report their findings in baby biographies. The scientific study of children did not emerge until nearly 1900 as G. Stanley Hall, in the United States, and Sigmund Freud, in Europe, began to collect data and to formulate theories about human growth and development. Soon other investigators were conducting research to evaluate and extend these theories, and the study of developmental psychology began to thrive.

    Developmental psychology today is truly an objective science. Gone forever are the days when the merits of a theory depended on the social or academic prestige of the theorist. Today a developmentalist determines the adequacy of a theory by deriving hypotheses and conducting research to see whether the theory can predict and explain the new observations that he or she has made. There is no room for subjective bias in evaluating ideas; theories of human development are only as good as their ability to account for the important aspects of children's growth and development.

III. **Research methods in developmental psychology**
    A.   The scientific method
    B.   Measuring behavior: Data-collection techniques
        1.   Self-report methodologies
        2.   Interviews and questionnaires
        3.   The case study
        4.   The clinical method
        5.   Observational methodologies
    C.   Detecting relationships: Correlational and experimental designs
        1.   The correlational design
        2.   The experimental design
        3.   A possible limitation of laboratory experiments
        4.   The field experiment
        5.   The natural (or quasi) experiment
    D.   Designs to measure developmental change
        1.   The cross-sectional design
        2.   Cohort effects
        3.   Data on individual development
        4.   The longitudinal design
        5.   The sequential design
    E.   The cross-cultural comparison

For research to be meaningful, the data that investigators collect must be reliable and valid. A research method is reliable if it produces consistent, replicable results. The method is valid if it measures precisely what it claims to measure. The most common methods of collecting data on developing children and adolescents include self-report measures such as interviews, questionnaires, case studies, and clinical procedures and direct behavioral observations that are made either in the natural environment or in structured laboratory settings.

Two general research designs--correlational and experimental--permit researchers to identify relationships among variables that interest them. Although correlational studies estimate the strength and the direction of associations among variables, they cannot specify whether variables are causally related. The experimental design, however, does point to cause-and-effect relationships; the experimenter manipulates one (or more) independent variables, controls all other extraneous variables that might affect participants' performance, and then observes the effect(s) of the manipulations(s) on one or more dependent variables. Experiments may be performed in the laboratory or, alternatively, in the natural environment, thereby increasing the generalizability of the results. The impact of real-world events that researchers cannot manipulate or control can be studied in natural (quasi) experiments. However, lack of control over natural events prevents the quasi-experimenter from drawing definitive conclusions about cause and effect.

Cross-sectional, longitudinal, and sequential designs are employed to detect developmental change. The cross-sectional design assesses developmental trends by studying participants of different ages at the same point in time. It is an expedient method but limited in that it observes each participant only once and cannot tell us how individuals develop. The longitudinal design detects developmental change by repeatedly examining the same participants as they grow older. Although it provides information on the development of individuals, the longitudinal design is costly, time consuming, and subject to problems such as cross-generational changes in environments and participant loss (resulting in biased samples). The sequential design, a combination of the cross-sectional and longitudinal approaches, offers the investigator the best features of both strategies.

Cross-cultural studies, in which participants from different cultures and subcultures are compared on one or more aspects of development, are becoming increasingly important. Only by comparing people from many cultures can we identify "universal" patterns of development and, at the same time, demonstrate that other aspects of development are heavily influenced by the social context in which they occur.

IV. Ethical considerations in developmental research

Research conducted with children raises some unique ethical considerations. No matter how important the knowledge that might be gained, a researcher is never justified in harming children. Care must be taken to gain the informed consent of children (and their parents), to keep in confidence the information obtained from research participants, and to carefully explain any deception that may have been necessary to collect data. The knowledge gained from research with children should benefit us all, but it is the responsibility of investigators to guarantee that this knowledge does not come at the expense of the participants who so generously provide it.

CHAPTER 1 VOCABULARY FILL-INS
(Definitions below are in order of appearance in text margins)

MATCH VOCABULARY WORD/PHRASE TO ITS DEFINITION.
THEN COVER YOUR ANSWERS TO TEST YOUR MASTERY.

development   learning
developmental psychology   maturation

1. _____development_____ The process by which organisms grow and change over the course of their lives.

2. _____ Developmental changes in the body or behavior that result from the aging process rather than from learning, injury, illness, or some other life experience.

3. _____ A relatively permanent change in behavior (or behavioral potential) that results from one's experiences or practice.

4. _____ The scientific study of how individuals change over time and the factors that produce these changes.

holistic perspective
innate purity
law of recapitulation

original sin
tabula rasa

5. _____ A unified view of the developmental process that emphasizes the important interrelationships among the physical, mental, social, and emotional aspects of human development.

6. _____ The idea that children are inherently negative creatures who must be taught to rechannel their selfish interests into socially acceptable outlets.

7. _____ The idea that infants are born with an intuitive sense of right and wrong that is often misdirected by the demands and restrictions of society.

8. _____ The idea that the mind of an infant is a "blank slate" and that all knowledge, abilities, behaviors, and motives are acquired through experience.

9. _____ The notion that the developmental phases that an individual displays (ontogeny) will retrace, or recapitulate, the evolutionary history of the species (phylogeny).

hypothesis
observer bias
reliability
scientific method

structured interview and
questionnaire
theory
validity

10. _____ A set of concepts and propositions designed to organize, describe, and explain an existing set of observations.

11. _____ A theoretical prediction about some aspect of experience.

12. _____ An attitude or value about the pursuit of knowledge that dictates that investigators must be objective and must allow their data to decide the merits of their theorizing.

13. _____ The extent to which a measuring instrument yields consistent results, both over time and across observers.

14. _____ The extent to which a measuring instrument accurately reflects what the researchers intended to measure.

15. _____ A tendency of an observer to over- or underinterpret naturally occurring experiences rather than simply recording the events that take place.

16. _____ A technique in which all participants are asked the same questions in precisely the same order so that the responses of different participants can be compared.

---

case study   questionnaire
clinical method   structured observation
naturalistic observation

17. _____ A research instrument that asks the persons being studied to respond to a number of written questions.

18. _____ A research method in which the investigator gathers extensive information about the life of an individual and then tests developmental hypotheses by analyzing the events of the person's life history.

19. _____ A type of interview in which a participant's response to each successive question (or problem) determines what the investigator will ask next.

20. _____ A method in which the scientist tests hypotheses by observing people as they engage in everyday activities in their natural habitats (for example, at home, at school, or on the playground).

21. _____ An observational method in which the investigator cues the behavior of interest and observes participants' responses in a laboratory.

---

correlation coefficient
correlational design
dependent variable
experimental control
experimental design

field experiment
independent variable
natural (or quasi) experiment
random assignment

22. _____ A type of research design that indicates the strength of associations among variables; though correlated variables are systematically related, these relationships are not necessarily causal.

23. _____ A numerical index, ranging from -1.00 to +1.00, of the strength and direction of the relationship between two variables.

24. _____ A research design in which the investigator introduces some change in the participant's environment and then measures the effect of that change on the participant's behavior.

25. _____ The aspect of the environment that an experimenter modifies or manipulates in order to measure its impact on behavior.

26. _____ The aspect of behavior that is measured in an experiment and assumed to be under the control of the independent variable.

27. _____ Steps taken by an experimenter to ensure that all extraneous factors that could influence the dependent variable are roughly equivalent in each experimental condition; these precautions must be taken before an experimenter can be reasonably certain that observed changes in the dependent variable were caused by the manipulation of the independent variable.

28. _____ A control technique in which participants are assigned to experimental conditions through an unbiased procedure so that the members of the groups are not systematically different from one another.

29. _____ An experiment that takes place in a naturalistic setting such as the home, the school, or a playground.

30. _____ A study in which the investigator measures the impact of some naturally occurring event that is assumed to affect people's lives.

cohort effect

cross-cultural comparison

cross-generational problem

cross-sectional design

longitudinal design

nonrepresentative sample

research ethics

sequential design

31. _____ A research design in which subjects from different age groups are studied at the same point in time.

32. _____ Age-related difference among cohorts that is attributable to cultural/historical differences in cohorts' growing-up experiences rather than true developmental change.

33. _____ A research design in which one group of subjects is studied repeatedly over a period of months or years.

34. _____ A subgroup that differs in important ways from the larger group (or population) to which it belongs.

35. _____ The fact that long-term changes in environment may limit conclusions of a longitudinal project to that generation of children who were growing up while the study was in progress.

36. _____ A research design in which subjects from different age groups are studied repeatedly over a period of months or years.

37. _____ A study that compares the behavior and/or development of people from different cultural or subcultural backgrounds.

38. _____ Standards of conduct that investigators are ethically bound to honor in order to protect their research participants from physical or psychological harm.

CHAPTER 1 STUDY QUESTIONS

THE CONCEPT OF DEVELOPMENT

1. What are three **goals of developmental psychologists?** (p. 6)

    (a)

    (b)

    (c)

2. According to the text author, which would most accurately **describe human development?** (*circle one*) (p. 6-7)

    (a) Early childhood events are very important in forecasting adult behavior and attitudes, so much so that after adolescence there is very little change.

    (b) Early childhood events are very important in forecasting adult behavior and attitudes, but many changes occur after adolescence; all phases of life involve development and change.

3. What is the emphasis of the **holistic perspective** of human development? (p. 8)

HUMAN DEVELOPMENT IN HISTORICAL PERSPECTIVE

4.   List three **child-rearing practices** used in premodern times that support the position that the **concept of childhood** may have been very different than now. (p. 9-12)

   (a)

   (b)

   (c)

5.   What conclusion does the text author reach in Box 1-1 regarding the **impact of culture and historical era** on the course of human development? (p. 11, Box 1-1)

6.   The views of Locke and Rousseau are seen as the **precursors of modern-day views** of childhood. Briefly characterize each view. (p. 11-12)

   LOCKE:

   ROUSSEAU:

Which view most closely matches your view of children's role in their development?

7. What **method** of studying children did each of the following individuals use in learning about development? What major **hypothesis** about the nature of development did each propose? (p. 12-14)

DARWIN:

FREUD:

HALL:

8. What is the yardstick by which a **theory's adequacy** must be measured? (p. 14)

RESEARCH METHODS IN DEVELOPMENTAL PSYCHOLOGY

(Questions 9-13 based on text and Table 1-2)

9. What are three potential **shortcomings** of **interviews and questionnaires** as strategies for obtaining information to answer questions about development? (p. 16-17 & Table 1-2)

   (a)

   (b)

   (c)

10.   What are three potential **limitations** of **case studies** as strategies for obtaining information to answer questions about development? (p. 17-18 & Table 1-2)

(a)

(b)

(c)

11.   What phrase describes a major **limitation** of the **clinical method,** a method used extensively by Jean **Piaget** in his study of children's intellectual development? (p. 18-19 & Table 1-2)

12.   What is a major **advantage** of the **naturalistic observation** method over the structured laboratory observation method? (p. 19-21 & Table 1-2)

13.   What is an **advantage** of the **structured laboratory observation** over the naturalistic observation method? (p. 19-21 & Table 1-2)

(*Questions 14-19 based on text and Table 1-3*)

14.   For each of the following correlation coefficients indicate what the **strength of the relationship** would be (strong, moderate, weak) and the **direction of the effect** (positive relationship, negative relationship). (p. 22 & Table 1-3)

+ .85

+ .40

+ .15

- .85

- .15

15.   What is the major, and very critical, **limitation** of the **correlational method**, one that markedly affects the conclusions that can be drawn? (p. 22-23 & Table 1-3)

16.   Describe one strength and one limitation of the **experimental method.** (p. 23-25 & Table 1-3)

        STRENGTH:

        LIMITATION:

17.   What is the major **advantage** of the **field experiment** over the laboratory experiment? (p. 25 & Table 1-3)

18.   What is the major **limitation** of the **natural (quasi) experiment?** (p. 25-26 & Table 1-3)

19.   Describe with a brief phrase the procedure used by each of the three **designs for studying developmental change** that are listed below. For each, give an example of a developmental question that would be best answered by use of that design. (p. 27-33 & Table 1-3)

CROSS-SECTIONAL DESIGN

Procedure:

Strengths:

Limitations:

Example:

LONGITUDINAL DESIGN

Procedure:

Strengths:

Limitations:

Example:

SEQUENTIAL DESIGN

Procedure:

Strengths:

Limitations:

Example:

20. **Cohort effects** (associated with the cross-sectional design) are more **likely to confound interpretation of** which of the following? *(circle one)* (p. 28)

    (a)   short-term developmental changes (e.g., a comparison between 3rd- and 5th-graders)

    (b)   long-term developmental changes (e.g., a comparison between 18- and 60-year-olds)

21. Describe how each of the following two **limitations** of **longitudinal** studies might affect the conclusions that could be drawn. (p. 29-30)

NONREPRESENTATIVENESS OF SAMPLE:

CROSS-GENERATIONAL PROBLEM:

22. What **type of comparison** is necessary in order to determine whether developmental findings are **universal** or only specific to one cultural group? (p. 32, 34)

23. What **conclusion** does the author reach regarding the **"best method"** for studying children and adolescents? (p. 33-34)

24.   What are the four **ethical guidelines** adopted to protect the rights of children from potential harm from participation in research? (p. 34-37 & Table 1-4)

   (a)

   (b)

   (c)

   (d)

25.   What **mechanism** has been set up in institutions that conduct research to **ensure "accountability"** and to **protect the welfare** of human subjects? (p. 36)

ACTIVITY 1-1

ASSUMPTIONS ABOUT CHILDREN AND HOW THEY AFFECT TREATMENT/PRACTICE

INTRODUCTION: This activity builds on the material presented in Chapter 1 (p. 4-13) on the concept of development and the changes in views and treatment of children over the centuries. It also is preparation for the section in Chapter 1 (p. 15-34) on research methods, where, in effect, you are reading about methods for determining whether the assumptions we make about children (assumptions that guide our practices) are indeed valid. In addition, this activity provides some preparation for the material presented in Chapter 2 (p. 43-46) on the major controversies about the nature of the child and of development (i.e., controversies about assumptions).

INSTRUCTIONS: For each of the following practices, identify the assumption(s) about children and the underlying beliefs concerning the nature of their development.

Practice A: Having ratings on movies (G, PG, PG-13, R, X)

Practice B: Having age-segregated classrooms

Practice C: (one of your own choosing; specify)

ACTIVITY 1-2

PRACTICE IN IDENTIFYING RESEARCH DESIGNS AND METHODS STUDYING DEVELOPMENTAL CHANGE

INTRODUCTION: This activity is related to material presented in Chapter 1 (p. 15-34) on the characteristics of experiments. It provides you with practice in applying what you have learned about research methods and will help you feel more confident about your mastery of the material.

INSTRUCTIONS: Titles and abstracts for three studies are presented on the next three pages. For each study do each of the following:

1. Indicate whether **developmental change** was studied, and if so, which of the following strategies was used for assessing change with age:
   - **a. longitudinal**
   - **b. cross-sectional**
   - **c. sequential**
   - **d. none of the above; developmental change was not studied**

2. Indicate the type of **research design** used.
   - **a. experimental-lab**
   - **b. experimental-field**
   - **c. quasi/natural-lab**
   - **d. quasi/natural-field**
   - **e. correlational-lab**
   - **f. correlational-field**
   - **g. none of the above; only developmental change was studied**

3. Specify what **type of conclusion** can be drawn.
   - **a. causal** (variable X caused Y to happen)
   - **b. relational** (variable X is related to, but did not necessarily cause Y)

4. Specify any **possible confounding** that could limit interpretation, e.g., lack of random assignment to group leaving open the possibility that some other factor associated with group membership might account for the results most likely to occur in quasi/natural studies.

STUDY 1: Haskett, M.E. (1991).   Social interactions and peer perceptions of young physically abused children. *Child Development, 62,* 979-990.

The peer interactions of 14 children with a history of physical abuse were compared with a closely matched group of 14 nonabused children. Behavioral ratings of peer interactions were made in the children's day care setting. In addition, peer sociometric ratings and teacher reports were obtained.

It was found that compared to nonabused children, abused children made fewer attempts to interact with peers, showed a higher proportion of negative (aggressive) behaviors when they did interact, were viewed as less desirable playmates, and were less likely to have their attempts to initiate play reciprocated. It was concluded that abused children are more likely to show disturbed peer interactions than nonabused children.

Developmental Change Strategy: _____

Research Design: _____

Type of Conclusion: _____

Possible Confounding: _____

STUDY 2: Rudy, L., & Goodman, G.S. (1991). Effects of participation on children's reports: Implications for children's testimony. *Developmental Psychology, 27,* **527-538.**

Pairs of 4-year-old and 7-year-old children participated in situations designed to allow for assessment of the accuracy of memory for events surrounding their interactions with a male university student confederate. One child played games (e.g., Simon Says, thumb wrestling) with the man while the other sat nearby and watched. Children were randomly assigned to the "participation" and "watch" conditions. The children were questioned 10-12 days later. Each child was asked to tell exactly what happened when she went into the trailer and was then asked specific questions (e.g., "what color was the man's hair?" "did the man kiss you?") that were potentially misleading (e.g., "what color was the hat that the man was wearing?").

It was found that, overall, older children remembered more than did younger children. Children who had actually participated in the games with the man did not differ from watchers in amount recalled but were more resistant to suggestive questions than watchers. Age differences in overall suggestibility were not found. The authors concluded that their research provided no evidence that young children who interacted with an adult are likely to inaccurately recall past events or that they are highly suggestible to leading questions. What children did recall was accurate, errors were ones of omission not of commission, and children were quite resistant to leading questions.

Developmental Change Strategy: _____

Research Design: _____

Type of Conclusion (regarding influence of participation versus watching):   _____

STUDY 3: Vandell, D.L., Henderson, V.K., & Wilson, K.S. (1988). A longitudinal study of children with day-care experiences of varying quality. *Child Development, 59,* 1286-1292.

The relationship between quality of day care and peer interaction was studied at age 4 and again at age 8 for 20 children. At age 4 the children were observed and their behavior coded during unstructured free play at their day care. At age 8 children were observed in groups of three in a laboratory play room.

In comparison to children from poor quality day care, children from better quality day care had more friendly interactions and fewer unfriendly ones with peers. In addition, observers rated those in better quality day care as more socially competent and happier. Considerable continuity was found between behavior at 4 years of age and 8 years of age. The authors concluded that quality of day care can play an important role in social behavior that carries over into later years.

Developmental Change Strategy: _____

Research Design: _____

Type of Conclusion: _____

Possible Confounding: _____

CHAPTER 1 ANSWERS TO STUDY QUESTIONS

THE CONCEPT OF DEVELOPMENT

1. (6)
   a) to describe
   b) to explain
   c) to optimize development

2. (6-7)   Alternative <u>b</u>

HUMAN DEVELOPMENT IN HISTORICAL PERSPECTIVE

3. (8)   Development is not piecemeal; changes in one area are dependent upon and affect changes in other areas.

4. (9-12)   In 9th century Sparta:
   1) weak or defective infants were executed
   2) children were not allowed to cry
   3) male children were separated from their families as early as age 7

5. (11)   We are largely products of the times and culture we live in.
   (Box 1-1)

6. (11-12)   LOCKE: believed children were neither inherently good nor bad, but were shaped by worldly experiences. He was in favor of disciplined child rearing to ensure development of good habits and few bad ones. Locke espoused the notion that the infant comes into the world a "blank slate" or <u>tabula rasa</u>.
   ROUSSEAU: believed children, themselves, were actively involved in the shaping of their intellects and personalities. He characterized children as busy, motivated, testing explorers.

7. (12-14)   DARWIN: baby biography; law of recapitulation
   FREUD: patient recall of childhood; there are shared developmental milestones and each milestone is meaningfully related to earlier events
   HALL: questionnaire; children's reasoning is quite deviant from logical thought

8. (14)   Its ability to predict and explain new observations, i.e., it must generate testable hypotheses and be able to explain obtained results

RESEARCH METHODS IN DEVELOPMENTAL PSYCHOLOGY

9. (16-17)
   (Tbl 1-2)
   a) limited to subjects able to read and comprehend speech
   b) subjects may not give honest, accurate answers
   c) subjects of different ages may have differing interpretations of the questions

10. (17-18) a) validity of conclusions is dependent
    (Tbl 1-2)   on accuracy of information received from the cases
            b) data from two or more individuals may not be comparable if any variation
               occurred in what questions were asked
            c) sample may lack generalizability

11. (18-19) Nonstandardized treatment of participants
    (Tbl 1-2)

12. (19-21) Naturalistic observation is the only method that tells how people behave in
    (Tbl 1-2) everyday life. It may be applied to infants and toddlers who cannot be studied
             through methods that require verbal skills.

13. (19-21) Lab observation allows the experimenter to control the subject's environment
    (Tbl 1-2) so each subject is exposed to the <u>same</u> stimuli and is given <u>equal opportunity</u> to
             perform the target behavior.

14. (22)   +.85 strong, positive
    (Tbl 1-3) +.40 moderate, positive
             - .15 weak, positive
             - .85 strong, negative
             - .15 weak, negative

15. (22-23) Does not permit determination of cause-and-effect relationships among variables
    (Tbl 1-3)

16. (23-25) STRENTGH: permits a precise assessment of the cause-and-effect relationships
    (Tbl 1-3) between two variables
             LIMITATION: laboratory environment may be too contrived and artificial

17. (25)   Combines naturalistic observation with the rigorous control of an experiment in
    (Tbl 1-3) a natural setting, allowing determination of cause-and-effect and generalization to
             the real world.

18. (25-26) Existing groups are used rather than random assignment. The investigator
    (Tbl 1-3) often has too little information about research participants and too little control
             over natural events to draw firm conclusions about cause and effect.

19. (27-33) CROSS-SECTIONAL DESIGN
    (Tbl 1-3)   Procedure: observes people of different ages (or cohorts) at one point in time
             Strengths: demonstrates age differences and hints at developmental trends;
                         relatively inexpensive; takes little time to conduct
             Limitations: age trends may reflect extraneous differences among cohorts
                         rather than true developmental change; provides no data on the
                         development of individuals because each participant is observed
                         at only one point in time
             Example: Are preschool children less proficient than 1st- and 2nd-graders
                         at learning new responses displayed by an adult model?

LONGITUDINAL DESIGN

Procedure: observes people of one cohort repeatedly over time

Strengths: provides data on the development of individuals; can reveal links between early experiences and later outcomes; indicates how individuals are alike and how they are different in the ways they change over time

Limitations: relatively time consuming and expensive; subject loss may yield nonrepresentative sample that limits the generalizability of one's conclusions; cross-generational changes may limit one's conclusions to the cohort that was studied

Example: How stable are individual differences from birth to 18 years?

SEQUENTIAL DESIGN

Procedure: combines the cross-sectional and the longitudinal approaches by observing different cohorts repeatedly over time

Strengths: discriminates true developmental trends from cohort effects; indicates whether developmental changes experienced by one cohort are similar to those experienced by other cohorts; often less costly and time consuming than the longitudinal approach

Limitations: more costly and time consuming than cross-sectional research; despite being the strongest design, may still leave questions about whether a developmental change is generalizable beyond the cohorts that were studied

Example: How enduring are decreases in racial prejudice resulting from a training program introduced at 2nd, 5th, and 8th grades and followed up for 3 years? Also, what is the optimal grade for introducing such training?

20. (28)   Alternative b, i.e., inferences about developmental differences of diverse age groups

21. (29-30)   a) NONREPRESENTATIVENESS OF SAMPLE: a nonrepresentative sample may occur due to subject loss over time and may limit the conclusions of the study to healthy, cooperative subjects whose parents do not move from the area.

b) CROSS-GENERATIONAL PROBLEM: children from one era may be exposed to very different kinds of experiences than children from another era. As a consequence, the patterns of development that characterize one generation of children may not apply to other generations.

22. (32,34)   Cross-cultural comparison

23. (33-34)   There is no "best" method for all research questions; all have contributed to our understanding.

24. (34-37) a) no procedure can be used that may harm the child either physically or
    (Tbl 1-4)   psychologically
             b) informed consent of parents or other responsible adult should be obtained
             c) confidentiality of identity of all data collected should be maintained
             d) children must be debriefed if there was any concealment of the purpose; they
                 also have a right to know the results of the research

25. (36)   Feedback on proposed research is provided by a human subjects ethics committee
             at the research institution.

CHAPTER 2

THEORIES OF HUMAN DEVELOPMENT

STUDY CHECKLIST

_____ Read Chapter Outline and Summary (Study guide)

_____ Read Chapter (Text)

_____ Completed Vocabulary Fill-Ins (Study guide)

_____ Re-Read Outline and Summary (Study guide)

_____ Reviewed Lecture Notes and Integrated with Text

_____ Reviewed Vocabulary, Study Questions, and Text Chapter

CHAPTER 2 OUTLINE AND SUMMARY

I.   **Questions and controversies about human development**
   A.   Assumptions about human nature
   B.   Nature versus nurture
   C.   Activity versus passivity
   D.   Continuity versus discontinuity
   E.   One path or many?

A theory is a set of concepts and propositions that helps to describe and explain observations one has made. Theories are particularly useful if they are concise and yet applicable to a wide range of phenomena. Good theories are also precise--that is, capable of making falsifiable predictions that can be evaluated in later research. Some of the basic issues addressed by theories of human development include questions about the inherent nature of human beings; the nature/nurture issue centering on the relative contributions of biology and environment to developmental outcomes; the question of whether people are actively involved in their own development; the continuity/discontinuity issue; and the question of whether people tend to follow universal or particularistic developmental paths. In this chapter we concentrated on four major theoretical perspectives on human development: psychoanalytic theory, learning theory (behaviorism), cognitive-developmental theory, and ethological theory.

II. **The psychoanalytic viewpoint**
   A.   Freud's psychoanalytic theory
      1.   Three components of personality: Id, ego, and superego
         a.   The id: legislator of the personality
         b.   The ego: executive of the personality
         c.   The superego: judicial branch of the personality
      2.   Stages of psychosexual development
         a.   The oral stage (birth to 1 year)
         b.   The anal stage (1-3 years)
         c.   The phallic stage (3-6 years)
         d.   The latency period (ages 6-12)
         e.   The genital stage (age 12 onward)
      3.   Contributions and criticisms of Freud's theory

B.   Erikson's theory of psychosocial development
      1.   Comparing Freud with Erikson
      2.   Eight life crises
      3.   Contributions and criticisms of Erikson's theory
C.   Psychoanalytic theory today

The psychoanalytic perspective originated from the work of Sigmund Freud, who depicted children as "seething cauldrons" driven by inborn erotic and destructive instincts. At birth the child's personality consists only of these instinctual forces (called the "id"). However, these id forces are gradually diverted into a system of rational thought, the "ego," and an irrational but ethical component of personality, the "super-ego." The child is thought to pass through five psychosexual stages--oral, anal, phallic, latency, and genital--that parallel the maturation of sex instinct. Each stage is characterized by conflicts that have lasting effects on the developing personality.

Erik Erikson revised and extended Freud's theory by concentrating less on the sex instinct and more on important sociocultural determinants of human development. According to Erikson, people progress through a series of eight psychosocial stages of conflict, beginning with trust versus mistrust in infancy and concluding with integrity versus despair in old age. Each conflict must be resolved in favor of the positive trait (trust, for example) if development is to be healthy.

III.   **The learning viewpoint (behaviorism)**
        A.   Watson's behaviorism
        B.   Skinner's operant-learning theory (radical behaviorism)
        C.   Bandura's cognitive social-learning theory
        D.   Social learning as a reciprocal process
        E.   Contributions and criticisms of learning theories

The learning, or behaviorist, viewpoint originated with John B. Watson, who argued that infants are _tabulae rasae_ who gradually change (develop) through their learning experiences. Development was viewed as a continuous process that could proceed in many different directions, depending on the kinds of environments to which a person is exposed. B. F. Skinner, who extended Watson's theory, claimed that development reflects the operant conditioning of children who are passively shaped by their experiences. By contrast, Albert Bandura's social-learning theory viewed children as active information processors who learn by observation and who have a hand in creating the environments that influence their growth and development.

IV.   **The cognitive-developmental viewpoint**
       A.   Piaget's view of intelligence and intellectual growth
       B.   Four stages of cognitive development
       C.   Contributions and criticisms of the cognitive viewpoint

The cognitive-developmental viewpoint of Jean Piaget stresses that children are active explorers who have an intrinsic need to adapt to their environments. Piaget described the course of intellectual development as an invariant sequence of four stages: sensorimotor, preoperational, concrete-operational, and formal-operational. According to Piaget, the child's stage of cognitive development determines how he or she will interpret various events and, thus, what the child will learn from the environment. The implication is that cognitive abilities play a central role in all aspects of development, particularly social and personality development.

V. The ethological viewpoint
    A. Ethology and human development
    B. Contributions and criticisms of the ethological viewpoint

The ethological viewpoint is that children are born with a number of adaptive responses that evolved over the course of human history and that serve to channel development along particular paths. Ethologists recognize that human beings are clearly influenced by their experiences (learning). However, they remind us that we are biological creatures whose innate characteristics affect the kind of learning experiences we are likely to have.

VI. Theories and world views

Although no single theoretical viewpoint offers a totally satisfactory explanation of human development, each of the theories reviewed in this chapter has contributed in meaningful ways to our understanding of developing children. Today, most contemporary developmentalists are eclectic, meaning that they borrow from many theories, attempting to integrate these contributions into a holistic portrait of the developing child.

CHAPTER 2 VOCABULARY FILL-INS
(Definitions below are in order of appearance in text margins)

MATCH VOCABULARY WORD/PHRASE TO ITS DEFINITION.
THEN COVER YOUR ANSWERS TO TEST YOUR MASTERY.

activity/passivity issues
behavior genetics
continuity/discontinuity issues
developmental stage
falsifiability

heuristic value
nature/nurture
   controversy
parsimony

1. _____ A criterion for evaluating the scientific merit of theories; a parsimonious theory is one that uses relatively few explanatory principles to explain a broad set of observation.

2. _____ A criterion for evaluating the scientific merit of theories. A theory is falsifiable when it is capable of generating predictions that could be disconfirmed.

3. _____ A criterion for evaluating the scientific merit of theories. An heuristic theory is one that continues to stimulate new research and new discoveries.

4. _____ The scientific study of how one's hereditary endowment interacts with environmental influences to determine such attributes as intelligence, temperament, and personality.

5. _____ The debate within developmental psychology over the relative importance of biological predispositions (nature) and environmental influences (nurture) as determinants of human development.

6. _____ A debate among developmental theorists about whether children are active contributors to their own development or, rather, passive recipients of environmental influence.

7. _____ A debate among theorists about whether developmental changes are best characterized as gradual, quantitative, and connected over time or, rather, are abrupt, qualitative, and often unconnected to earlier developments.

8. _____ A distinct phase within a larger sequence of development; a period characterized by a particular set of abilities, motives, behaviors, or emotions that occur together and form a coherent pattern.

ego	reality principle
Eros	superego
id	Thanatos
instinct	unconscious motives
pleasure principle	

9. _____ An inborn biological force that motivates a particular response or class of responses.

10. _____ Freud's name for instincts such as respiration, hunger, and sex that help the individual (and the species) to survive.

11. _____ Freud's name for inborn, self-destructive instincts that were said to characterize all human beings.

12. _____ Freud's term for feelings, experiences, and conflicts that influence a person's thinking and behavior, but lie outside the person's awareness.

13. _____ Psychoanalytic term for the inborn component of the personality that is driven by the instincts.

14. _____ Tendency of the id to seek immediate gratification for instinctual needs, even when realistic methods for satisfying these needs are unavailable.

15. _____ Psychoanalytic term for the rational component of the personality.

16. _____ Tendency of the ego to defer immediate gratification in order to find rational and realistic methods for satisfying the instincts.

17. _____ Psychoanalytic term for the component of the personality that consists of one's internalized moral standards.

anal stage	Oedipus complex
Electra complex	oral stage
genital stage	phallic stage
latency period	repression
libido	

18. _____ A type of motivated forgetting in which anxiety-provoking thoughts and conflicts are forced out of conscious awareness.

19. _____ Freud's term for the biological energy of the sex instinct.

20. _____ Freud's first stage of psychosexual development (from birth to 1 year), in which children gratify the sex instinct by stimulating the mouth, lips, teeth, and gums.

21. _____ Freud's second stage of psychosexual development (from 1 to 3 years of age), in which anal activities such as defecation become the primary methods of gratifying the sex instinct.

22. _____ Freud's third stage of psychosexual development (from 3 to 6 years of age), in which children gratify the sex instinct by fondling their genitals and developing an incestuous desire for the parent of the other sex.

23. _____ Freud's term for the conflict that 4- to 6-year-old boys experience when they develop an incestuous desire for their mothers and, at the same time, a jealous and hostile rivalry with their fathers.

24. _____ Female version of the Oedipus complex, in which a 4- to 6-year-old girl was said to envy her father for possessing a penis and would choose him as a sex object in the hope of sharing the organ that she lacks.

25. _____ Freud's fourth stage of psychosexual development (age 6 to puberty), in which sexual desires are repressed and the child's available libido is channeled into socially acceptable outlets such as school work or vigorous play.

26. _____ Freud's final stage of psychosexual development (from puberty onward), in which the underlying aim of the sex instinct is biological reproduction.

---

autonomy versus shame and doubt   **initiative versus guilt**
basic trust versus mistrust

27. _____ The first of Erikson's eight psychosocial stages, in which infants must learn to trust their closest companions or else run the risk of mistrusting other people later in life.

28. _____ The second of Erikson's psychosocial stages, in which toddlers either assert their wills and attend to their own basic needs or else become passive, dependent, and lacking in self-confidence.

29. _____ The third of Erikson's psychosocial stages, in which preschool children either develop goals and strive to achieve them or feel guilty when their ambitions are thwarted by others.

---

behaviorism
habits
observational learning

operant learning
punishment
reinforcer

30. _____ A school of thinking in psychology that holds that conclusions about human development should be based on controlled observations of overt behavior rather than speculation about unconscious motives or other unobservable phenomena; the philosophical underpinning for the early theories of learning.

31. _____ Well-learned associations between various stimuli and responses that represent the stable aspects of one's personality.

32. _____ Any consequence of an act that increases the probability that the act will recur.

33. _____ Any consequence of an act that suppresses that act and/or decreases the probability that it will recur.

34. _____ A form of learning in which freely emitted acts (or operants) become either more or less probable, depending on the consequences they produce.

35. _____ Learning that results from observing the behavior of others.

ecological perspective
environmental determinism

reciprocal determinism

36. _____ The notion that children are passive creatures who are molded by their environments.

37. _____ The notion that the flow of influence between children and their environments is a two-way street; the environment may affect the child, but the child's behavior will also influence the environment.

38. _____ Bronfenbrenner's view emphasizing that the developing person is embedded in a series of environmental systems that interact with each other and with the person to influence development.

accommodation
assimilation
cognitive development

disequilibrium
scheme

39. _____ Age-related changes that occur in mental activities such as attending, perceiving, learning, thinking, and remembering.

40. _____ An organized pattern of thought or action that a child develops to make sense of some aspect of his or her experience; Piaget sometimes uses the term *cognitive structures* as a synonym for schemes.

41. _____ Piaget's term for the process by which children interpret new experiences by incorporating them into their existing schemata.

42. _____ Imbalances or contradictions between one's thought processes and environmental events. By contrast, *equilibrium* refers to a balanced, harmonious relationship between one's cognitive structures and the environment.

43. _____ Piaget's term for the process by which children modify their existing schemata in order to incorporate or adapt to new experiences.

critical period
ethology
mechanistic model

organismic model
social cognition

44. _____ The study of children's thinking about the thoughts, motives, intentions, and behaviors of themselves and other people.

45. _____ The study of the bioevolutionary bases of behavior.

46. _____ A brief period in the development of an organism when it is particularly sensitive to certain environmental influences; outside this period, the same influences will have little if any effect.

47. _____ View of children as passive entities whose developmental paths are primarily determined by external (environmental) influences. Represented by learning theorists.

48. _____ View of children as active entities whose developmental paths are primarily determined by forces from within themselves. Represented by psychoanalytic, ethological, and cognitive-developmental theorists.

CHAPTER 2 STUDY QUESTIONS

THEORIES

1.   One characteristic of a **good theory** is that it be concise (parsimonious) yet able to explain a broad range of phenomena. What else must a good theory do? (p. 42-43)

    (a)   parsimonious

    (b)

    (c)

QUESTIONS AND CONTROVERSIES ABOUT HUMAN DEVELOPMENT

2.   What is the contemporary developmentalist view of the **nature versus nurture controversy**? (p. 43-44)

3.   A teacher who plans a school environment where there are learning stations, learning is self-paced, questioning is encouraged, etc., probably holds the view that children play a/an _____ (active, passive) **role** in their own development. (p. 44)

4. The transformation of a caterpillar into a butterfly or moth would most closely parallel the _____ (continuity, discontinuity) **view of development,** i.e., that developmental changes are changes in _____ (degree, kind). (p. 44)

5. **Stage theorists** generally assume that all individuals proceed through the same progression of stages; hence, these stages are assumed to be _____ (universal, particularistic). (p. 45-46)

FREUD'S PSYCHOANALYTIC VIEWPOINT

6. According to **Freud,** in the mature, healthy personality a dynamic balance operates between what **three components of personality?** Give a brief description of the role of each component. (p. 47-48)

   (a)

   (b)

   (c)

7. Freud called the five major stages of personality **"psychosexual" stages** because he believed the maturation of the _____ _____ led to a shift of energy from one part of the body to another, thereby, indirectly shaping the personality. (p. 49)

List the **order** in which body parts give pleasure. (p. 49-51)

8.   What role do **defense mechanisms** acquired in childhood play in adults' lives? (p. 50, Box 2-2)

9.   If development is normal, how does Freud suggest that boys resolve the **Oedipal complex**? (p. 50)

10.   What consequence for the **superego** does resolution of the Oedipal complex have? (p. 50)

11.   Freud's theory has had a marked impact on psychology. What are three **major contributions** made by Freud? (p. 52)

(a)

(b)

(c)

ERIKSON'S THEORY OF PSYCHOSOCIAL DEVELOPMENT

12.   List three ways in which **Erikson's theory differs from Freud's.** (p. 52-53)

(a)

(b)

(c)

13.   Each of Erikson's eight stages is believed to occur as a result of **conflicts/crises** that arise from what? (p. 53)

14.   Freud emphasized a caregiver's feeding practices as influential in personality development during infancy, whereas **Erikson emphasized** _____ _____ of the caregiver. (p. 53)

15.   Read through each of the paragraphs in Table 5-2 describing Erikson's viewpoint of what is learned at each of his psychosocial stages. Pick out a key word or phrase that captures the essence of what he views to be the outcome of each phase, i.e., provide a label for each stage. (p. 54)

Stage 1:   _____   Stage 5:   _____

Stage 2:   _____   Stage 6:   _____

Stage 3:   _____   Stage 7:   _____

Stage 4:   _____   Stage 8:   _____

16.   Erikson's theory offers an interesting description of human social and emotional development but does **not meet** what important **criterion** of an adequate theory? (p. 55)

17.   What **shortcoming** of the psychoanalytic theories has led to their abandonment by most contemporary developmentalists? (p. 56)

THE LEARNING VIEWPOINT

18.   **B. F. Skinner** argues that behavior is motivated by _____ _____ rather than by internal forces such as drives or instincts. This view is an example of a theory that emphasizes _____ (nature, nurture) as the primary determinant of behavior. (p. 57)

19.   In applying operant-learning principles to humans, Bandura stresses that our behavior is not shaped just by immediate reinforcers, but that we are often influenced by long-term consequences. He has also demonstrated that observational learning plays a central role in learning, yet the individual does not actually receive a reward. **What does Bandura believe distinguishes human learners from animals?** (p. 58-59)

20.   **Early learning theory** viewed the learner as playing an/a _____ (active, passive) role in his or her own development and viewed development as occurring in _____ (stages, small incremental steps). (p. 59)

21.   The notion of **reciprocal determinism** differs from environmental determinism in its reflection of the belief that not only does the environment affect the child but _____. (p. 59-60)

22.   One of the **contributions of learning theory** was the behavior change technique known as incompatible-response technique. What are two other contributions noted by your text author? (p. 60-62)

(a) incompatible-response technique

(b)

(c)

23.   List three **limitations/criticisms** of behavioral learning theories. (p. 60-62)

(a)

(b)

(c)

24.   **Ecological theory** suggests that children must be studied in _____ rather than the lab. Why? (p. 60-61, Box 2-3)

THE COGNITIVE-DEVELOPMENTAL VIEWPOINT

25.   **Piaget's cognitive developmental theory** is a theory that claims that development occurs in _____ (distinctive stages, small increments) and that the child plays an/a _____ (active, passive) role in her own development. (p. 62-64)

26.   What answer did Piaget give to the question, "**How do children develop increasingly complex knowledge or understanding of their world**"? (p. 63)

27.   What two **complementary processes** did Piaget suggest are involved in the child's interactions with the environment? (p. 64)

(a)

(b)

28.   Piaget maintained that our experiences are organized into **cognitive structures** that he called _____ . (p. 63-64)

29. Note three **criticisms** that have been made of Piaget's theory. (p. 66)

(a)

(b)

(c)

THE ETHOLOGICAL VIEWPOINT

30. The **ethological view** emphasizes the role of _____ (environmental, biological) influences on development. (p. 67)

31. What would be an ethologist's response to the question: "**How important are an individual's early experiences**"? (p. 67-68)

32. Does the ethological view portray infants as passive or active in their interactions with their environment? Give an example. (p. 68-70)

THEORIES AND WORLD VIEWS

33. List the **characteristics** of mechanistic and organismic theories. (p. 70)

MECHANISTIC THEORIES

(a)

(b)

(c)

ORGANISMIC THEORIES

(a)

(b)

(c)

34. Place an **M** in front of those theories that ascribe to the **mechanistic view** and an **O** in front of those basing their theory on an **organismic model.** (p. 70)

_____ Freud's psychoanalytic theory

_____ Erikson's psychosocial theory

_____ Learning theory: Skinner's version

_____ Learning theory: Bandura's version

_____ Piaget's cognitive-developmental theory

_____ Ethological perspective

35. Explain what the author meant by the statement: "The plan for the remainder of the book is to take an **eclectic** approach..." (p. 70-71)

ACTIVITY 2-1

ASSUMPTIONS MADE BY MAJOR THEORIES

INSTRUCTIONS: Below are each of the major theories discussed in Chapter 2. For each theory indicate with a checkmark on the appropriate line what assumption that theory makes about (1) the major determinant of behavior (nature, nurture), (2) the role of the child in her own development (active, passive), and (3) the nature of developmental change (continuous, discontinuous). If a particular theory seems to be "middle of the road" on an assumption, put the checkmark between lines.

THEORY	(1) MAJOR DETERMINANT OF BEHAVIOR		
	NATURE	**NURTURE**	**BOTH**
Freud's Psychoanalytic	_____	_____	_____
Erikson's Psychosocial	_____	_____	_____
Skinner's Behaviorism	_____	_____	_____
Bandura's Social Learning	_____	_____	_____
Piaget's Cognitive- 　Developmental	_____	_____	_____
Ethological (e.g., Bowlby)	_____	_____	_____

THEORY	(2) ROLE OF CHILD IN OWN DEVELOPMENT	
	ACTIVE	**PASSIVE**
Freud's Psychoanalytic	_____	_____
Erikson's Psychosocial	_____	_____
Skinner's Behaviorism	_____	_____
Bandura's Social Learning	_____	_____
Piaget's Cognitive-Developmental	_____	_____
Ethological (e.g., Bowlby)	_____	_____

THEORY	(3) NATURE OF DEVELOPMENTAL CHANGE	
	CONTINUOUS (small increments)	**DISCONTINUOUS** (stages)
Freud's Psychoanalytic	_____	_____
Erikson's Psychosocial	_____	_____
Skinner's Behaviorism	_____	_____
Bandura's Social Learning	_____	_____
Piaget's Cognitive-Developmental	_____	_____
Ethological (e.g., Bowlby)	_____	_____

CHAPTER 2 ANSWERS TO STUDY QUESTIONS

THEORIES

1. (42-43)   a) A good theory is <u>falsifiable</u>, i.e., capable of making explicit predictions about future events so that the theory can be supported or disconfirmed.
   b) A good theory is also <u>heuristic</u>, i.e., builds on existing knowledge by continuing to generate testable hypotheses that, if confirmed by future research, will lead to a much richer understanding of the phenomena under investigation.

QUESTIONS AND CONTROVERSIES ABOUT HUMAN DEVELOPMENT

2. (43-44)   Relative contributions of nature and nurture depend on the aspect of development in question. Complex human attributes (intelligence, temperament, personality) are the end products of a long and involved interplay between biological predispositions and environmental forces.

3. (44)   Active

4. (44)   Discontinuity; kind

5. (45-46)   Universal

FREUD'S PSYCHOANALYTIC VIEWPOINT

6. (47-48)   a) id: seeks to satisfy instinctual needs
   b) ego: rational component of the personality that helps the individual find realistic ways of gratifying instincts
   c) superego: one's internalized moral standards that help the individual decide whether the ego's modes of gratifying instincts are morally acceptable

7. (49)   Sex instinct
   Mouth, anus, genitals

8. (50)   Defenses acquired in childhood may influence adult interests, behavior, and
   (Box 2-2)   personalities.

9. (50)   Resolution comes through identification with the father figure, adopting a preference for the male sex role, becoming a male psychologically.

10. (50)   Resolution results in repression of taboo motives (murder, incest), allowing internalization of moral standards.

11. (52)   a) the concept of unconscious motivation
   b) drawing attention to the importance of early experience for later development
   c) his focus on emotions and the defense mechanisms used to cope with emotions

ERIKSON'S THEORY OF PSYCHOSOCIAL DEVELOPMENT

12. (52-53)   a) Erikson stresses children that are active rather than passive learners.
               b) Erikson assumes that humans are basically rational creatures whose personalities are largely controlled by the ego rather than through conflicts between the id and superego.
               c) Erikson places less emphasis on sexual urges and more emphasis on social influences and cultural aspects.

13. (53)   Biological maturation and social demands

14. (53)   Overall responsiveness

15. (54)   Stage 1: trust   Stage 5: identity
               Stage 2: autonomy   Stage 6: intimacy
               Stage 3: initiative   Stage 7: productivity
               Stage 4: industry   Stage 8: ego integrity

16. (55)   It does not explain how or why development takes place.

17. (56)   The propositions of psychoanalytic theory are difficult to verify. Other theories seem more compelling.

THE LEARNING VIEWPOINT

18. (57)   External stimuli, nurture

19. (58-59)   Humans are cognitive beings, i.e., active information processors, able to consider the relationships between their behavior and its consequences.

20. (59)   Passive, small incremental steps

21. (59-60)   The child's behavior will also influence the environment.

22. (60-62)   b) a wealth of information regarding developing children through research and observation
               c) learning theorists stress objectivity; units of analysis are objective rather than subjective, concepts are carefully defined, hypotheses tested, and experiments tightly controlled

23. (60-61)   a) oversimplified account of human development
               b) the "environment" that so powerfully influences development is really a series of social systems that interact with one another in complex ways that are impossible to simulate in a laboratory
               c) underestimation of role of maturation and heredity

24. (60-61)   Natural settings so we can understand how individuals influence and are influenced
    (Box 2-3) by their environments

THE COGNITIVE-DEVELOPMENTAL VIEWPOINT

25. (62-64)   Stages, active

26. (63)   Children <u>actively construct</u> new understanding of the world based on their own experiences.

27. (64)   a) assimilation
                b) accommodation

28. (63-64)   Schemes

29. (66)   a) the influence of motivation and emotion on human thought processes is largely ignored
                b) some critics argue that the role of basic biological processes in human development is overemphasized
                c) some argue children's behavior is not as stagelike as he maintained

THE ETHOLOGICAL VIEWPOINT

30. (67)   Biological influences

31. (67-68)   Very important; ethologist's argue that there may be early-occurring "critical periods" when individuals are more sensitive or responsive to environmental influences that affect attributes and behaviors.

32. (68-70)   Ethologists portray infants as active in their interactions with their environment. Socialization is one example; it is believed that infants promote and maintain social interactions from the day they are born.

THEORIES AND WORLD VIEWS

35. (70)   a) people are a collection of behaviors
                b) people are passive
                c) people change gradually/continuously

                a) people are whole beings
                b) people are active in the developmental process
                c) people evolve through discontinuous stages

34. (70)   O,O,M,M,O,O

35. (70-71)   An <u>eclectic</u> developmental approach borrows the strong points of many theories to help explain the developing child.

CHAPTER 3

HEREDITARY INFLUENCES
ON DEVELOPMENT

STUDY CHECKLIST

_____ Read Chapter Outline and Summary (Study guide)

_____ Read Chapter (Text)

_____ Completed Vocabulary Fill-Ins (Study guide)

_____ Re-Read Outline and Summary (Study guide)

_____ Reviewed Lecture Notes and Integrated with Text

_____ Reviewed Vocabulary, Study Questions, and Text Chapter

CHAPTER 3 OUTLINE AND SUMMARY

I. Heredity in historical perspective
   A. The work of Gregor Mendel
   B. The discovery of chromosomes

Since the dawn of recorded history, people have tried to understand how characteristics are transmitted from parents to offspring. Early theories of heredity claimed that the germ cells of either the father or the mother contained tiny preformed embryos that would begin to develop after a mating. However, biologists eventually discovered that each parent contributes equally to the creation of a child by passing hereditary "characters," or genes, to the offspring.

II. Principles of hereditary transmission
   A. Conception
   B. Growth of the zygote and production of body cells
   C. Germ cells and hereditary transmission
      1. Genetic uniqueness and relatedness
      2. Determination of sex
   D. Patterns of genetic expression
      1. Dominant and recessive alleles
      2. Incomplete dominance
      3. Codominance
      4. Sex-linked characteristics
      5. Modifier genes and polygenic inheritance
      6. A final note on genetic transmission

Development begins at conception, when a sperm cell from the father penetrates the wall of an ovum from the mother, forming a zygote. A normal zygote contains 46 chromosomes (23 from each parent), each of which consists of approximately 20,000 genes. Thus each zygote may have as many as 500,000 pairs of genes that provide the hereditary blueprint for the development of this single cell into a recognizable human being.

Human beings consist of two kinds of cells: (1) body cells, which make up our bodies and organs, and (2) germ cells, which produce gametes--sperm in males and ova in females. Our body cells each contain duplicates of the 46 chromosomes (23 pairs) that we inherited at conception. Germs cells, which also have 23 pairs of chromosomes, divide by a process called meiosis to produce gametes that each contain 23 single (unpaired) chromosomes. Since individual gametes do not contain all the parent's chromosomes, the genetic composition of each sperm or ovum will differ. Therefore each child inherits a unique combination of genes. The one exception is identical twins, who are formed from a single zygote that divides, creating two individuals with identical genes.

There are many ways in which one's genotype may affect phenotype--the way one looks, feels, thinks, or behaves. At least one phenotypic characteristic--gender--is determined by the 23rd pair of chromosomes (that is, the sex chromosomes). Normal females have inherited one relatively large sex chromosome (called an X chromosome) from each parent, whereas males have inherited an X chromosome and a smaller Y chromosome. An adult female (XX) can pass only X chromosomes to her offspring. However, an adult male (XY) can transmit either an X chromosome or a Y chromosome to his offspring. Thus the father, not the mother, determines the sex of a child.

Some characteristics are determined by a single pair of genes, one of which is inherited from each parent. In dominant/recessive pairs, the individual will exhibit the phenotype of the dominant gene. If a gene pair is codominant or incompletely dominant, the individual will develop a phenotype in between those ordinarily produced by the dominant and the dominated (or recessive) genes. Sex-linked characteristics are caused by recessive genes that appear on only one of the two kinds of sex chromosomes (usually the X chromosome). Females must inherit two of these recessive genes (one on each X chromosome) in order to exhibit a sex-linked characteristic. However, males need only inherit one recessive gene to show the characteristic, because they have only one X chromosome.

Most complex human attributes such as intelligence and personality are polygenic, meaning that they are influenced by several pairs of genes rather than a single pair. In addition, the action or expression of one set of genes may be altered by the presence of modifier genes.

III. Chromosomal and genetic abnormalities
    A. Chromosomal abnormalities
        1. Abnormalities of the sex chromosomes
        2. Autosomal abnormalities
        3. Causes of chromosomal abnormalities
    B. Genetic abnormalities
    C. Applications: Genetic counseling and the treatment of hereditary disorders
        1. Genetic counseling
        2. Establishing the likelihood of a defect
        3. Prenatal detection of hereditary abnormalities
        4. Treating hereditary disorders
        5. How do I obtain more information?

Occasionally children inherit abnormal genes and chromosomes. In most cases of chromosome abnormalities, the child has inherited too few or too many sex chromosomes. In about 1 in 600 births, a child inherits an extra 21st chromosome. The resulting phenotype is known as Down syndrome, in which the child has a number of distinctive physical features and will be mentally retarded.

There are also a number of genetic diseases that children may inherit from parents who themselves are not affected but who carry the abnormal genes. Genetic counseling can help people to calculate the odds that they might bear a child with a genetic disorder. Family histories and blood tests can often identify the carriers of many disorders caused by a single gene pair, and abnormalities in the fetus can be detected through amniocentesis, chorionic villus sampling, and ultrasound. Harmful effects of several hereditary disorders can now be minimized by medical interventions. And, because knowledge of human genetics is rapidly increasing, many more genetic defects are likely to become detectable and treatable in the near future.

Behavior genetics is the study of how genes and environment contribute to individual variations in development. Although animals can be studied in selective-breeding experiments, human behavior geneticists must conduct family studies, estimating hereditary contributions to various attributes from the similarities and differences among family members who differ in kinship. These family studies reveal that the genes people inherit exert an important influence on their intellectual performances, temperaments, personality, and tendencies to display abnormal patterns of behavior. However, family studies also show that the environment contributes in important ways to individual variations in development and that all behavioral attributes of lasting developmental significance are products of a long and involved interplay between the forces of nature and nurture.

V. Another look at the nature/nurture controversy
    A.   Waddington's canalization principle
    B.   Gottesman's range of reaction principle
    C.   A new look at genotype/environment interactions
          1.   Passive gene influences
          2.   Evocative gene influences
          3.   Active gene influences (niche picking)
          4.   How do genotype/environment interactions influence development?
          5.   A final comment

Several theories have been proposed to explain how heredity and environment might combine to produce developmental change. For example, the canalization principle implies that genes channelize development along predetermined pathways that are sometimes difficult for the environment to alter. The range of reaction principle adds that, for most traits, heredity sets a range of developmental potentials and the environment determines the extent of development. A more recent theory is that our genotypes influence the environments we are likely to experience-- environments that then shape our conduct and character. So the current view is that heredity and environment interact to produce developmental change and that these two important influences are completely (and perhaps inseparably) intertwined.

CHAPTER 3 VOCABULARY FILL-INS
(Definitions below are in order of appearance in text margins)

MATCH VOCABULARY WORD/PHRASE TO ITS DEFINITION.
THEN COVER YOUR ANSWERS TO TEST YOUR MASTERY.

preformationist theories	**ovulation**
genes	**zygote**
chromosome	**mitosis**
conception	**meiosis**

1. _____ Early hereditary theories specifying that fathers' sperm or mothers' ova contain preformed human embryos.

2. _____ Hereditary blueprints for development that are transmitted unchanged from generation to generation.

3. _____ A threadlike structure made up of genes; in humans there are 46 chromosomes in the nucleus of each body cell.

4. _____ The moment of fertilization, when a sperm penetrates an ovum, forming a zygote.

5. _____ The process in which a female gamete (ovum) matures in one of the ovaries and is released into the fallopian tube.

6. _____ A single cell formed at conception from the union of a sperm and an ovum.

7. _____ The process in which a cell duplicates its chromosomes and then divides into two genetically identical daughter cells.

8. _____ The process in which a germ cell divides, producing gametes (sperm or ova) that each contain half of the parent cell's original complement of chromosomes; in humans, the products of meiosis contain 23 chromosomes.

===

crossing over
dizygotic (or fraternal)
            twins
genotype
independent assortment
karyotype

monozygotic (or
            identical) twins
phenotype
X chromosome
Y chromosome

9. _____ The Mendelian principle stating that each pair of chromosomes segregates independently of all other chromosome pairs during meiosis.

10. _____ A process in which genetic material is exchanged between pairs of chromosomes.

11. _____ Twins that result when a single zygote divides into two separate but identical cells that each develop independently. As a result, each member of a monozygotic twin pair has inherited exactly the same set of genes.

12. _____ Twins that result when a mother releases two ova at roughly the same time and each is fertilized by a different sperm, producing two zygotes that are genetically different.

13. _____ A chromosomal portrait created by staining chromosomes and then photographing them under a high-power microscope.

14. _____ The longer of the two sex chromosomes; normal females have two X chromosomes, whereas normal males have but one.

15. _____ The shorter of the two sex chromosomes; normal males have one Y chromosome, whereas females have none.

16. _____ The genetic endowment that an individual inherits.

17. _____ The ways in which a person's genotype is expressed in observable or measurable characteristics.

---

alleles	modifier gene
codominance	polygenic
dominant alleles	recessive allele
heterozygous	sex-linked characteristics
homozygous	sickle-cell anemia
incomplete dominance	

18. _____ Alternative forms of a gene that are coded for a particular trait.

19. _____ A relatively powerful gene that is expressed phenotypically and masks the effect of a less powerful gene.

20. _____ A less powerful gene that is not expressed phenotypically when paired with a dominant allele.

21. _____ Having inherited two alleles for an attribute that are identical in their effects.

22. _____ Having inherited two alleles for an attribute that have different effects.

23. _____ Condition in which a stronger allele fails to mask all the effects of a weaker allele; a phenotype results that is similar but not identical to the effect of the stronger gene.

24. _____ A genetic blood disease that causes red blood cells to assume an unusual sickled shape and to become inefficient at distributing oxygen throughout the body.

25. _____ Condition in which two heterozygous but equally powerful alleles produce a phenotype in which both genes are fully and equally expressed.

26. _____ An attribute determined by a gene that appears on only one of the two types of sex chromosomes, usually the X chromosome.

27. _____ A gene that influences the expression of other alleles.

28. _____ A characteristic that is influenced by the action of many genes rather than a single pair.

---

aging-ova hypothesis
congenital defect
Down syndrome

fragile-X syndrome
Huntington's chorea
mutation

29. _____ A problem that is present (though not necessarily apparent) at birth; such defects may stem from genetic and prenatal influences or from complications of the birth process.

30. _____ A genetic disease caused by a dominant allele that typically appears later in life and causes the nervous system to degenerate (see Box 3-1).

31. _____ A sex chromosome abnormality in which individuals have a compressed or broken X chromosome; affected individuals (particularly males) may show mild to severe mental retardation.

32. _____ A chromosomal abnormality (also known as trisomy-21) caused by the presence of an extra 21st chromosome; people with this syndrome have a distinct physical appearance and are moderately to severely retarded.

33. _____ The hypothesis that an older mother is more likely to have children with chromosomal abnormalities because her ova are degenerating as she nears the end of her reproductive years.

34. _____ A change in the chemical structure or arrangement of one or more genes that has the effect of producing a new phenotype.

---

amniocentesis
chorionic villus sampling
genetic counseling
muscular dystrophy

phenylketonuria (PKU)
Tay-Sachs disease
ultrasound

35. _____ A service designed to inform prospective parents about genetic diseases and to help them determine the likelihood that they would transmit such disorders to their children.

36. _____ A genetic disease that attacks the muscles and results in a gradual loss of motor capabilities (see Table 3-3).

37. _____ A genetic disease that attacks the nervous system, causing it to degenerate (see Table 3-3).

38. _____ A method of extracting amniotic fluid from a pregnant woman so that fetal body cells within the fluid can be tested for chromosomal abnormalities and other genetic defects.

39. _____ An alternative to amniocentesis in which a catheter is inserted through the cervix to withdraw fetal cells for prenatal tests.

40. _____ Method of detecting gross physical abnormalities by scanning the womb with sound waves, thereby producing a visual outline of the fetus.

41. _____ A genetic disease in which the child is unable to metabolize phenylalanine; if left untreated, it soon causes hyperactivity and mental retardation.

---

adoption study
behavior genetics
concordance rate
heritability

heritability coefficient
kinship
twin study

42. _____ The scientific study of how genotype interacts with environment to determine behavioral attributes such as intelligence, temperament, and personality.

43. _____ The amount of variability in a trait that is attributable to hereditary factors.

44. _____ The extent to which two individuals have genes in common.

45. _____ Study in which sets of twins that differ in zygosity (kinship) are compared to determine the heritability of an attribute, or attributes.

46. _____ The percentage of cases in which a particular attribute is present for both members of a twin pair if it is present for one member.

47. _____ Study in which adoptees are compared to their biological relatives and their adoptive relatives to estimate the heritability of an attribute, or attributes.

48. _____ A numerical estimate, ranging from .00 to +1.00, of the amount of variation in an attribute that is due to hereditary factors.

---

behavioral inhibition
empathic concern
"goodness of fit" model
introversion/extraversion

nonshared environmen-
tal influence
temperament

49. _____ A person's characteristic modes of response to the environment, including such attributes as activity level, irritability, fearfulness, and sociability.

50. _____ A temperamental characteristic reflecting one's tendency to withdraw from unfamiliar people or situations.

51. _____ Thomas and Chess's notion that development is likely to be optimized when parents' child-rearing practices are adapted to (or are compatible with) the child's temperamental characteristic.

52. _____ The opposite poles of a personality dimension; introverts are shy, anxious around others, and ready to withdraw from social situations; extraverts are highly sociable and enjoy being with others.

53. _____ A measure of the extent to which an individual recognizes the needs of others and is concerned about their welfare.

54. _____ An environmental influence that people living together do not share and that makes these individuals different from one another.

manic depression
neurotic disorder

schizophrenia

55. _____ A serious form of mental illness characterized by disturbances in logical thinking, emotional expression, and interpersonal behavior.

56. _____ A psychotic disorder characterized by extreme fluctuations in mood.

57. _____ An irrational pattern of thinking or behavior that a person may use to contend with stress or to avoid anxiety.

active genotype/environment
    interactions
canalization
evocative genotype/
    environment interactions

passive genotype/
    environment
    interactions
range of reaction
    principle

58. _____ Genetic restriction of phenotype to a small number of developmental outcomes; a highly canalized attribute is one for which genes channel development along predetermined pathways, so that the environment has little effect on the phenotype that emerges.

59. _____ The idea that genotype sets limits on the range of possible phenotypes that a person might display in response to different environments.

60. _____ The notion that the rearing environments that biological parents provide are influenced by the parents' own genes, and hence are correlated with the child's own genotype.

61. _____ The notion that our heritable attributes will affect others' behavior toward us and thus will influence the social environment in which development takes place.

62. _____ The notion that our genotypes affect the types of environments that we prefer and will seek out.

CHAPTER 3 STUDY QUESTIONS

HEREDITY IN HISTORICAL PERSPECTIVE

1.   In the 17th century **Swammerdam** proposed the theory of the homunculus and another group espoused the ovist view of heredity. What **erroneous assumption** did both of these views make? (p. 78)

2.   In 1865 **Mendel** reported his remarkable discovery that each parent contributes half of the genes that each child receives from the parents. Beyond this, one of Mendel's important contributions has to do with how each pair of genes works to determine characteristics--the notion of **genetic dominance**. Describe this principle. (p. 79)

3.   In 1933 **Morgan** discovered that genes, thousands of them, lie like beads on a string along **what structure**? (p. 79)

PRINCIPLES OF HEREDITARY TRANSMISSION

4.   **Mitosis** involves a cell duplicating its chromosomes and then dividing into two genetically identical daughter cells. **How does meiosis differ?** (p. 81-82)

Draw a schematic illustrating each process. (p. 81-82, Fig. 3-3, Fig. 3-4)

5.   What **two processes** account for the fact that no two children look exactly the same (unless they are identical twins)? (p. 82-83)

(a)

(b)

6.   **Most twins** result from the mother releasing **two ova** at the same time and each being fertilized by a different sperm. These twins _____ (are, are not) identical. (p. 83)

Can these twins differ in sex?

What are two names for this type of twinning?

What is the less common type of twinning called and how does it occur?

7.   Sex of an individual is determined by the 23rd chromosome pair and is designated by Xs and Ys because of the shape of the chromosomes. What **pattern of Xs and Ys** is found in normal males and which in normal females? (p. 83-84)

MALES:

FEMALES:

8.   For many centuries women were blamed for the failure to produce male offspring. What do we now know about **hereditary determination of sex** that makes this accusation unfair? (p. 83-84)

9.   For recessive traits such as cystic fibrosis, PKU, and Tay-Sachs disease is it possible for two normal parents to have a child who displays one of these recessive traits? (p. 85-86)

Explain how this could be.

10.   The dominance/recessive pattern of genetic transmission has been found to be only one pattern of transmission. Describe each of the others and give an example of a characteristic showing each **type of transmission.** (p. 86-88)

INCOMPLETE DOMINANCE:

EXAMPLE:

CODOMINANCE:

EXAMPLE:

SEX-LINKED CHARACTERISTICS:

EXAMPLE:

MODIFIER GENE INFLUENCE:

EXAMPLE:

POLYGENIC INHERITANCE:

EXAMPLE:

CHROMOSOMAL AND GENETIC ABNORMALITIES

11.   Most chromosomal abnormalities result in failure to develop or in spontaneous abortion. Some are not lethal, however, resulting in 1 in 200 children being born with one too many or too few chromosomes. For each of the six chromosomal abnormalities discussed in the text and Table 3-1 indicate **how the chromosomes are abnormal**. Also indicate whether appearance and intelligence are typically normal or abnormal for each disorder. (*circle or underline*) (p. 89-92 & Table 3-1)

FRAGILE-X SYNDROME
chromosomal abnormality (specify):
appearance (normal, abnormal)
intelligence (normal, abnormal)

TURNER'S SYNDROME
chromosomal abnormality (specify):
appearance (normal, abnormal)
intelligence (normal, abnormal)

POLY-X, SUPERFEMALE SYNDROME
chromosomal abnormality (specify):
appearance (normal, abnormal)
intelligence (normal, abnormal)

KLINEFELTER'S SYNDROME
chromosomal abnormality (specify):
appearance (normal, abnormal)
intelligence (normal, abnormal)

SUPERMALE SYNDROME
chromosomal abnormality (specify):
appearance (normal, abnormal)
intelligence (normal, abnormal)

DOWN SYNDROME
chromosomal abnormality (specify):
appearance (normal, abnormal)
intelligence (normal, abnormal)

12.   **Fragile-X syndrome** has recently (Zigler & Hodapp, 1991) been **linked with** what serious **emotional disorder?** (p. 89)

13.   What is the most basic **cause of chromosomal abnormalities?** (p. 91-92)

What is the relationship between mother's age and likelihood of producing a child with chromosomal abnormalities? (p. 91-92)

What three explanations have been proposed for this relationship? (p. 92)

   (a)

   (b)

   (c)

14.   List three examples of **defects** that are **attributable to a single pair of genes** rather than to chromosomal abnormalities. (p. 92-94 & Table 3-3)

   (a)

   (b)

   (c)

15.   Explain **how it is possible** for diseases such as cystic fibrosis and Tay-Sachs to be fatal and to occur in the offspring of two normal parents. (p. 85-86, 92-94)

16. We typically associate **mutations** with maladaptive outcomes, but evolutionary theorists believe some might even be beneficial. Give an example. (p. 93-94)

17. Many but not all **disorders** can now be detected early in pregnancy. What **three tests** are described in the text? Note any limitations or advantages. (p. 95-96)

(a)

(b)

(c)

18. One might assume that if a child inherits a genetic defect that there is not much that can be done since genes cannot be altered at will. However, scientists have discovered how some genetic abnormalities affect physiological functioning and found that they can counter the impact by **normalizing physiological functioning**. (p. 96-97)

How are each of the following disorders treated?

PKU:

DIABETES:

TURNER'S SYNDROME:

CYSTIC FIBROSIS:

HEREDITARY INFLUENCES ON BEHAVIOR

19.   **Genotype** refers to _____, whereas **phenotype** refers to _____. (p. 97)

20.   How do **behavior geneticists differ from ethologists**? (p. 97-98)

21.   What is the **rationale behind selective breeding studies**, i.e., what can be concluded if individuals increase on some trait (e.g., aggressiveness) over generations when aggressive individuals are bred with other aggressive individuals? (p. 98)

22.   Human behavior genetics usually relies on two types of family studies in determining the role of heredity on a trait. Describe what comparisons are made and the **rationale** behind the use of the **two main types of family studies** used today. (p. 98-99)

    TWIN STUDY:

    ADOPTION STUDY:

23.   Calculate the heritability coefficient of a double chin when the correlation between identical twins is +.70 and the correlation between fraternal twins is +.40. Interpret the coefficient. (p. 100)

If the **heritability** of a characteristic (e.g., sense of humor) were **estimated to be .83**, which of the following would be appropriate to conclude? (*circle one*) (p. 99-100)

    (a)   the differences we observe in people's sense of humor are influenced to a large extent by hereditary factors.

    (b)   83% of your (an individual's) sense of humor is due to heredity.

24.   List two findings that provide supportive evidence for the **role of heredity on intellectual performance.** (p. 101-102)

    (a)

    (b)

25.   List two findings that provide supportive evidence for the **role of environment on intellectual performance.** (p. 102)

    (a)

    (b)

26.   What characteristic modes of response are believed to be **components of temperament?** (p. 103)

    (a)

    (b)

    (c)

    (d)

    (e)

Alexander **Thomas** and associates have identified **three temperament profiles** in their longitudinal studies, the _____ child, the _____ child, and the _____ child. (p. 104)

They found these temperament profiles to be quite stable over time. Does that mean that environmental influences cannot modify these patterns (i.e., is there nothing a parent can do to improve on a child's unpleasant temperament?)? What answer have Thomas and Chess given to this question? Explain. (p. 103-105)

27.   List two examples of **personality attributes for which comparisons of identical and fraternal twins have indicated a hereditary component.** (p. 105)

(a)

(b)

Table 3-5 presents correlations for different levels of kinship on **personality attributes.** Identical twins showed a correlation of .50, with correlations decreasing as kinship decreases. What correlations and comparisons of correlations in the table provide evidence for a role of heredity? Explain. What correlations and comparisons of correlations provide evidence for a role of environment? Explain. (p. 105-107, & Table 3-5)

EVIDENCE FOR HEREDITY:

EXPLANATION:

EVIDENCE FOR ENVIRONMENT:

EXPLANATION:

28.   How does the concept of "nonshared environmental influence" help to account for the relatively low personality resemblances among siblings reared in the same home? (p. 106-107)

How do we know that people do not experience different environments solely because they have different genes? (p. 107)

29.   By calculating concordance rates it has been shown that **heredity** does play a role in many **psychiatric disorders. Does this mean that it is inevitable** a child will be schizophrenic or depressed or manic-depressive if a parent is? if an identical-twin sibling is? Explain. (p. 107-108)

THE NATURE/NURTURE CONTROVERSY

30.   The **onset of babbling** during infancy and the **onset of walking** are both characteristics that **Waddington** would describe as _____ **canalized.** For these characteristics, the number of outcomes occurring in response to variations in environment are quite limited. For other characteristics such as **intelligence**, the range of outcomes is greater, since the characteristic is _____ **canalized.** (p. 109)

Gottesman's range of reaction principle is similar in suggesting that heredity serves to set limits on the range or number of possible variations in outcomes for a given genotype. *To illustrate these notions, answer the following questions based on Fig. 3-10, a graphic representation of Gottesman's range of reaction notion.* (p. 109-110 & Fig. 3-10)

        A.   What is the range of reaction, i.e., the possible IQ scores, for a child with genotype C?

B.   What is the range of reaction, i.e., the possible IQ scores, for a child with genotype B?

C.   What is the range of reaction, i.e., the possible IQ scores, for a child with genotype A?

D.   If a child takes an IQ test and scores 100, what conclusions can be made about that child's genetic potential for intellectual development?

E.   If one child obtains a score of 80 and another a score of 100, what conclusion can be drawn about whether these children differ in genetic potential for intellectual development; i.e., what conclusion, if any, can we draw in absence of information about environment? (*Select one answer after checking Fig. 3-9 to see what genotype a child with a score of 80 and one of 100 could have.*)

(a)   they are both genotype A
(b)   they are both genotype B
(c)   that one is A and the other B
(d)   no inference about genotype can be made without knowing about type of environment; the child could be either genotype A or B or anything in between

31.   Recently, **Scarr and McCartney** (1983) and others have argued that our **genetic makeup may influence the kinds of environments that we are likely to experience.** Characterize each of the **three ways** described in the text.
(p. 110-111)

PASSIVE GENE INFLUENCE:

EVOCATIVE GENE INFLUENCE:

ACTIVE GENE INFLUENCE (NICHE PICKING):

32.   How does Scarr and McCartney's theory of genotype/environment interactions **explain the fact that fraternal twins and other non-twin siblings become increasingly dissimilar on many attributes as they mature?** (p. 111)

(a)

(b)

33.   How does the notion of **active gene influence** help to explain the sometimes uncanny **similarities between identical twins' habits and lifestyles even when they have been reared apart?** (p. 111-112 & Box 3-2)

ACTIVITY 3-1

DETERMINANTS OF SIMILARITIES AND DIFFERENCES

INTRODUCTION: This activity relates to the material in Chapter 3 on the interdependent role of heredity and environment in determining physical characteristics, personality, intelligence, etc. As a resource for this activity you are asked to tap what you know best--yourself. It is suggested that you complete this activity before reading the text material, and then look back over your responses after reading the text to see if you might have a different perspective on possible determinants.

INSTRUCTIONS:

1. Describe yourself in <u>two</u> of the following areas:

    SOCIABILITY, AGGRESSION, PERSONALITY, TEMPERAMENT, INTELLIGENCE

2. Speculate about what factors you think may have contributed to your being the way you are in those two areas.

HEREDITY IN HISTORICAL PERSPECTIVE

1. (78)   HOMUNCULUS: believed each sperm cell contains a tiny <u>preformed embryo</u> that grows only if deposited in the mother's womb

                OVIST: believed that <u>preformed embryos</u> are in the mother's ova and that the father's sperm acts as a catalyst for growth

2. (79)   According to the genetic dominance theory, one of the parental genes will completely dominate the other (rather than producing a blend) and the child will resemble the parent who contributed the dominant gene.

3. (79)   Chromosome

PRINCIPLES OF HEREDITARY TRANSMISSION

4. (81-82)   Meiosis is the process in which a germ cell divides to produce gametes (sperm or ova) that each contain 23 single, unpaired chromosomes (see Fig. 3-4, p. 82).

                Mitosis is the process in which a cell duplicates its chromosomes and then divides into two genetically identical daughter cells, each containing 46 chromosomes (see Fig. 3-3, p. 81).

5. (82-83)   a) independent assortment
                b) crossing over

6. (83)   <u>Are not</u> identical
                Yes
                Dizygotic, fraternal
                Monozygotic, identical; a single zygote splits into two identical cells

7. (83-84)   Males: XY
                Females: XX

8. (83-84)   The male sperm carries the sex-determining chromosome. All ova contain X.

9. (85-86)   Yes, if both parents are heterozygous and therefore carry both the dominant (N) and recessive (n) gene. There are four possible combinations passed to the child: NN, nN, Nn, and nn. Therefore, there is a 1 in 4 possibility that the recessive nn characteristic will be displayed.

10. (86-88)   INCOMPLETE DOMINANCE: some "dominant" alleles fail to mask all the effects of a "recessive" gene.
Example: sickle-cell trait

CODOMINANCE: neither form of the gene is able to dominate the other.
Example: blood types A and B

SEX-LINKED CHARACTERISTICS: determined by recessive genes located on the sex chromosomes. The majority are found only in the X chromosomes. Males are most often affected because they are missing the corresponding genes on the Y chromosome.
Example: red/green color blindness

MODIFIER GENE INFLUENCE: influences the action or expression of other genes
Example: sex differences in pattern baldness

POLYGENIC INHERITANCE: attributes are influenced by many genes rather than a single pair
Example: intelligence

CHROMOSOMAL AND GENETIC ABNORMALITIES

11. (89-92)   FRAGILE-X SYNDROME: an X chromosome is brittle in places and may even
    (Tbl. 3-4)   have separated into two or more pieces; normal appearance; low IQ

TURNER'S SYNDROME: no X or Y chromosome was present in the sperm (XO); abnormal appearance (small, underdeveloped female); normal in verbal intelligence, low in spatial abilities

POLY-X, SUPERFEMALE SYNDROME: females with extra X chromosomes (XXX, XXXX, or XXXXX); normal appearance; low IQ

KLINEFELTER'S SYNDROME: males with extra X chromosomes (XXY or XXXY); abnormal appearance (female); about 20-30% have low IQ

SUPERMALE SYNDROME: males with extra Y chromosomes (XYY, XYYY, or XYYYY); abnormal appearance (tall, large teeth, acne); normal IQ range

DOWN SYNDROME: there is an extra 21st chromosome; abnormal appearance (distinctive facial features); low IQ

12. (89)   Infantile autism

13. (91-92)   Uneven segregation of chromosomes

Positive relationship

    (92)   a) aging-ova hypothesis
    b) environmental hazards
    c) greater likelihood of abnormal sperm from older father

14. (92-94)   a) cystic fibrosis
    (Tbl. 3-3) b) muscular dystrophy
               c) phenylketonuria
               d) Tay-Sachs disease
               e) hemophilia
               f) diabetes

15. (85-86)   These diseases are caused by recessive genes carried by the two healthy
    (92-94)   heterozygous parents. The affected children receive a recessive gene from both
               parents.

16. (93-94)   Sickled cells are protective against malaria.

17. (95-96)   a) amniocentesis; cannot be performed before 14th to 16th week of pregnancy and
                  it takes an additional two weeks to obtain the test results
               b) chorionic villus sampling; can be performed earlier in pregnancy, 6th to 10th
                  week, and results are known in 48 hours
               c) ultrasound; can only detect gross abnormalities

18. (96-97)   PKU: diet low in phenylalanine
    (Tbl. 3-3) DIABETES: insulin
               TURNER'S SYNDROME: estrogen
               CYSTIC FIBROSIS: no known treatment yet for the missing enzyme

HEREDITARY INFLUENCES ON BEHAVIOR

19. (97)   Genes one inherits

               Observable characteristics and behaviors

20. (97-98)   Behavior geneticists focus on understanding individual differences, whereas
               ethologists are interested in identification of inherited attributes that are common
               across all members of a species.

21. (98)   If get an increase in expression of the trait, there must be a genetic contribution

22. (98-99)   TWIN STUDIES: compare identical twins reared apart to fraternal twins reared
               together. A higher correlation between identical twins must reflect shared genetic
               makeup since they were reared separately.
               ADOPTION STUDIES: a higher correlation between the adopted child and her
               biological parents than between the adopted child and her adoptive parents can be
               interpreted as evidence for genetic influence. A correlation with the adoptive parents
               or genetically related siblings can be interpreted as evidence for an environmental
               influence. A difference between adoptees and controls reared in less favorable
               conditions also can be interpreted as evidence for an environmental influence.

23. (100) $H = (.70 - .40) \times 2 = .30 \times 2 = \underline{.60}$, meaning that this characteristic is influenced to
               a moderate degree by heredity and, by inference, to a moderate but lesser degree by
               environment.

    (99-100)   Alternative a

24. (101-102)   a) when reared together, the intellectual resemblance between pairs of individuals increases as a function of their degree of kinship.
    b) identical twins reared apart are more similar in IQ than fraternal twins reared together.

25. (102)   a) genetically unrelated individuals living together are more intellectually similar than individuals living apart.
    b) in the Scarr and Weinberg interracial adoptee study the IQ scores of Black children adopted into higher socioeconomic environments were substantially higher (20 IQ points) than the IQs of nonadopted controls.

26. (103-105)   a) activity level
    b) irritability
    c) soothability
    d) fearfulness
    e) sociability

    Easy, difficult, slow-to-warm-up

    No, temperament is highly modifiable by environmental influence; one factor influencing whether change occurs is "goodness of fit" between a child's temperament and parental child-rearing patterns.

27. (105-106)   a) introversion/extroversion
    (Tbl. 3-5)   b) empathic concern

    HEREDITY: the correlation for identical twins is +.52, whereas the correlation for unrelated children in the same household is only +.07. This difference would indicate that heredity contributes to personality attributes. Also the higher correlation for identical twins than for fraternal twins or siblings provides evidence for heredity.
    ENVIRONMENT: the moderate correlation of +.52 for identical twins also indicates that although there are personality similarities there are also many differences that would be attributable to nonshared environmental influences
        (NSE = 1 - .52 = .48).

28. (106-107)   One or both parents may respond very differently to different children (e.g., sons and daughters, first-born and later-born), which has the effect of exaggerating differences due to heredity.

    Because the correlation between identical twins on personality attributes is considerably less than +1.0

29. (108)   No, it is not inevitable. Parenting factors and stress make a difference. This is consistent with the range of reaction principle, which maintains one's genotype sets a range of possible outcomes for any particular attribute and the environment largely determines the point within the range where the individual will fall.

30. (109)   highly, less

   (Fig 3-10)   a)   25 to 65
                 b)   45 to 100
                 c)   70 to 145
                 d)   either A or B, depending on the type of environment in which the child was reared
                 e)   alternative <u>d</u>

31. (110-111)   PASSIVE GENE INFLUENCE: the environment parents provide is a product of their genotype, which is correlated with their children's genotype (i.e., parents who enjoy physical activity may be predisposed to enjoying physical activity and create an environment where their children are both exposed to physical activity and are possibly predisposed genetically to enjoy it).
                 EVOCATIVE GENE INFLUENCE: the inherited attributes a child possesses affect how others respond to him. For example, smiley, active babies may receive more attention than moody, passive babies.
                 ACTIVE GENE INFLUENCE (NICHE PICKING): children seek out environments compatible with their genetic predisposition. For example, shy children may avoid large social groups and prefer activities that may be done alone such as coin collecting.

32. (111)   a)   they evoke different responses from others by virtue of having different genotypes
                 b)   their different genotypes predispose them to select different environments

33. (111-112)   Identical twins reared apart may be genetically predisposed to choose
   (Box 3-2)   similar environments. Their "different" environments may provide them with similar experiences, allowing the development of similar habits, mannerisms, abilities, and interests.

CHAPTER 4

PRENATAL DEVELOPMENT
AND BIRTH

STUDY CHECKLIST

_____ Read Chapter Outline and Summary (Study guide)

_____ Read Chapter (Text)

_____ Completed Vocabulary Fill-Ins (Study guide)

_____ Re-Read Outline and Summary (Study guide)

_____ Reviewed Lecture Notes and Integrated with Text

_____ Reviewed Vocabulary, Study Questions, and Text Chapter

CHAPTER 4 OUTLINE AND SUMMARY

I. **From conception to birth**
    A. The germinal period
    B. The period of the embryo
    C. The period of the fetus

During the 266 days between conception and birth, the unborn child passes through three successive phases. Within the first two weeks, or germinal period, the single-celled zygote becomes a multicelled blastula that travels down the fallopian tube, implants itself in the uterine lining, and begins to grow.

The second phase of prenatal development lasts from the third through the eighth week of pregnancy and is called the period of the embryo. By the end of this phase the unborn child is only about an inch long and weighs about 1/10 of an ounce. However, it already bears some resemblance to a human being because most of its organs and body parts have formed and begun to function.

From the end of the eighth week until birth is the period of the fetus. As the fetus rapidly grows, the genitals appear, the muscles and bones develop, and all organ systems become integrated in preparation for birth. Between the 24th and 28th weeks the brain and respiratory system mature to an extent that the fetus attains the age of viability--the point at which survival outside the uterus may be possible. At the beginning of the seventh month the fetus weighs 2 pounds and is 14-15 inches long. By the end of the ninth month the full-term fetus will have grown to 19 or 20 inches and will weigh about 7 - 7 1/2 pounds.

II. **Environmental influences on prenatal development**
    A. Maternal characteristics
        1. Maternal age
        2. The mother's emotional state
        3. The mother's diet (nutrition)
    B. Teratogens
        1. Maternal diseases
        2. Drugs
        3. Environmental hazards
    C. On the prevention of birth defects

Many environmental influences can complicate prenatal development and the birth process. Among these influences are characteristics of the mother such as age, emotional state, and quality of diet. If a mother is malnourished, particularly during the last three months of pregnancy, she runs an increased risk of having a stillborn infant or a premature baby who may fail to survive. In addition, the fetally malnourished infant may be sluggish, irritable, and neurologically immature--liabilities that could contribute to long-term deficits in social and intellectual development.

Prenatal development may also be disrupted by teratogens (drugs, diseases, chemicals, and radiation), which can attack the developing embryo or fetus and produce serious birth defects. Teratogens are dangerous throughout pregnancy; however, many of these agents are especially troublesome during the first eight weeks, when the major organs and body parts are developing. Many diseases may produce birth defects; rubella, syphilis, herpes, and toxoplasmosis are particularly harmful. A large number of drugs, including thalidomide, alcohol, tobacco, hormones, narcotics, and even some antibiotics, are known to cause congenital malformations and complications at birth. In addition, radiation and chemical pollutants such as mercury, lead, and PCBs may have adverse effects on an unborn child.

III. **Birth and the perinatal environment**
   A. The birth process
   B. The social environment surrounding birth
      1. The parents' experience
      2. The baby's experience
      3. The older child's experience
   C. Perinatal hazards and complications
      1. Perinatal screening
      2. Anoxia
      3. Abnormal positioning of the fetus
      4. Effects of obstetric medication
      5. Complications of low birth weight
   D. On reproductive risk and infants' capacity for recovery
   E. Ecological considerations: Should you have your baby at home?

Childbirth is a three-step process that begins when the uterus contracts and prepares to push the fetus through the cervical opening and ends a few minutes after birth of the baby, when the afterbirth is expelled from the body. Many women feel exhilarated after giving birth, particularly if the baby's father is present or nearby to provide emotional support. Fathers who watch or participate in the birth process are likely to feel more positive about childbirth and to be more involved with their babies than are nonparticipating fathers.

Some developmentalists believe that babies are insensitive creatures who experience little if any discomfort when they are born. Others believe that birth is extremely traumatic, and they suggest "gentle birthing" as a way of making the process less terrifying.

A new baby is a mixed blessing for an older child, who may feel neglected. Parents can make this period easier by spending time with their older children and inviting them to help in caring for the baby.

Complications of birth such as anoxia, breech deliveries, overuse of obstetric medication, and low birth weight may make a baby irritable and unresponsive and may lead to adverse developmental outcomes. Fortunately, the problems stemming from prenatal and perinatal complications are often overcome, provided that the child (1) is not brain damaged and (2) has a stable and supportive postnatal environment in which to grow.

An increasing number of couples are choosing to forgo hospital deliveries and have their babies within the familiar surroundings of their own homes. However, many obstetricians are critical of the home birth movement, arguing that home deliveries may jeopardize the mother and her infant should complications arise. Today many hospitals maintain birthing rooms--delivery areas furnished like typical bedrooms that provide many of the comforts of home within the protective confines of a hospital.

CHAPTER 4 VOCABULARY FILL-INS
(Definitions below are in order of appearance in text margins)

MATCH VOCABULARY WORD/PHRASE TO ITS DEFINITION.
THEN COVER YOUR ANSWERS TO TEST YOUR MASTERY.

blastocyst	**period of the embryo**
blastula	**period of the fetus**
germinal period	**prenatal development**
implantation	**trophoblast**

1. _____ Development that occurs between the moment of conception and the beginning of the birth process.

2. _____ First phase of prenatal development, lasting from conception until the developing organism becomes attached to the wall of the uterus.

3. _____ Second phase of prenatal development, lasting from the third through the eighth prenatal week, during which the major organs and anatomical structures take shape.

4. _____ Third phase of prenatal development, lasting from the ninth prenatal week until birth; during this period, all major organ systems begin to function and the fetus grows rapidly.

5. _____ A hollow sphere of about 100-150 cells that results from the rapid division of the zygote as it moves through the fallopian tube.

6. _____ Inner layer of the blastula, which becomes the embryo.

7. _____ Outer cells of the blastula, which eventually develop into tissues that serve to protect and nourish the embryo.

8. _____ The burrowing of the blastula into the lining of the uterus.

age of viability
allantois
amnion
chorion
indifferent gonad

neonate
placenta
umbilical cord
yolk sac

9. _____ A watertight membrane that develops from the trophoblast and surrounds the developing embryo, serving to regulate its temperature and to cushion it against injuries.

10. _____ A balloonlike structure that develops from the trophoblast and produces blood cells until the embryo is capable of manufacturing its own.

11. _____ A membrane that develops from the trophoblast and becomes attached to the uterine tissues to gather nourishment for the embryo.

12. _____ An organ, formed from the lining of the uterus and the chorion, that provides for respiration and nourishment of the unborn child and the elimination of its metabolic wastes.

13. _____ A membrane that develops from the trophoblast and forms the umbilical cord.

14. _____ A soft tube containing blood vessels that connects the embryo to the placenta.

15. _____ Undifferentiated tissue that produces testes in males and ovaries in females.

16. _____ A point between the 24th and 28th prenatal weeks when a fetus may survive outside the uterus if excellent medical care is available.

17. _____ A newborn infant from birth to approximately 1 month of age.

acquired immune deficiency
     syndrome (AIDS)
Cesarean section
diethylstilbestrol (DES)
fetal alcohol syndrome (FAS)
genital herpes

phocomelia
rubella (German
     measles)
syphilis
teratogens
thalidomide

18. _____ External agents such as viruses, drugs, chemicals, and radiation that can cross the placental barrier and harm a developing embryo or fetus.

19. _____ A disease that has little effect on a mother but may cause a number of serious birth defects in unborn children who are exposed in the first 3-4 months of pregnancy.

20. _____ A common venereal disease that may cross the placental barrier in the middle and later stages of pregnancy, causing miscarriages or serious birth defects.

21. _____ A sexually transmitted disease that can infect infants at birth, causing blindness, brain damage, or even death.

22. _____ Surgical delivery of a baby through an incision made in the mother's abdomen and uterus.

23. _____ A viral disease that can be transmitted from a mother to her fetus or neonate and that results in a weakening of the body's immune system and, ultimately, death.

24. _____ A mild tranquilizer that, taken early in pregnancy, can produce a variety of malformations of the limbs, eyes, ears, and heart.

25. _____ A prenatal malformation in which all or parts of the limbs are missing.

26. _____ A synthetic hormone, formerly prescribed to prevent miscarriage, that can produce cervical cancer in adolescent female offspring.

27. _____ A group of congenital problems commonly observed in the offspring of mothers who abuse alcohol during pregnancy.

first stage of labor
perinatal environment
prepared or natural childbirth

second stage of labor
third stage of labor

28. _____ The environment surrounding birth, including influences such as childbirth medication, obstetrical practices, and the social stimulation a baby may receive.

29. _____ The period of the birth process lasting from the first regular uterine contractions until the cervix is fully dilated.

30. _____ The period of the birth process during which the fetus moves through the vaginal canal and emerges from the mother's body (also called the delivery).

31. _____ Expulsion of the placenta (afterbirth).

32. _____ A delivery in which physical and psychological preparations for the birth are stressed and medical assistance is minimized.

anoxia
Apgar test
birthing room
breech birth
engrossment

gentle birthing
hyaline membrane disease
postpartum depression
short-gestation (preterm) babies
small-for-date babies

33. _____ Parents' fascination with their neonate; a desire to touch, hold, caress, and talk to the newborn baby.

34. _____ Feelings of sadness, resentment, and depression that mothers may experience following a birth (also called the "baby blues").

35. _____ Leboyer's method of childbirth, in which the neonate is comforted, massaged, shielded from unpleasant sensory stimulation, and bathed in warm water in an attempt to reduce any traumas associated with birth.

36. _____ A quick assessment of the newborn's heart rate, respiration, color, muscle tone, and reflexes that is used to gauge perinatal stress and to determine whether a neonate requires immediate medical assistance.

37. _____ A lack of sufficient oxygen to the brain; may result in neurological damage or death.

38. _____ A delivery in which the fetus emerges feet first or buttocks first rather than head first.

39. _____ Babies born close to their due dates but weighing less than 2500 grams.

40. _____ Babies born more than three weeks before their due dates.

41. _____ A serious respiratory condition in which the neonate breathes very irregularly and is at risk of dying (also called respiratory distress syndrome).

42. _____ A hospital delivery area that is furnished like a typical bedroom to provide a homelike atmosphere for childbirth.

CHAPTER 4 STUDY QUESTIONS

FROM CONCEPTION TO BIRTH

1. The **germinal** period of prenatal development lasts from **conception** until _____. At what point during this period does **cell differentiation** begin? (*select one*) (p. 119)

    (a)   within the first 3 days after conception

    (b)   after implantation in the lining of the uterus (at 8-14 days)

2. **What proportion of zygotes survive** the **germinal phase** of prenatal development? (p. 119)

3. The **placenta** provides the developing embryo with a(an) _____ (direct; indirect) **link to the mother's bloodstream.** Describe just what the relationship is. (p. 120, 127)

4. About 14 days after conception a portion of the ectoderm folds into a _____ that soon **becomes the head, brain, and spinal cord.** (p. 120)

5. By the end of the _____ week the **heart is formed** and has begun **to beat.** (p. 120)

6. What **triggers the differentiation** of the **indifferent gonad** during the 7th and 8th prenatal weeks? (p. 121)

   (a)   in males:

   (b)   in females:

7. At 9 weeks of prenatal development all the major organs have begun to form and the organism changes status from **embryo to** _____. (p. 121 & Fig. 4-3)

8. By the end of the **first trimester** (3 months) of pregnancy, the fetus is still only _____ long and weighs _____ (p. 122 & Fig. 4-4); however, all organ systems and body structures are present, many operational. List examples of the body structures and organ systems that are present and describe any motor capabilities. (p. 119-122)

   BODY STRUCTURES:

   ORGAN SYSTEMS:

   MOTOR CAPABILITIES:

9.   When the brain and respiratory system are sufficiently mature to allow for **survival outside the uterus**, the fetus is said to have reached the **age of** _____. (p. 122)

How many weeks after conception is this point reached on the average? (p. 122)

The majority of infants born weighing less than _____ **do not survive.** (p. 122-123, Table 4-1)

10.   During the **last trimester** of pregnancy what main change is occurring? (p. 123)

ENVIRONMENTAL INFLUENCES ON PRENATAL DEVELOPMENT

11.   The **risk of complications** during pregnancy or birth are greatest for what two age groups of women? Why? (p. 123-124)

(a)

(b)

Are older women's pregnancies "doomed" from the start? (p. 124)

12.   What relationship has been found between **mother's emotional state** and **pregnancy complications?** (p. 124-125)

After birth, babies of distressed mothers tend to be more irritable and "difficult." Recent research (**Vaughn** et al.) suggests that these **negative characteristics are due to** _____ (*select one:* abnormal hormonal levels during pregnancy stress periods, innate temperament of the infant, mother's child rearing approach). (p. 125)

13.   Malnourishment during the _____ trimester of pregnancy has been shown to affect birth weight, infant mortality, and responsiveness of infants. What two kinds of **intervention** have been found to **minimize the long-term effect of prenatal malnutrition**? (p. 125-126 & Box 4-1)

(a)

(b)

14.   Teratogens are any agents (disease, drugs, chemicals, etc.) that can interfere with prenatal development and produce defects. The **first trimester** (first 12 weeks) of pregnancy is sometimes called a critical period, a time when the fetus is most sensitive to teratogenic agents. Why is the embryo/fetus so **susceptible to teratogenic effects** during this period? (p. 127)

15.   Based on Figure 4-7 and the text, list at least six body parts, organs, or systems that are particularly **vulnerable** during the **first trimester** (first 12 weeks). (p. 127-128 & Fig. 4-7)

(a)   (d)

(b)   (e)

(c)   (f)

16.   Based on Figure 4-7 and the text, list three body parts or systems that are **sensitive to teratogens throughout** the second and third trimester of pregnancy as well as the first (see the lightly shaded bars that run to far right of the graph to 38 weeks). (p. 128 & Fig. 4-7)

(a)

(b)

(c)

17.   List three (or more) additional **"anytime malformations."** (p. 127)

(a)

(b)

(c)

18.   Studies have shown that the percent of babies who are born with defects associated with rubella drops from 60% to 85% in the first eight weeks to about 16% during weeks 13-20. This **decrease in vulnerability** with advancing weeks and maturity **illustrates what principle?** (p. 128)

19.   One of the generalizations the author makes about the effects of teratogens is that **a variety of defects can result from a single teratogen.** Provide examples of the defects that have been found to be associated with each of the following teratogens:

RUBELLA (p. 128-129):

(a)   (c)

(b)   (d)

GENITAL HERPES (p. 129):

(a)   (b)

ALCOHOL (p. 134):

(a)   (d)

(b)   (e)

(c)   (f)

20.   Another generalization made by the author about teratogens is that **not all embryos and fetuses are adversely affected by exposure to a particular teratogen.** What two factors determine whether or not serious harm will occur (*see generalizations #2 and #5 in the text*, p. 127)?

(a)

(b)

21.   What outcomes have been found to be associated with taking **medications containing sex hormones** during pregnancy? (p. 132-133, Table 4-3)

22.   What is the relationship of **amount of alcohol** consumed to abnormalities in children? (p. 134)

23.   What relationship has been found between **cigarette smoking** and developmental outcomes? (p. 134)

24.   Regular **cocaine use** by the mother during pregnancy has been linked to short- and long-term effects on infants and children. Indicate the effects below. (p. 135-136)

SHORT-TERM EFFECTS:

LONG-TERM EFFECTS (2-3 YEARS):

25.   **Radiation, chemicals, and pollutants** have been found to affect the developing fetus _____. *(select one)* (p. 136-137)

   (a)   only if the fetus and the mother are exposed

   (b)   only if the father has been exposed and suffered chromosomal damage

   (c)   both <u>a</u> and <u>b</u> can result in birth defects or spontaneous abortion

What **adverse outcomes** have been linked to pregnant women's consumption of fish contaminated with **PCBs**? (p. 136-137)

BIRTH AND THE PERINATAL ENVIRONMENT

26.   Although going to prepared childbirth classes and having the father present during the birth is not essential, some benefits have been documented. List **benefits** found for participation in prepared childbirth and for having the father present. (p. 139-140)

   PREPARED CHILDBIRTH:

   FATHER PRESENT:

27.   What factors contribute to **postpartum depression?** (p. 141)

28.   **Leboyer** claims there are long-term advantages associated with "**gentle birthing.**" What does research evidence indicate? (p. 142)

29. Of the **complications** that can occur **during the birth process**, what is the **greatest hazard** to the infant? (p. 143)

30. What are the pros and cons of administration of **medications** to the mother **during the birth process**? (p. 144-145)

    PROS:

    CONS:

31. Most likely to jeopardize **short-gestation** (preterm) babies' health is the **immaturity of the** _____ **system.** (p. 145-146)

32. What kinds of experiences have been found to **optimize** the **development of low-birth weight infants**? (p. 146-147)

33. What variable did **Wilson** find to **moderate the long-term effects of low birth weight on later intellectual performance**? (p. 147 & Fig. 4-10)

34. According to the text, what conclusion is warranted regarding the **long-term consequences of low birth weight and other perinatal complications**? (p. 147-150)

What did **Werner and Smith's longitudinal data** show that supports this conclusion? (p. 148)

35.   What do mortality statistics tell us about the **relative safety of home birthing versus hospital birth**?   (p. 149-150)

Why might the infant mortality statistics be **misleading**?   (p. 149)

ACTIVITY 4-1

GIVING ADVICE ON PRENATAL CARE--YOU BE THE EXPERT

This activity relates to the material presented in Chapter 4 (p. 123-137) on factors influencing prenatal development such as maternal diet, smoking, drug use, diseases, etc.   Assume that you were asked to give a talk to a group of teenagers who are in the early weeks of pregnancy and planning on having their babies. What advice could you give them regarding factors that might influence the course of their pregnancy?   Try to think about how you can give advice that will not just scare them but will also help them make healthy choices for themselves and their babies.

RELATED REFERENCES

Aaronson, L.S., & MacNee, C.L. (1989).   Tobacco, alcohol, and caffeine use during pregnancy. *Journal of Obstetrics, Gynecology, and Neonatal Nursing, 18,* 279-287.

Moore, K.L. (1989).   *Before we are born.*   (3rd ed.).   Philadelphia: Saunders.

ACTIVITY 4-2

EVERYDAY MEDICATIONS AND THEIR TERATOGENIC EFFECTS

INTRODUCTION: This activity relates to the material presented in Chapter 4 (p. 127, 133-134) on the potentially harmful effects of over-the-counter and prescription medications on prenatal development. One purpose is to increase your awareness of the potential for harm to the fetus from a pregnant woman's ingestion of medications. Most gynecologists caution pregnant women to not take any kind of drug without first consulting them. Why? What's the big deal? How can a medication that is not harmful to the mother, but therapeutic, cause damage to a developing fetus? Reasons include:

1. The dose that is therapeutic for a 135-pound woman may be a massive overdose for a developing embryo or fetus.

2. The mother is not undergoing organogenesis (differentiation of the organ systems) but the fetus is.

3. The placenta and immature fetal lever may be unable to convert the medication into a harmless or therapeutic substance.

4. The mother's physiology may be altered, compromising the intrauterine environment.

INSTRUCTIONS: Go through your medicine cabinet and look for those drugs (prescription and nonprescription) that have a warning about taking them when pregnant or nursing. This warning may appear on the bottle, the package insert, or on the original box. Include such medications as aspirin, antibiotics, birth control pills, allergy medicines, cold or flu symptom medications, acne medications, antidepressants, nicotine patches, diuretics, blood pressure medication, PMS drugs, etc. Look up each type of drug in Table 4-3 (p. 133) of the text to see the possible effects. Then write down each medication and its teratogenic effects (if given in text, Table 4-3, or on the package insert). (Note--if you do not take any medications, visit a friend who does and ask to read the labels, or go to a drug store and read the labels on several over-the-counter drugs.) Put together a list of at least five medications and their teratogenic effects.

CHAPTER 4 ANSWERS TO STUDY QUESTIONS

FROM CONCEPTION TO BIRTH

1. (119)   Implantation; alternative <u>a</u>

2. (119)   1 in 4 (25%)

3. (120,127) Indirect; the placenta forms a semipermeable barrier between the bloodstream of the mother and the developing embryo, allowing gases such as oxygen and carbon dioxide, salts, and various nutrients, such as sugars, proteins and fats, to cross.

4. (120)   Neural tube

5. (120)   4th week

6. (121)   a) Males: testosterone
              b) Females: nothing

7. (121)   Fetus

8. (199-122) 3 inches; less than an ounce

              BODY STRUCTURES: head, brain, spinal cord, eyes, ears, nose, mouth, arms, legs
              ORGAN SYSTEMS: heart, sexual organs, other organ systems allowing the fetus to swallow, digest nutrients, and urinate
              MOTOR CAPABILITIES: arm movement, leg movement, hand movement, twisting, turning, somersaulting

9. (122)   Viability

              24th to 28th week

              2 1/4 pounds (1000 grams)

10. (123)   Weight gain

ENVIRONMENTAL INFLUENCES ON PRENATAL DEVELOPMENT

11. (123-124) a) <u>Mothers under 17</u> years of age are at risk for stillbirths, infants who fail to live, and obstetrical complications <u>because</u> the uterus may be immature and pregnant teenages often do not receive adequate prenatal care.
              b) <u>Mothers over 35</u> years of age are at risk for spontaneous abortion, chromosomal abnormalites, and obstetrical complications <u>because</u> they are more likely to suffer from chronic illnesses, to not have sought adequate prenatal care, and because of aging ova.

              No; the majority of older mothers have normal pregnancies and healthy babies.

12. (124-125)   Prolonged, severe stress is associated with pregnancy complications.
                Mother's child-rearing approach. Prenatal levels of activating hormones, such as
                adrenalin, did <u>not</u> predict infants' later temperamental characteristics.

13. (125-126)   Last (3rd) trimester

                a) adequate postnatal diet
                b) stimulating, responsive environment

14. (127)   The infant's body parts and organ systems are evolving and taking shape.

15. (127-128)   a) central nervous system
    (Fig.4-2)   b) heart
                c) arms, legs
                d) eyes, mouth
                e) external genitalia
                f) ears
                g) teeth
                h) palate

16. (128)   a) central nervous system
    (Fig. 4-7) b) eyes
                c) external genitalia

17. (127)   a) hip dislocation
                b) hernias
                c) cataracts
                d) benign tumors

18. (128)   Critical-period principle

19. (128-129)   RUBELLA
                    a) blindness
                    b) deafness
                    c) cardiac abnormalities
                    d) mental retardation
    (129)   GENITAL HERPES
                    a) blindness
                    b) brain damage
    (134)   ALCOHOL
                    a) microcephaly
                    b) malformed heart
                    c) malformed limbs, joints
                    d) excessive irritability/hyperactivity
                    e) seizures
                    f) tremors

20. (134)   a) genetic make up
                b) dosage

21. (132-133)   Small increase in risk of heart malformations, cervical cancer, sterility in males,
    (Tbl 4-3)   masculinization of the fetus

22. (134)   Symptoms are most severe when "doses" are highest, but no amount is considered safe for the developing fetus.

23. (134)   Retards fetal growth, increases risk of spontaneous abortion and newborn death

24. (135-136)   SHORT-TERM EFFECTS: vomiting, dehydration, convulsions, extreme irritability, weak sucking, high-pitched crying, restlessness, tremors, sleep disturbance
LONG-TERM EFFECTS (2-3 years): hyperactivity, attention deficit

25. (136-137)   Alternative c

Smaller, less responsive, less neurologically mature, lag in recognition memory and information processing

BIRTH AND THE PERINATAL ENVIRONMENT

26. (139-140)   PREPARED CHILDBIRTH: greater relaxation in childbirth
FATHER PRESENT: shorter labors, less pain, less medication; more positive toward themselves, families, and the birth process

27. (141)   Postpartum depression is just as likely among mothers of healthy babies as among mothers whose babies died or were abnormal. Factors found to contribute to postpartum depression include hormonal changes that occur after birth, drugs given during delivery, feeling ignored, and having negative feelings toward the pregnancy or marriage.

28. (141-142)   Shows no clear evidence of positive or negative outcomes, although some obstetricians are concerned that complications could get overlooked

29. (143)   Anoxia (oxygen deprivation)

30. (144-145)   PROS: greater comfort for the mother and may reduce chances of anoxia
CONS: may adversely affect infants by making them unresponsive to social stimulation, by making them weak suckers at feedings, or irritable and difficult to comfort. Babies of heavily medicated mothers may show deficits in physical and intellectual development for months.

31. (145-146)   Respiratory; a deficiency of surfactin may result in respiratory distress

32. (146-147)   Touching, rocking, mother's voice, responsive care once home

33. (147)   Postnatal environment; children in unstable, disadvantaged homes remained below average in mental development, whereas children in more advantaged homes scored within the normal range by age 6 years.

34. (147-150)   The long-term consequences depend critically on the postnatal environment in which they are raised. Twin studies from middle-class homes showed these infants eventually made up their intellectual deficits, whereas their counterparts from lower socioeconomic backgrounds remained below average in intellectual performance.

By age 10 home environment was a better predictor of intellectual performance than perinatal complications; poor environment was a much more powerful variable than severe perinatal complication.

35. (149-150)   A Dutch study showed lower mortality rate for home births than for hospital births.

Because mothers who were at risk for complications were instructed to give birth in the hospital

CHAPTER 5

THE PHYSICAL SELF: DEVELOPMENT OF THE BRAIN, THE BODY, AND MOTOR SKILLS

STUDY CHECKLIST

_____ Read Chapter Outline and Summary (Study guide)

_____ Read Chapter (Text)

_____ Completed Vocabulary Fill-Ins (Study guide)

_____ Re-Read Outline and Summary (Study guide)

_____ Reviewed Lecture Notes and Integrated with Text

_____ Reviewed Vocabulary, Study Questions, and Text Chapter

CHAPTER 5 OUTLINE AND SUMMARY

I. **The neonate**
   A. Is my baby all right?
      1. Agpar scale
      2. Brazelton scale
   B. The neonate's "preparedness" for life
      1. Survival reflexes
      2. Primitive reflexes
   C. Living with an infant
      1. A description of infant states
         a. Regular sleep
         b. Irregular sleep
         c. Drowsiness
         d. Alert inactivity
         e. Waking activity
         f. Crying
      2. Developmental changes in state
         a. Sleep patterns
         b. Crib death
         c. The course and functions of crying
      3. Methods of soothing a fussy baby

Neonates are remarkably capable organisms who emerge from the womb prepared for life. They have functioning sense organs; they display some capacity for learning; and they come equipped with a repertoire of inborn reflexes (breathing, sucking, swallowing, and so on) that help them to adapt to their new surroundings. One of the first tests many babies take is the Brazelton Neonatal Behavioral Assessment Scale, an instrument designed to measure their reflexes, social responsiveness, and neurological well-being. This scale is particularly useful for identifying infants who are likely to experience later emotional difficulties.

The infant's state (that is, state of consciousness) changes many times during a typical day. Newborns spend nearly 70% of their time asleep; but as they mature, they spend less time sleeping and more time awake, alert, and attending to the environment. Crying is a state that tells us much about the baby. If a neonate's cries are high pitched and nonrhythmic, he or she may be premature, malnourished, or brain damaged. Normal, healthy infants emit at least three different cries (hunger, anger, and pain) to communicate their wants and discomforts. However, crying usually diminishes over the first year as parents learn how to soothe their crying infants and infants learn to use other methods of communciating with their close companions.

II. An overview of maturation and growth
- A. Changes in height and weight
- B. Changes in body proportions
- C. Skeletal development
- D. Muscular development

The body is constantly changing between infancy and adulthood. Height and weight increase rapidly during the first two years. Growth then becomes more gradual until early adolescence, when there is a rapid "growth spurt." The shape of the body also changes, because various body parts grow at different rates and different times. For example, the head and trunk grow rapidly during the prenatal period and infancy, the limbs are growing fastest in late childhood, and the trunk is once again the fastest-growing segment of the body during adolescence.

Skeletal and muscular development parallel the changes occurring in height and weight. The bones become longer and thicker, and they gradually harden, completing their growth and development by the late teens. Muscles increase in density and size, particularly during the growth spurt of early adolescence. Development of the skeletal, muscular, and nervous system follows a cephalocaudal (head downward) and proximodistal (center outward) pattern: structures in the upper and central regions of the body mature before those in the lower and peripheral regions.

III. Development of the brain and nervous system
- A. Neural development and plasticity
  - 1. An early "reserve capacity"
  - 2. Plasticity of neural development
  - 3. Experiential effects on neural development
- B. Brain differentiation and growth
  - 1. Myelinization
  - 2. Cerebral laterlization

The brain and nervous system develop very rapidly during the last three months of the prenatal period, when neurons proliferate, and the first two years of life, when neurons become organized into interconnected pathways and are encased in myelin--a waxy material that acts like an insulator to speed the transmission of neural impulses. Many neurons and synapses are formed, but only those that are often used are likely to survive. The brain has a great deal of plasticity--a characteristic that allows it to change in response to experience and to recover from many injuries. Although the brain may be organized from birth so that its two cerebral hemispheres serve different functions, children come to rely more and more on one hemisphere to perform specific tasks, and they become increasingly proficient at integrating the respective functions served by their two cerebral hemispheres.

IV.   **Motor development**
    A.   Basic trends in locomotor development
        1.   Evidence for the maurational viewpoint
        2.   Evidence for practice effects
        3.   Motor skills as dynamic, goal-directed systems
    B.   Early Manipulatory Skills and Visual/Motor Coordination
        1.   Locating and grasping objects
    C.   Beyond infancy--Motor development in childhood

Like the physical structures of the body, motor development proceeds in a cephalocaudal and proximodistal direction. As a result, motor skills evolve in a definite sequence: infants gain control over their head, neck, and upper arms before they become proficient with their legs, feet, and hands. As the nervous system and muscles mautre, children gradually acquire more control over their bodies. Yet the increasingly complex motor skills that children display do not simply "unfold" according to a maturational timetable; each emerging skill represents a complex reorganization of several developing capabilities--a reorganization that is perfected through practice as a means of coping with environmental demands or achieving important objectives.

V.   **Puberty--The physical transition from child to adult**
    A.   The adolescent growth spurt
    B.   Sexual maturation
        1.   Sexual development in girls
        2.   Sexual development in boys
        3.   Individual differences in sexual maturation
        4.   Secular trends--Are we maturing earlier?
    C.   Psychological impact of adolescent growth and development
        1.   Reactions of adolescents to puberty
        2.   Does the timing of puberty matter?

At about age 10 1/2 for females and age 13 for males, the adolescent growth spurt begins. Weight increases first, followed some four to six months later by a rapid increase in height. The muscles undergo a period of rapid growth about a year after the greatest growth in height.

Sexual maturation begins about the same time as the adolescent growth spurt and follows a predictable sequence for members of each sex. For females, the onset of breast and pubic-hair development is followed by a widening of the hips, enlarging of the uterus and vagina, menarche (first menstruation), and completion of breast and pubic hair growth. For males, development of the testes and scrotum is followed by the emergence of pubic hair, the growth of the penis, the ability to ejaculate, the appearance of facial hair, and lowering of the voice. Over the past 100 years, males and females have been growing taller and heavier and reaching sexual maturity earlier-- possibly because of improved nutrition and health care. Yet there are wide individual variations in the timing of sexual maturation and growth. Early-maturing males experience fewer psychological and social problems than late maturers. Among females the psychological correlates of early or late maturing are less apparent although early-maturing girls seem to be less popular than prebuscent classmates in grade school but tend to become more popular and self-assured later in adolescence.

VI. **Causes and correlates of physical development**
   A. Biological mechanisms
      1. Effects of individual genotypes
      2. Hormonal influences--The endocrinology of growth
   B. Environmental influences
      1. Nutrition
         a. Problems of undernutrition
         b. Problems of overnutrition
      2. Illness
      3. Climatic effects
      4. Emotional stress and lack of affection

The course of physical development represents a complex interplay between biological and environmental influences. Individual genotypes set limits for stature, shape, and the tempo of growth. Growth is also heavily influenced by hormones released from the endocrine glands. Pituitary growth hormone and thyroxine regulate growth throughout childhood. At adolescence the pituitary stimulates other endocrine glands to secrete their hormones, most notably estrogen from the ovaries (which triggers sexual development in females) and testosterone from the testes (which instigates sexual development in males).

Adequate nutrition is essential for normal growth and development, as is freedom from prolonged and serious illness. Undernutrition makes children more susceptible to the growth-retarding effects of disease; in turn, chronic diseases can interfere with nutrition. Climate affects growth, as differences in the body builds of people from different cultures are adaptations to the varying climates in which these groups live. Finally, the growth disorder known as failure to thrive (deprivation dwarfism) illustrates that emotional traumas can inhibit growth and that sensitive, responsive caregiving is important for normal growth and development.

CHAPTER 5 VOCABULARY FILL-INS
(Definitions below are in order of appearance in text margins)

MATCH VOCABULARY WORD/PHRASE TO ITS DEFINITION.
THEN COVER YOUR ANSWERS TO TEST YOUR MASTERY.

autostimulation theory	REM sleep
cephalocaudal development	skeletal age
fontanelles	sudden infant death
primitive reflexes	syndrome (SIDS)
proximodistal development	survival reflexes

1. _____ Inborn responses such as breathing, sucking, and swallowing that enable the newborn to adapt to the extrauterine environment.

2. _____ Reflexes controlled by subcortical areas of the brain that gradually disappear over the first year of life.

3. _____ A state of active or irregular sleep in which the eyes move rapidly beneath the eyelids and brain-wave activity is similar to the pattern displayed when awake.

4. _____ A theory proposing that REM sleep in infancy is a form of self-stimulation that helps the central nervous system to develop.

5. _____ The unexplained death of a sleeping infant who suddenly stops breathing (also called crib death).

6. _____ A sequence of physical maturation and growth that proceeds from the head to the tail.

7. _____ A sequence of physical maturation and growth that proceeds from the center of the body to the extremities.

8. _____ The six soft spots in a baby's skull where the bones are not fully joined.

9. _____ A measure of physical maturation based on the child's level of skeletal development.

brain growth spurt
cerebral cortex
cerebral lateralization
corpus callosum
dyslexia
equipotentiality hypothesis

glia
multiple sclerosis
myelinization
neurons
plasticity
synapse

10. _____ The connective space (juncture) between one nerve cell (neuron) and another.

11. _____ Nerve cells that receive and transmit neural impulses.

12. _____ Nerve cells that nourish neurons and encase them in insulating sheaths of myelin.

13. _____ The period between the seventh prenatal month and two years of age when more than half of the child's eventual brain weight is added.

14. _____ Capacity for change; a developmental state that has the potential to be shaped by experience.

15. _____ The process by which neurons are enclosed in waxy myelin sheaths that will facilitate the transmission of neural impulses.

16. _____ A crippling loss of muscular control that occurs when the myelin sheaths surrounding individual neurons begin to disintegrate.

17. _____ The bundle of neural fibers that connects the two hemispheres of the brain and transmits information from one hemisphere to the other.

18. _____ The outer layer of the brain's cerebrum that is involved in voluntary body movements, perception, and higher intellectual functions such as learning, thinking, and speaking.

19. _____ The specialization of brain functions in the left and the right cerebral hemispheres.

20. _____ The notion that the cerebral hemispheres are extremely plastic early in life, so that each hemisphere can assume functions normally served by the other.

21. _____ A general label used to describe the abnormal impairments that some seemingly normal individuals experience when learning to read.

pincer grasp
reaction time
ulnar grasp

22. _____ An early manipulatory skill in which an infant grasps objects by pressing the fingers against the palm.

23. _____ A grasp in which the thumb is used in opposition to the fingers, enabling an infant to become more dexterous at lifting and fondling objects.

24. _____ A measure of the time it takes for a person to respond motorically to a test stimulus (for example, the time between seeing a flash and pressing a button).

estrogen
follicle-stimulating
      hormone (FSH)
growth hormone (GH)
luteinizing hormone (LH)
menarche

pituitary
puberty
secular trend
testosterone
thyroxine

25. _____ The point at which a person reaches sexual maturity and is physically capable of fathering or conceiving a child.

26. _____ The first occurrence of menstruation.

27. _____ A trend in industrialized societies toward earlier maturation and greater body size now than in the past.

28. _____ A hormone produced by the thyroid gland, essential for normal growth of the brain and the body.

29. _____ A "master gland" located at the base of the brain that regulates the endocrine glands and produces growth hormone.

30. _____ The pituitary hormone that stimulates the rapid growth and development of body cells; primarily responsible for the adolescent growth spurt.

31. _____ A pituitary hormone that activates the gonads, causing the ovaries to produce estrogen and the testes to produce sperm; helps to regulate the female menstrual cycle.

32. _____ A pituitary hormone that activates the gonads, causing the ovaries to release ova and to produce progesterone and the testes to produce testosterone; helps to regulate the female menstrual cycle.

33. _____ Female sex hormone, produced by the ovaries, that is responsible for female sexual maturation.

34. _____ Male sex hormone, produced by the testes, that is responsible for male sexual maturation.

CHAPTER 5 STUDY QUESTIONS

THE NEONATE

1. Characterize the difference between the **Agpar test** (Chapter 4, p. 142-143 & Table 4-4) and the **Brazelton Neonatal Behavioral Assessment Scale** as assessments of neonatal health status. (Chapter 5, p. 155)

2. The Brazelton Neonatal Behavioral Assessment Scale has been used to train parents of newborns. **What effects has the training been found to have on parenting?** (p. 155, Box 5-1)

    (a)

    (b)

    (c)

3.   List three **survival reflexes** and describe the **significance** of each for survival. (p. 157, Table 5-1)

   (a)

   (b)

   (c)

4.   **Primitive reflexes** such as the Babinski or stepping reflex are short-lived, in part, because they have no clear adaptive function. However, **the absence of one of these reflexes in early infancy or its failure to disappear at the appropriate age is important because:** (p. 156-157, Table 5-1)

5.   **Wolff** mentions two types of sleep, **regular sleep** and **irregular sleep,** in his list of six states of consciousness. How do they differ? (p. 158)

About what **percent** of a **newborn's sleep is irregular** sleep? (p. 159)

6.   What **function** does the **autostimulation theory** and research by **Boismier suggest REM sleep plays** in early development? (p. 159)

7.   What two **symptoms** have been found to **precede death** in 50-70% of **SIDS victims?** (p. 160)

   (a)

   (b)

Is the **cause of SIDS** known? (p. 160)

Is there any reliable means of **prevention**? (p. 160)

8.   What important **function** is **crying** believed to serve? (p. 160)

Has the claim that infants have **discriminably different crys** been supported?
(p. 160-161)

9.   How did **Ainsworth** et al. explain the finding that mothers who were quick
to respond to their young infants' crying, later had infants who cried less? (p. 161)

10.   What methods in addition to feeding have been found to be effective in
soothing a fussy baby? (p. 161-162)

Do **all** babies respond to soothing methods? (p. 161-162)

11.   What does **Brazelton** suggest can be done to **help parents** who have a baby
who is difficult to soothe? (p. 162 & p. 156, Box 5-1)

12.   During what two age periods is **growth the most rapid?** (p. 162)

13.   The **disproportionate size of the neonate's head** (1/4 of the body length) **and the earlier maturation of muscles in the neck** than those in the trunk and limbs are both indicative that early development has taken place in a _____ direction. (p. 163)

The trend of **faster/earlier maturation of the heart and lungs** than of the hands is indicative of the _____ trend of maturation. (p. 163)

14.   What is the name of the **process of gradual change of soft cartilage tissue into bone?** (p. 163-164)

15.   What **method** is sometimes used to **estimate physical maturation?** (p. 164)

How do **males and females compare** on this measure of maturation? (p. 164)

16.   What actually changes with **muscular development** (the number of muscle fibers or muscle mass)? (p. 164)

During adolescence how great is the divergence in muscle mass of males and females? (p. 164)

DEVELOPMENT OF THE BRAIN AND THE NERVOUS SYSTEM

17.   How fully developed is the **brain at birth?** (p. 164-165)

18.   **During what period** of development is **adequate protein** in the diet particularly important for supporting the **rapid brain growth** that occurs? (p. 165)

What is changing during this spurt? (p. 165)

19.   What **relationship** does **Huttenlocher** suggest exists **between the infant's "reserve capacity" of neurons and plasticity** of the young brain? (p. 166)

20.   **Young children** typically **recover more quickly** and fully from brain injury than do adults. Why? (p. 165-166)

21.   What effect have researchers found **experience and environmental stimulation** to have on **neural development?** (p. 166-167 & Box 5-2)

22.   What is the **relationship between brain maturation and maturation of function** in the motor, sensory, and cognitive domains of behavior? (p. 166-167)

23.   What does the disease **multiple sclerosis** (MS) tell us about the **importance of the myelin sheath** that encases the axons of nerves? (p. 167-168)

24.   What does it mean to say that the **brain** is a **lateralized organ?** (p. 168-169)

How early does recent evidence (Kinsbourne) indicate **lateralization** is present? (p. 169)

What phrase characterizes **developmental changes in lateralization?** (p. 169)

Is there any evidence of **integration** or coordination of information from the two hemispheres **in infants? in older children?** (p. 168-169)

What **relationship between dyslexia and cerebral lateralization** has been found (Witelson)? (p. 169)

MOTOR DEVELOPMENT

25.   **Motor development** follows what **two fundamental "laws"** or trends in development (those same trends that muscular development, organ development, and myelinization also follow)? (p. 170-171)

(a)

(b)

26.   What does research evidence suggest regarding the **importance of experience relative to maturation** as a determinant of **locomotor development?** (p. 170-173 & Box 5-3)

27.   What does **Goldfield's** research suggests **motivates** infants to engage in **crawling motions** initially? (p. 173)

28.   Infants come into the world with functioning visual systems and a reflexive palmar grasp. What occurs at approximately **three months** and continues to mature thereafter that reflects increasing **coordination of the motor and visual systems?** (p. 173)

What motor development around 4 months is an important **precursor to exploration of objects using both hands,** one to hold and one to finger the object? (p. 173)

29.   Is development of **motor abilities** completed by school age or is there further maturation of motor abilities into adolescence? Explain your answer. (p. 174-176)

30.   **How do boys and girls compare in physical abilities** such as running speed, broad jump, softball throw, etc. during childhood? during adolescence? (p. 174-176)

CHILDHOOD:

ADOLESCENCE:

31.   What **explanation** has research by **Herkowitz** and by **Dyer** suggested for the **decline in physical performance** of many **girls at adolescence?** (p. 174-176)

PUBERTY--THE PHYSICAL TRANSITION FROM CHILD TO ADULT

32.   What year does **growth peak for males?**   **for females?**   (p. 176)

How variable is the age of the **growth spurt** and of sexual maturation? (p. 176-178)

What is the **average age of menarche?** (p. 177)

33. To what does **Tanner** (1990) attribute the **secular trend** of earlier sexual maturation and greater height and weight of children today? (p. 178-179)

34. **Early sexual maturation** has been found to have **social advantages** for which sex? How is this effect explained? (p. 179-182)

35. Box 5-4 describes two **eating disorders** about which much is being written. **How common and how serious** are these two disorders? (p. 180, Box 5-4)

ANOREXIA:

BULIMIA:

CAUSES AND CORRELATES OF PHYSICAL DEVELOPMENT

36. Why is the **pituitary** sometimes referred to as the "**master gland**"? (p. 183-185)

What two hormones **regulate growth in childhood**? (p. 183)

(a)

(b)

What hormone change is responsible for the adolescent **growth spurt** in males? in females? (p. 184)

37.   What is believed to be responsible for the **greater growth of muscle, bone, and height at adolescence for males** than females? (p. 184)

38.   Distinguish between the causes and the outcomes of the **three types of malnutrition.** Note effects of each type of malnutrition. (p. 186-187)

        MARASMUS

                CAUSE:

                EFFECTS:

        KWASHIORKOR

                CAUSE:

                EFFECTS:

        VITAMIN/MINERAL DEFICIENCY

                CAUSE:

                EFFECTS:

39.   In addition to physical growth, **malnutrition has been found to influence** what other aspects of development either directly or indirectly? (p. 186-187)

40. What **factors** have been found to contribute to many obese children's having a **lifetime weight problem**? (p. 187-189)

(a)

(b)

(c)

41. Some people claim that **climate** is related to body build, height, weight, lung capacity, etc. Is there any evidence supporting this claim? (p. 189-190)

42. Sometimes children who have a potentially adequate diet and no major illness show **"failure to thrive"** syndrome. What is the current view on the **cause of growth retardation in these children**? (p. 190-191)

ACTIVITY 5-1

MY LOOKS AND MY PHYSICAL CAPABILITIES

INTRODUCTION: This activity relates to the material in Chapter 5, particularly the material on the psychological implications of maturation. "Ho-hum, boring" is the reaction of most people when they open up a text to a chapter on physical development. "So kids grow and they get stronger and they lose and gain teeth and they spurt at adolescence...so?" The "so" is that what is going on physically does matter a great deal to the person undergoing the development. The first couple of loose teeth are <u>very</u> significant events to the child losing those teeth. The child may talk about little else for days, may be very concerned about losing a piece of herself and may not want to give up the tooth for the tooth fairy, may be very excited about reaching this milestone that indicates, "I'm getting pretty grownup," etc. Similarly, not being able to make it across the monkey bars is very significant to the child who can not do it. Being able to do the best cartwheel in the class is very significant to the child who can do it. Being the first or last in your grade to wear a bra is very significant to the girls who are first or last. These are just a few examples of changes and abilities that can affect how a child is reacted to by others and how that child feels about himself.

The purpose of this activity is to bring up <u>feelings</u>--not just the descriptions--associated with your appearance and physical capabilities as a child and now. Reading Chapter 5 will be anything but "ho-hum" when you can look at the topic from the perspective of how physical growth and development impacts the individual doing the growing and developing.

INSTRUCTIONS: Write about how you felt about your LOOKS and your PHYSICAL CAPABILITIES at each of the following times in your life:
   a. grade school years
   b. middle school/junior high school years
   c. high school years
   d. now

CHAPTER 5 ANSWERS TO STUDY QUESTIONS

THE NEONATE

1. (143-155)   Brazelton Neonatal Assessment Scale is sensitive to more subtle neurological and behavioral problems.

2. (155)   a) helps parents become more aware of what the infant can do
   (Box 5-1)   b) demonstrates ways of being responsive in their interactions even with at-risk infants
      c) increases both parents' confidence in their caretaking abilities

3. (157)   See Table 5-1 for survival reflexes and their significance

4. (156)   Irregularity of timing of appearance or disappearance of a primitive reflex can be an indication of neurological abnormality.

5. (158)   Irregular sleep is characterized by irregular breathing, the eyes frequently moving beneath closed lids, grimacing, twitching, and movement in response to noise or light.
   Regular sleep is characterized by the opposite, i.e., regular breathing, no eye movement, no response to noise or light.

   50%

6. (159)   REM sleep may provide a source of stimulation to the central nervous system that enables higher brain centers to mature.

7. (160)   a) effortful respiration
      b) feeding changes

   No, although SIDS victims typically have a respiratory infection leading some researchers to suggest a virus as the cause. Other possible causes include chilling, overheating, allergic reactions, and blockage of the nasal passages that is not struggled against.

   No; apnea monitoring is not 100% effective

8. (160-161)   Signaling or communicating needs to caregivers

   Results are mixed; what is clear is that cries signal distress

9. (161)   Because these responsive mothers also were responsive to other, more mature forms of communication when the infant became more capable, such as smiling, talking, etc.

10. (161-162)   Soft rhythmic stimulation (e.g., motion, music, pacifier, being picked up and put to the shoulder)

   No; some are readily soothed, while others are not easily quieted by any methods of soothing

11. (156, 162)   Parents can be trained using the Brazelton Neonatal Behavioral Assessment
    (Box 5-1)   Scale to elicit more positive responses from difficult children.

AN OVERVIEW OF MATURATION AND GROWTH

12. (162)   Infancy, adolescence

13. (163)   Cephalocaudal; proximodistal

14. (163-164)   Ossification

15. (164)   Skeletal age

                 Females are 4-6 weeks ahead of males in skeletal growth at birth and 2 years ahead
                 by age 12.

16. (164)   Muscle mass; infants are born with all the muscle fibers they will ever have

                 Before adolescence, muscle mass is 18-24% of body weight. After adolescence,
                 males' increase to about 40% and females' only slightly to about 24%.

DEVELOPMENT OF THE BRAIN AND NERVOUS SYSTEM

17. (164-165)   About 25% of adult weight

18. (165)   Last three months prenatally and first two years

                 Size of neurons, number of glia cells

19. (166)   Huttenlocher suggests that excess neurons provide "standby" circuits for the young
                 brain that can take over functions of an injured part of the brain.

20. (165-166)   Reserve capacity and plasticity of brain early in development

21. (166-167)   Rats raised in highly stimulating environments have brains with larger neurons,
                 more extensive connections between neurons, and brains that are biochemically
                 different.

22. (166-167)   A direct relationship; the earlier maturing areas of the brain are those controlling
                 the earlier-maturing sensory, motor, and cognitive capabilities.

23. (167-168)   Tells us that myelin is not just facilitory but essential for normal brain functioning

24. (168-169)   The two hemispheres are specialized

At birth, but increases with age

Increasing <u>reliance</u> on a particular hemisphere for certain tasks

Yes, there is evidence of some integration at birth, but integration also increases with age.

Dyslexia was found to be associated with an abnormal pattern of lateralization for spatial tasks.

MOTOR DEVELOPMENT

25. (170-171)   Cephalocaudal trend; proximodistal trend

26. (170-173)   Evidence supports a role of experience (e.g., Dennis; Thelan; Zelazo et al.) and of
    (Box 5-3)   maturation (e.g., Dennis & Dennis; McGraw) in locomotor development;
                 maturation alone is not sufficient.

27. (173)   Out-of-reach visual stimuli

28. (173)   Development of visually-guided reaching

Reaching to midline precedes grasping an object with one hand while fingering it with the other.

29. (174-176)   No; eye/hand coordination, small-muscle coordination, reaction times, large-muscle skills, and strength all improve

30. (174-176)   CHILDHOOD: males and females are similar
                 ADOLESCENCE: females decline slightly in performance while males increase dramatically

31. (174-176)   Sex-role socialization

PUBERTY--THE PHYSICAL TRANSITION FROM CHILD TO ADULT

32. (176-178)   Females, 12 years; males, 14 1/2 years

   (Fig 5-5)   Quite variable, e.g., <u>onset</u> of growth spurt in males may be as early as 10 1/2 years or as late as 16 years.

                 Menarche: 12 1/2 to 13 years

33. (178-179)   Improved medical care, better nutrition

34. (179-182)   Males; greater size and strength often makes him more capable athletically; he may be granted more privileges and responsibilities; his parents are likely to have higher achievement aspirations for him; and he is likely to have less conflict with parents about curfew

35. (180)   ANOREXIA: 1 in 200 females; can be fatal
   (Box 5-4)   BULIMIA: more common than anorexia; about 5% of women suffer from bulima; can have serious side-effects such as heart attacks

CAUSES AND CORRELATES OF PHYSICAL DEVELOPMENT

36. (183-185)   Pituitary plays a triggering role for all other endocrine glands

   a) thyroxine
   b) growth hormone

   An increase in testosterone in males and estrogen in females

37. (184)   Testosterone

38. (186-187)   MARASMUS: too few calories and insufficient protein; remain small in stature; show impaired social and intellectual development
   KWASHIORKOR: get sufficient calories, but little protein; more likely to develop after weaning; characterized by a swollen stomach, thin hair, and skin lesions
   VITAMIN/MINERAL DEFICIENCY: iron deficiency causes irritability, inattentiveness, and listlessness, retards growth, impairs motor and intellectual performance

39. (186-187)   Social development; intellectual development

40. (187-189)   a) fat cells remain in body for life
   b) obese individuals tend to be less active
   c) eating patterns are established early in life

41. (189-190)   Yes; e.g., individuals living at high elevations develop greater lung capacity

42. (190-191)   Severe emotional traumas may cause a growth slowdown by inhibiting the production of pituitary growth hormone.

CHAPTER 6

PERCEPTUAL DEVELOPMENT

STUDY CHECKLIST

_____ Read Chapter Outline and Summary (Study guide)

_____ Read Chapter (Text)

_____ Completed Vocabulary Fill-Ins (Study guide)

_____ Re-Read Outline and Summary (Study guide)

_____ Reviewed Lecture Notes and Integrated with Text

_____ Reviewed Vocabulary, Study Questions, and Text Chapter

CHAPTER 6 OUTLINE AND SUMMARY

I. Controversies about perceptual development

Sensation refers to the detection of sensory stimulation, whereas perception is the interpretation of what is sensed. Philosophers and developmentalists have debated whether basic perceptual skills are innate (the nativist position) or acquired (the empiricist position) and whether perception involves detection of the distinctive aspects of different sensations (differentiation theory) or the cognitive embellishment of sensory input (enrichment theory). Today most theorists have rejected extreme nativist or empiricist positions in favor of an interactionist viewpoint, and many would concede that both detection and embellishment of sensory information contribute to the growth of perceptual skills.

II. "Making sense" of the infant's sensory (and perceptual) experiences
A. The preference method
B. The habituation method
C. Evoked potentials
D. High-amplitude sucking

III. Infant sensory capabilities
A. Vision
B. Audition
C. Taste and Smell
D. Touch, Temperature, and Pain

Researchers have devised several creative methods of persuading infants to tell us what they might be sensing or perceiving. Among the more useful of these approaches are the preference method, the habituation paradigm, the method of evoked potentials, and the high-amplitude sucking procedure. Applying these methods, researchers have learned that the sensory equipment of young infants is in reasonably good working order. Neonates can see patterns and colors and can detect changes in brightness. Their visual acuity is poor by adult standards but improves rapidly over the first six months. Moreover, young infants can hear very well; even newborns can discriminate sounds that differ in loudness, direction, duration, and frequency. The senses of taste and smell are also well developed at birth. Babies are born with definite taste preferences, favoring sweet over sour, bitter, or salty substances. They avoid unpleasant smells and will soon come to recognize their own mother by odor alone if they are breast fed. Newborns are also quite sensitive to touch, temperature, and pain.

IV. Visual perception in infancy
A. Perception of patterns and forms
B. Spatial perception
1. Early research on depth perception-Infants' avoidance of dropoffs
2. Experiments on visual looming and other kinetic cues
3. Experiments on size constancy
4. Experiments on pictorial depth cues
5. Conclusions

Visual perception develops rapidly during the first year. For the first two months of life, babies are "stimulus seekers" who prefer to look at moderately complex, high-contrast targets, particularly those that move. Between 3 and 6 months of age, infants are perceiving forms and beginning to recognize familiar faces. Spatial perception also improves as 3-6-month-olds begin to respond to looming objects, to display size constancy, to recognize pictorial cues to depth, and to fear heights. During the latter half of the first year, infants become increasingly proficient at interpreting visual forms and at estimating size, depth, and distance relations.

V. Auditory perception in infancy
A. Voice recognition
B. Reactions to speech and language
C. The sound of music

The neonate's auditory capabilities are truly remarkable. In the first three days of life an infant can already recognize its mother's voice. Neonates are quite responsive to human speech, and they place the auditory components of language into roughly the same vowel and consonant categories that adults do. Finally, babies prefer music to unpatterned auditory stimulation, and they begin to "bounce" to music and to recognize changes in melody and tempo by 4-6 months of age.

VI. Intersensory perception
A. Theories of intersensory perception
B. Are the senses integrated at birth?
C. Development of cross-modal perception
D. Another look at the enrichment/differentiation controversy
E. Infant perception in perspective

Apparently the senses are integrated at birth, for neonates will look in the direction of sound-producing sources, reach for objects they can see, and expect to see the source of sounds or to feel objects for which they are reaching. As soon as sensory information is readily detectable through two or more senses, infants are likely to display cross-modal perception--the ability to recognize by one sensory modality an object or experience that is already familiar through another modality.

VII. **Perceptual learning and development in childhood**
    A.   Development of attention
        1.   Changes in attention span
        2.   Changes in visual search
        3.   Changes in selective attention
    B.   Development of form perception
        1.   Unmasking visual forms
        2.   Gibson's differentiation theory

Several important perceptual changes take place between infancy and adolescence. Attentional abilities improve as children begin to examine sensory inputs more systematically. Children also become more selective in what they will attend to and more proficient at concentrating on objects and tasks for long periods. As they become more attentive, they begin to identify the distinctive features that differentiate objects and events. This "perceptual learning" is a continuing process that enables the child to gradually become more proficient at interpreting the broad array of stimuli that impinge on the sensory receptors.

VIII. **Environmental influences on perception**
    A.   What kinds of experiences are important?
        1.   Neurological effects of visual deprivation
        2.   Effects of movement on perception
    B.   Social and cultural influences
        1.   Perception of physical stimuli
        2.   Social values and perception
        3.   Social environments and perceptual styles

The environment influences perceptual development in many ways. Deprivation experiments suggest that young animals (and presumably children) must be exposed to patterned visual stimuli that capture their attention if their visual perception is to develop normally. Moreover, our social/cultural environments may influence our auditory perception, our interpretation of artwork, and our judgments about the physical characteristics of objects. Finally, it appears that our cultural and family environments contribute to the development of broad perceptual "styles" (field dependence or field independence) that may have important implications for many other aspects of development.

CHAPTER 6 VOCABULARY FILL-INS
(Definitions below are in order of appearance in text margins)

MATCH VOCABULARY WORD/PHRASE TO ITS DEFINITION.
THEN COVER YOUR ANSWERS TO TEST YOUR MASTERY.

---

differentiation theory
distinctive features
enrichment theory
evoked potential
habituation
high-amplitude sucking
    method

looking chamber
perception
preference method
pupillary reflex
sensation

1. _____ Detection of stimuli by the sensory receptors and transmission of this information to the brain.

2. _____ The process by which we categorize and interpret sensory input.

3. _____ The reflexive action by which the pupils constrict in bright light and dilate in dark or dim surroundings.

4. _____ A theory of perception specifying that we must "add to" sensory stimulation by drawing on stored knowledge in order to perceive a meaningful world.

5. _____ A theory specifying that perception involves detecting distinctive features or cues that are contained in the sensory stimulation we receive.

6. _____ Dimensions on which two or more objects differ and can be discriminated.

7. _____ A method used to gain information about infants' perceptual abilities by presenting two (or more) stimuli and observing which stimulus the infant prefers.

8. _____ An enclosed criblike apparatus used to study infants' visual preferences.

9. _____ A decrease in one's response to a stimulus that has become familiar through repetition.

10. _____ A change in patterning of the brain waves that indicates that an individual detects (senses) a stimulus.

11. _____ A method of assessing infants' perceptual capabilities that capitalizes on the ability of infants to make interesting events last by increasing the rate at which they suck on a special pacifier.

---

cross-modal perception   virtual object
kinesthetic sense   visual acuity
pictorial (perspective) cues   visual cliff
size constancy   visual contrast
social referencing   visual looming
stereopsis

12. _____ A person's ability to see small objects and fine detail.

13. _____ The amount of light/dark transition in a visual stimulus.

14. _____ The use of others' emotional expressions to infer the meaning of otherwise ambiguous situations.

15. _____ Fusion of two flat images to produce a single image that has depth.

16. _____ Depth and distance cues; including linear perspective, texture gradients, sizing, interposition, and shading, that are monocular-- that is, detectable with only one eye.

17. _____ An elevated platform that creates an illusion of depth; used to test the depth perception of infants.

18. _____ The expansion of the image of an object to take up the entire visual field as it draws very close to the face.

19. _____ The tendency to perceive an object as the same size from different distances despite changes in the size of its retinal image.

20. _____ The ability to use one sensory modality to identify a stimulus or pattern of stimuli that is already familiar through another modality.

21. _____ An intangible object (optical illusion), produced by a shadow caster, that appears to occupy a particular location in space.

22. _____ Sensations of motion produced by movements of the muscles, joints, and tendons.

---

attention deficit-
    hyperactivity disorder
attention span

myelinization
reticular formation
selective attention

23. _____ A person's capacity for sustaining attention to a particular stimulus or activity.

24. _____ An area of the brain that serves to activate the organism and is thought to be important in the regulation of attention.

25. _____ The process by which neurons are encased in waxy myelin sheaths that facilitate transmission of neural impulses.

26. _____ The focusing of attention on certain aspects of experience while ignoring irrelevant or distracting sensations.

27. _____ A childhood disorder involving inattentiveness, impulsive behavior, and hyperactivity that often leads to academic difficulties, low self-esteem, and social/emotional problems.

embedded-figures test
field dependence/independence
motion hypothesis

perceptual learning
visual astigmatism
visual cortex

28. _____ A measure of the ability to locate hidden objects in a distracting visual context.

29. _____ Changes in the ability to extract information from sensory stimulation that occur as a result of experience.

30. _____ The area of the brain that receives and interprets visual impulses.

31. _____ A refractive defect of the lens of the eye that prevents the formation of clear, distinct images.

32. _____ The notion that individuals must attend to objects that move in order to develop a normal repertoire of visual/spatial skills.

33. _____ A dimension of perceptual style--namely, the extent to which the surrounding context (the field) affects a person's perceptual judgments.

CHAPTER 6 STUDY QUESTIONS

1.   **Sensation** refers to the _____ by which information about external events is _____ by the sensory receptors and transmitted to the brain.

   Perception refers to the _____ of sensory input by the brain.
(p. 198)

CONTROVERSIES ABOUT PERCEPTUAL DEVELOPMENT

2.   Developmental theorists today take which view regarding the **role of heredity and environment** in perceptual development? (*Circle the correct answer below*) (198-199)

   (a)   heredity is the predominant factor
   (b)   environment is the predominant factor
   (c)   heredity and environment work in an interactive fashion

3.   **Enrichment theory** specifies that we must _____ _____ sensory stimulation by drawing on stored knowledge in order to perceive a meaningful world.

   Differentiation theory specifies that perception involves _____ _____ _____ that are _____ in the sensory stimulation we receive. (p. 199, see margin definitions)

Note: Your text author concludes that there is evidence supporting BOTH theories.

MAKING SENSE OF THE INFANT'S SENSORY CAPABILITIES

4.   Below are listed four **methods for studying infant sensory and perceptual capabilities.** *Match the procedure description to the method.* (p. 199-200)

(P) PREFERENCE   (H) HABITUATION

(EV) EVOKED POTENTIAL   (HAS) HIGH-AMPLITUDE SUCKING

____ The infant hears the sound "ba" repeatedly until his initially elevated heart rate (on another response) has returned to baseline. Then the infant is presented the sound "ga." If the infant cannot tell the difference between "ba" and "ga," heart rate will remain constant. If the infant can detect the difference, heart rate should increase.

____ The infant is provided a pacifier that allows for recording of her rate of sucking. The infant's sucking rate controls the delivery of a series of "BA" sounds on a tape recorder. After the baby's interest decreases and sucking is at baseline, another sound, e.g., "ga," is played when the baby sucks. If the baby can detect the difference between "ba" and "ga," renewed interest will be shown and sucking rate will increase until the baby habituates.

____ The infant is shown a picture of an X and an O simultaneously.   An observer records the amount of time the infant looks at each target. It is assumed that a difference in amount of time viewing the stimuli indicates the ability to detect a difference.

____ Electrodes are placed on the infant's scalp above the temporal lobe of the brain. The sound "ga" is presented and the brain's electrical activity recorded. Then the sound "ba" is presented. If the infant perceives "ba" to be different from "ga," the pattern of electrical activity will differ.

INFANT SENSORY CAPABILITIES

5.   Every new parent wonders: How much can my baby really see, hear, feel, etc? Before techniques were developed for studying infant sensory capabilities it was thought that infants were functionally blind, deaf, and could not feel pain at birth. We now know different. For each of the senses below, characterize in a phrase or sentence what is known about the **infant's sensory capabilities.** (p. 201-204)

VISION:

AUDITION:

TASTE AND SMELL:

TOUCH, TEMPERATURE, AND PAIN:

VISUAL PERCEPTION IN INFANCY

6.   Your text author notes three **properties of visual stimuli** that have been shown to attract infants' attention (p. 205). They are:

(a)

(b)

(c)

7.   Researchers (e.g., Banks & Ginsburg, 1985) report that very **young** infants spend more time looking at a **moderately complex visual pattern** than a highly detailed one. What **explanation** do **Banks and Salapatek** give for this preference? (p. 205)

8.   **Kellman and Spelke** used the habituation procedure to assess whether 4-month-old infants can infer the presence of a whole object when only a part is visible (e.g., rods partially hidden by a block). They found that **4-months-olds were able to infer the object's wholeness only when the rod had been** _____ (moving, stationary) (p. 207 & Fig. 6-4)

9.   One question researchers have asked is whether the infant shows evidence of recognizing forms when only given **partial information**. Stimuli such as those presented in Fig. 6-5 and 6-6 have been presented to infants. It has been found that **before 12 months of age infants** _____ (can, cannot) **interpret "representations" of forms**, i.e., they _____ (do, do not) need all the cues of an actual form to recognize its squareness or humanness, or whatever is its identity. (p. 208)

10.   An intriguing question that many parents ask is, "How early can my infant **discriminate** (tell the difference) **between mom and a stranger** or the difference between two strangers with no other cues than pictures of the face?" **Barrera and Maurer** have demonstrated that these **discriminations can be made as early as** _____ (1, 3, 6, 9, 12) **months.** (p. 209)

A somewhat **older infant** needs less time to make the same discriminations and is less likely to forget the face even after two weeks. This ability to remember a face even after **brief exposure** has been found as early as _____ months (Fagan, 1979). (p. 209)

NOTE: How have researchers demonstrated the above? By using the habituation procedure, which involves presenting a second stimulus after the infant has ceased responding to the first. If the infant responds (indexed by changes in heart rate, respiration, etc.), it is concluded that the infant discriminated the two stimuli.

11.   Researchers have found that before the age of 12 months infants can **distinguish a happy face** from a sad one or an angry one, even when there are no other cues. Indicate below how early with: (p. 209)

STATIC VISUAL CUES ONLY: _____ months

NATURAL DISPLAYS OF EMOTION: _____ months

12.   By 8-12 months many infants begin to take their cues as to what they should be afraid of or what they should laugh at and what they can approach from the people around them, i.e., they **"read" the emotional expressions** of their parents, siblings, and others around them and respond in kind. Developmentalists call this milestone _____ _____. (p. 210)

13.   **Perceiving objects in space** (spatial perception) involves being sensitive to the cues that tell us about size, distance, and depth in the world around us, a 3-D world. Researchers have asked whether the infant is born with the ability to detect and use cues that indicate depth, size, etc. Your text describes research using a visual cliff, looming objects, objects at different distances to assess size constancy, pictures that appear near but are actually far to reach, etc. From this research, it has been concluded that **infants** _____ (do, do not) **show the ability to detect and utilize these cues from birth.** If not, then when do they show these abilities? (p. 214)

DEPTH PERCEPTION   (visual cliff):   _____ months
                    (looming objects):   _____ weeks, sometimes
                                           _____ months, reliably

SIZE CONSTANCY: _____ months

PICTORIAL CUES TO DEPTH
AND DISTANCE: _____ months

Infants initially rely on _____ cues to perceive form, depth, and distance relations. (p. 213)

When an object moves in very close to the face (looms), Yonas and others have shown that infants 3 weeks of age sometimes blink and do so more reliably over the next 3 months. What finding led **Yonas** to argue that **neurological maturation plays a role** in this acquisition? (p. 212)

AUDITORY PERCEPTION IN INFANCY

14.   How early has it been demonstrated that infants prefer their **mother's voice** (and therefore must be discriminating it from other voices)? Why might this be possible? (p. 215)

15.   The **ability to hear the difference between the sounds that make up languages** has been shown to be present as early as _____ for vowel sounds and _____ for consonant sounds. (p. 215)

Why is the **ability to discriminate certain sounds** later **lost**? (p. 215)

16.   In Fig. 6-10 infants are shown to have a higher amplitude of sucking to music than to noise. What does this data tell us about infant ability to perceive the difference between **music and noise** and about their preference in sounds? (p. 216, Fig. 6-10)

INTERSENSORY PERCEPTION

17.   Researchers have shown that the **senses are integrated at birth** by assessing infants' reactions to sensory incongruities such as not being able to touch something that looks touchable (e.g., the illusion of a bubble) or a voice coming from the wrong place. What reaction do infants as young as 8 days show to these situations that illustrates that their senses are integrated? (p. 217)

The text author concluded that the **data** _____ (support, do not support) **the differentiation view** that the senses are integrated at birth? (p. 217)

18.   What about **cross-modal perception**; is it present at birth?   If not, when, for: (p. 217-218)

ORAL-TO-VISUAL TRANSFER: ____ months

VISUAL-AUDITORY TRANSFER: ____ months

What factor has been found to determine **when cross-modal perception will be evident?** (p. 219)

What finding by **Bahrick** provides **support for the differentiation theory?** Explain. (p. 218-219, Fig. 6-11)

PERCEPTUAL LEARNING AND DEVELOPMENT IN CHILDHOOD

19.   What **change in the central nervous system** has been hypothesized to lie behind the gradual improvement of **attention span** throughout childhood? (p. 220)

20.   List three **developmental changes in the deployment of attention** and characterize each. (p. 220-221)

(a)

(b)

(c)

21.   Box 6-2 describes a disorder of the attention system, **attention deficit-hyperactivity disorder** (ADHD). It has been found that ADHD **affects not only the visual and auditory experience of the child but the child's** _____, _____, and _____ development as well. Many ADHD individuals _____ (continue, do not continue) to have more problems in adolescence and adulthood than other individuals. (p. 222, Box 6-2)

22. What three **types of treatments** have been utilized with some success to improve self-esteem and academic performance of **ADHD** children? (p. 222, Box 6-2)

(a)

(b)

(c)

DEVELOPMENT OF FORM PERCEPTION

23. What explanation does Gollin's research suggest for the difficulty a 5-year-old might have in identifying a white rabbit on a white snowy background? (p. 224 & Fig. 6-14)

24. According to **Gibson** perceptual learning is a process of **differentiation**, i.e., children must discover the _____ _____ that differentiate one object (e.g., cat) from others (e.g., dog, squirrel, rat, rabbit, etc.). (p. 224-225)

25. Gibson has found that by age _____ years children are showing the ability to detect the **distinctive features that differentiate letters**, an ability that would greatly facilitate learning to read. (p. 224-225)

ENVIRONMENTAL INFLUENCES ON PERCEPTION

26. Research by **Riesen** with chimpanzees indicates that normal **pattern perception** _____ (is, is not) dependent on some minimal amount of exposure to patterns during the first months of life. (p. 226-227)

Describe how being born with cataracts or visual astigmatisms offers a **human parallel** to Riesen's chimpanzee research. (p. 227)

27. Held and Hein found that kittens who had no chance for self-produced movement in their environment showed perceptual deficits. Later research with both kittens (Walk, 1981) and human infants (**Acredolo, Adams, & Goodwyn**, 1984) indicates that self-produced movement is not as essential as Held and Hein had believed. Their findings indicate that **exposure to** _____ **objects in the environment is what is most critical.** (p. 227-228)

SOCIAL AND CULTURAL INFLUENCES

28. List three types of **social/cultural influences** on perception. (p. 229-230)

(a)

(b)

(c)

29. Witkin has found that individuals differ in their characteristic **style of processing** perceptual information. Some are _____ _____, meaning that **they tend to not be distracted by contextual information** that is not central to a task. Others are _____ _____, meaning that they are **readily influenced by irrelevant or distracting information** in perceptual situations. (p. 230-231)

What child-rearing practices are thought to contribute to a child's characteristic style of processing? (p. 230)

People from **hunter/gatherer societies** tend to be **field** _____, whereas those from **farming and pastoral societies** tend to be more **field** _____ because: (p. 231)

ACTIVITY 6-1

DEVELOPMENT OF SYSTEMATIC ATTENTIONAL/SEARCH STRATEGIES

INTRODUCTION: This activity relates to material in Chapter 6 (p. 221-223) and Chapter 8 (p. 299) on the development of the ability to carry out systematic visual searches. Young children characteristically do not gather information needed for making judgments in a systematic way. We can see the effects of their unsystematic visual search in the errors young children make on word match tests, in finding a needed puzzle piece from an assortment of a dozen possibilities, in finding a lost sock, etc.

INSTRUCTIONS:

Children. Locate two children between 3 and 8 years of age. Ask parental permission for the children to help you with your homework for a developmental psychology class.

Material. Two identical apartment houses are pre-printed for you at the end of this activity description. Cover each window with a piece of index card cut to fit. Put a loop of tape on top of each cover so they can be picked up with the touch of an index finger.

Procedure.
1. Place the two house pages side by side on a table or on the floor. All windows should be individually covered when the child first sees the apartment houses.

2. Introduce the task to the child by saying, **"There are two apartment houses in front of us. The windows are all covered up. I would like to you to find out if the windows are all just the same on the two houses or if some are different. Uncover the windows one at a time. Leave uncovered. Tell me when you know whether the apartment houses are just the same or not--when you know that all the windows are just alike."**

3. Record each child's sequence of lifting the covers by recording the order (1, 2, 3....) in the blanks provided. Also indicate the child's verbalizations, record the number of windows opened before making a conclusion, and record the child's conclusion.

CHILD 1   age ____   **CHILD 2**   age ____

— —   — —   — —   — —
— —   — —   — —   — —
— —   — —   — —   — —
— —   — —   — —   — —

Number of windows opened before concluding that the houses are the same;
Child 1 ____   Child 2 ____

Verbalizations of interest:
Child 1   Child 2

Question. How did the two children differ in their approach to the task and in the accuracy of their conclusions?

RELATED REFERENCES

Vliestra, A.G. (1982). Children's responses to task instructions: Age changes and training effects. *Child Development, 53,* 534-542.

Vurpilloit, E. (1968). The development of scanning strategies and their relation to visual differentiation. *Journal of Experimental Child Psychology, 6,* 632-650.

CHAPTER 6 ANSWERS TO STUDY QUESTIONS

1. (198)   Process, detected

            Interpretation

CONTROVERSIES ABOUT PERCEPTUAL DEVELOPMENT

2. (198)   Alternative c

3. (199)   a) add to
            b) detecting distinctive features, contained

MAKING SENSE OF THE INFANT'S SENSORY CAPABILITIES

4. (199-200)   H, HAS, P, EV

INFANT SENSORY CAPABILITIES

5. (201-203)   a) At birth, vision is about 20/300, meaning that newborns require sharper visual contrasts than adults. Infants see in color.
   (202-203)   b) Newborns hear very well. Infants startle at loud noises and seem to prefer softer sounds. Young infants are particularly responsive to human voices.
   (203)   c) Infants are born with some very definite taste preferences and are capable of detecting a variety of odors.
   (203-204)   d) There is less research in this area; however, evidence indicates that newborns are sensitive to a variety of tactile experiences, to temperature, and to pain.

VISUAL PERCEPTION IN INFANCY

6. (205)   a) high-contrast patterns
            b) moderately complex patterns
            c) things that move

7. (205)   Babies prefer to look at whatever they see well.

8. (207)   Moving

9. (208)   Can, do not

10. (209)   3 months

            5-7 months

11. (209)   a) 7-10 months
            b) 3-5 months

12. (210)   Social referencing

13. (211-214)   Do not

> DEPTH PERCEPTION (visual cliff): 2 months
>   (looming object): 3 weeks, sometimes; 4 months, reliably
> SIZE CONSTANCY: 4 1/2 months
> PICTORIAL CUES TO DEPTH AND DISTANCE: 7 months

Motion

Preterm infants do not begin to blink at looming objects until several weeks after full-term infants do.

AUDITORY PERCEPTION IN INFANCY

14. (215)   During the first 3 days of life <u>because</u> some auditory learning occurs before birth.

15. (215)   2 days for vowels

2-3 months for consonants

Lose ability to discriminate sounds that do not signal meaning differences in their own language

16. (216)   Because infants <u>avoided</u> listening to nonrhythmic noice, and sucked to hear music, it was concluded that infants can perceive the difference between noise and music <u>and</u> that they prefer music.

17. (217-218)   Infants often became frustrated to tears when they failed to touch the object.

Support

18. (217)   ORAL-TO-VISUAL TRANSFER: 1 month, increasing to higher proficiency by 5-6 months
VISUAL-AUDITORY TRANSFER: 4-5 months

(219)   Maturation; infants show cross-modal transfer when the slower maturing of the two modalities has developed sufficiently.

(218-219)   Infants were able to link sights with synchronous, appropriate sounds after only a single exposure.

PERCEPTUAL LEARNING AND DEVELOPMENT IN CHILDHOOD

19. (220)   Myelination of the "reticular formation," the area of the brain responsible for the regulation of attention

20. (220-221)   a) changes in attention span (increase)
b) changes in visual search (more planful and systematic)
c) changes in selective attention (improvement in selectivity)

21. (223)   Academic, social, and emotional development

Continue

22. (222)   a)   drug treatment
    (Box 6-2)   b)   behavior intervention
                   c)   drug treatment and behavior intervention

DEVELOPMENT OF FORM PERCEPTION

23. (224)   There may not be enough distinctive features to provide sufficient visual cues to differentiate the white form of the rabbit from the snow; young children require more cues for differentiation than do adults.

24. (224)   Distinctive features

25. (225)   6-8 years

ENVIRONMENTAL INFLUENCES ON PERCEPTION

26. (227)   Is

                   Even after correction, form perception shows deficits from lack of early exposure.

27. (228)   Moving

SOCIAL AND CULTURAL INFLUENCES

28. (229-230)   a)   culturally-based expectations
                   b)   social values (i.e., a valued object)
                   c)   social environment, particularly parenting style, may promote either a field-dependent or field-independent style of information processing

29. (230)   Field independent, field dependent

    (230-231)   Restrictive, rigid rules linked to field dependence; less restrictive, rule-oriented rearing linked to field independence

    (231)   Field independent, field dependent; because they stress different skills and values (assertiveness and independence for the hunter/gatherer; cooperation and obedience for the farming and pastoral societies)

CHAPTER 7

COGNITION AND COGNITIVE DEVELOPMENT: A PIAGETIAN PERSPECTIVE

STUDY CHECKLIST

_____ Read Chapter Outline and Summary (Study guide)

_____ Read Chapter (Text)

_____ Completed Vocabulary Fill-Ins (Study guide)

_____ Re-Read Outline and Summary (Study guide)

_____ Reviewed Lecture Notes and Integrated with Text

_____ Reviewed Vocabulary, Study Questions, and Text Chapter

CHAPTER 7 OUTLINE AND SUMMARY

I. **What are cognition and cognitive development?**
II. **Piaget's basic ideas about cognition**
    A.   What is intelligence?
    B.   Cognitive schemes: The structural aspects of intelligence
    C.   How is knowledge gained? The functional basis of intelligence

In this chapter we considered Piaget's broad "structural-functional" theory of intellectual development--a theory that evolved from his naturalistic observations and conversations (clinical interviews) with developing children. Influenced by his early training in zoology, Piaget defined intellectual activity as a basic life function that helps the child to adapt to the environment. He described children as active, inventive explorers who construct knowledge (schemes) and modify these cognitive structures through the processes of organization and adaptation. Organization is the process by which children rearrange their existing knowledge into higher-order structures, or schemes. Adaptation consists of two complementary activities: assimilation and accommodation. Assimilation is the process by which the child attempts to fit new experiences into existing schemes. Accommodation is the process of modifying existing schemes in response to new experiences. Presumably, cognitive growth results from the interplay of these intellectual functions: assimilations stimulate accommodations, which induce the reorganization of schemes, which allows further assimilations, and so on.

III. **Piaget's stages of cognitive development**
    A.   The sensorimotor stage (birth to 2 years)
        1.   Growth of problem-solving skills
        2.   Development of imitation
        3.   Object permanence: Out of sight is no longer out of mind
        4.   An overview of sensorimotor development
    B.   The preoperational stage (2 to 7 years)
        1.   The preconceptual period
        2.   The intuitive period
        3.   Does Piaget underestimate the preoperational child?
    C.   The concrete-operational stage (7 to 11 years)
        1.   Some characteristics of concrete-operational thinking
        2.   The sequencing of concrete operations
        3.   Piaget on education

Piaget believed that intellectual growth proceeds through an invariant sequence of stages that can be summarized as follows:

Sensorimotor period (0-2 years). Over the first two years, infants come to know and understand objects and events by acting on them. The sensorimotor schemes that a child creates to adapt to his or her surroundings are eventually internalized to form mental symbols enabling him or her to understand the permanence of objects, to imitate the actions of absent models, and to solve simple problems at a mental level without resorting to trial and error. Although Piaget's general sequences of sensorimotor development have been confirmed, recent evidence indicates that infants achieve such milestones as deferred imitation and object permanence earlier than Piaget had thought.

Preoperational period (roughly 2 to 7 years). Symbolic reasoning becomes increasingly apparent during the preoperational period as children begin to use words and images in inventive ways in their play activities. Although 2- to 7-year-olds are becoming more and more knowledgeable about the world around them, Piaget described their thinking as animistic, egocentric, and unidimensional. Consequently, he claimed that preschool children cannot think logically and will fail to solve problems that require them to consider the implications of several pieces of information or to assume another person's point of view. Yet recent research has challenged Piaget's characterization by illustrating that 3 to 7-year-olds are much more logical and less egocentric when thinking about familiar issues or taking simplified versions of Piaget's tests. Moreover, preoperational children can be trained to solve complex problems such as Piaget's conservation tasks. So preschool children possess an early capacity for logical reasoning that Piaget had overlooked.

Concrete-operational period (roughly 7 to 11 years). During the period of concrete operations, children can think logically and systematically about concrete objects, events, and experiences. They can now add and subtract in their heads, and they recognize that the effects of many physical actions are reversible. The acquisition of these and other cognitive operations permits the child to conserve, seriate, make transitive inferences, and construct mental representations of a complex series of actions. However, concrete operators can apply their logic only to real or tangible aspects of experience and cannot reason abstractly.

Formal-operational period (age 11 to 12 and beyond). Formal-operational reasoning is rational, abstract, and much like the hypothetical-deductive reasoning of a scientist. Attainment of formal operations is associated with other developmental changes and may sometimes contribute to confusion, idealism, rebellion, and adolescent egocentrism. However, not all adolescents and adults reason at this level. Formal operations may elude those who score below average on intelligence tests or who have not been exposed to the kinds of educational experiences that promote this highest form of intellect. Yet intellectual performance, even at this level, is uneven. Adults are most likely to display formal-operational reasoning in their areas of expertise. And some adults may even go beyond formal operations, displaying problem-finding abilities, dialectical thinking, and the ability to construct innovative supersystems.

IV. Language and thought
    A.   Piaget's viewpoint on language and thought
    B.   Vygotsky's theory of language and thought
    C.   Which viewpoint should we endorse?

Piaget argued that language development reflects cognitive development and plays little if any role in the construction of new knowledge. Lev Vygotsky challenged this idea, noting that what Piaget called egocentric speech was really a private "speech for self" that helped children to plan and regulate their problem-solving activities. According to Vygotsky, private speech is eventually internalized to become verbal thought. Recent research supports Vygotsky's position rather than Piaget's and suggests that language plays a very important role in children's intellectual development.

V. An evaluation of Piaget's theory
    A.   The issue of timing
    B.   The competence/performance issue
    C.   Does cognitive development occur in stages?
    D.   Does Piaget explain intellectual development?

Although Piaget has adequately described the general sequencing of intellectual development, his tendency to infer underlying competencies from children's intellectual performance often led him to underestimate and occasionally to overestimate the child's cognitive capabilities. Some investigators have challenged Piaget's assumption that development occurs in stages, and others have criticized his theory for failing to specify how children progress from one "stage" of intellect to the next. Although the Piagetian approach remains the most comprehensive statement on intellectual growth that currently exists, contemporary researchers generally agree that many of Piaget's theoretical propositions simply must be revised if this theory is to retain its influence.

CHAPTER 7 VOCABULARY FILL-INS
(Definitions below are in order of appearance in text margins)

MATCH VOCABULARY WORD/PHRASE TO ITS DEFINITION.
THEN COVER YOUR ANSWERS TO TEST YOUR MASTERY.

clinical method
cognition
cognitive development

cognitive equilibrium
constructivist
intelligence

1. _____ The activity of knowing and the processes through which knowledge is acquired.

2. _____ Changes that occur in mental activities such as attending, perceiving, learning, thinking, and remembering.

3. _____ A type of interview in which a child's response to each successive question or problem determines what the investigator will ask next (see Chapter 1 for an extended discussion of this technique).

4. _____ In Piaget's theory, a basic life function that enables an organism to adapt to its environment.

5. _____ Piaget's term for the state of affairs in which there is a balanced, or harmonious, relationship between one's thought processes and the environment.

6. _____ One who gains knowledge by acting or otherwise operating on objects and events to discover their properties.

accommodation
adaptation
assimilation
behavioral schemes
cognitive operation

invariant developmental
sequence
organization
scheme
symbolic schemes

7. _____ An organized pattern of thought or action that one constructs to interpret some aspect of one's experience (also called cognitive structure).

8. _____ Organized patterns of behavior that are used to represent and respond to objects and experiences.

9. _____ Internal mental symbols (such as images or verbal codes) that one uses to represent aspects of experience.

10. _____ An internal mental activity that one performs on objects of thought.

11. _____ One's inborn tendency to combine and integrate available schemes into coherent systems or bodies of knowledge.

12. _____ One's inborn tendency to adjust to the demands of the environment.

13. _____ The process of interpreting new experiences by incorporating them into existing schemes.

14. _____ The process of modifying existing schemes in order to incorporate or adapt to new experiences.

15. _____ A series of developments that occur in one particular order because each development in the sequence is a prerequisite for those appearing later.

A--not B--error
deferred imitation
inner experimentation
object permanence
primary circular reaction

secondary circular
reaction
sensorimotor stage
tertiary circular
reaction

16. _____ Piaget's first intellectual stage, from birth to 2 years, when infants are relying on behavioral schemes as a means of exploring and understanding the environment.

17. _____ A pleasurable response, centered on the infant's own body, that is discovered by chance and performed over and over.

18. _____ A pleasurable response, centered on an external object, that is discovered by chance and performed over and over.

19. _____ An exploratory scheme in which the infant devises a new method of acting on objects to reproduce interesting results.

20. _____ The ability to solve simple problems on a mental, or symbolic, level without having to rely on trial-and-error experimentation.

21. _____ The ability to reproduce a modeled activity that has been witnessed at some point in the past.

22. _____ The realization that objects continue to exist when they are no longer visible or detectable through the other senses.

23. _____ Tendency of 8- to 12-month-olds to search for a hidden object where they first found it even after they have seen it moved to a new location.

===

animism   precausal or transductive
appearance/reality distinction   reasoning
centered thinking (centration)   preconceptual period
egocentrism   preoperational stage
intuitive period   symbolic function

24. _____ Piaget's second stage of cognitive development, lasting from about age 2 to age 7, when children are thinking at a symbolic level but are not yet using cognitive operations.

25. _____ The early substage of preoperations, from age 2 to age 4, characterized by the appearance of primitive ideas, concepts, and methods of reasoning.

26. _____ The ability to use symbols (for example, images and words) to represent objects and experiences.

27. _____ Attributing life and lifelike qualities to inanimate objects.

28. _____ Reasoning from the particular to the particular, so that events that occur together are assumed to be causally related.

29. _____ The tendency to view the world from one's own perspective while failing to recognize that others may have different points of view.

30. _____ Ability to keep the true properties or characteristics of an object in mind despite the deceptive appearance the object has assumed; notably lacking among young children during the preconceptual period.

31. _____ The later substage of preoperations, from age 4 to age 7, when the child's thinking about objects and events is dominated by salient perceptual features.

32. _____ The tendency to focus on only one aspect of a problem when two or more aspects are relevant.

class inclusion

compensation

concrete operations

conservation

horizontal decalage

identity training

reversibility

seriation

transitivity

zone of proximal
    development

33. _____ The ability to compare a class of objects with its subclasses without confusing the two.

34. _____ The recognition that the properties of an object or substance do not change when its appearance is altered in some superficial way.

35. _____ The ability to reverse, or negate an action by mentally performing the opposite action.

36. _____ The ability to consider more than one aspect of a problem at a time (also called decentration).

37. _____ An attempt to promote conservation by teaching nonconservers to recognize that a transformed object or substance is the same object or substance, regardless of its new appearance.

38. _____ Piaget's third stage of cognitive development, lasting from about age 7 to age 11, when children are acquiring cognitive operations and thinking more locally about real objects and experiences.

39. _____ A cognitive operation that allows one to order a set of stimuli along a quantifiable dimension such as height or weight.

40. _____ The ability to recognize relations among elements in a serial order for example, if A > B and B > C, then A > C.

41. _____ Piaget's term for a child's uneven cognitive performance; an inability to solve certain problems even though one can solve similar problems requiring the same mental operations.

42. _____ Vygotsky's term for the range of tasks that are too complex to be mastered alone but can be accomplished with guidance and encouragement from a more skillful partner.

dialectical reasoning	imaginary audience
egocentric speech	personal fable
formal operations	private speech
hypothetical-deductive reasoning	problem-finding stage
	systematic reasoning

43. _____ Piaget's fourth and final stage of cognitive development, from age 11 or 12 and beyond, when the individual begins to think more rationally and systematically about abstract concepts and hypothetical events.

44. _____ A style of problem solving in which the possible solutions to a problem are generated and then systematically evaluated to determine the correct answer.

45. _____ A form of adolescent egocentrism that involves confusing your own thoughts with those of a hypothesized audience and concluding that others share your preoccupations.

46. _____ A form of adolescent egocentrism that involves thinking that oneself and one's thoughts and feelings are special or unique.

47. _____ According to Arlin, a stage beyond formal operations in which the individual is now capable of using knowledge to ask questions and define new problems.

48. _____ The ability to resolve logical inconsistencies or paradoxes; thought by some to be a stage of reasoning beyond formal operations.

49. _____ The ability to operate on abstract systems to construct higher-order structures (or supersystems).

50. _____ Piaget's term for the subset of a young child's utterances that are nonsocial--that is, neither directed to others nor expressed in ways that listeners might understand.

51. _____ Vygotsky's term for the subset of a child's verbal utterances that serve a self-communicative function and guide the child's thinking.

CHAPTER 7 STUDY QUESTIONS

1.   **Cognition** refers to the activity of knowing, or the mental processes by which knowledge is _____, _____, _____, _____, and _____ _____ _____
_____. (p. 236)

PIAGET'S BASIC IDEAS ABOUT COGNITION

2.   According to Piaget's view of intelligence, **intellectual growth** is stimulated by mismatches between _____ and _____. (p. 237)

3.   Piaget describes the child as a **constructivist**. What does he mean by this assumption? (p. 237-238)

4.   What does Piaget call the models or **mental structures** that a person creates to represent, organize, and interpret experience? (p. 238)

5.   Piaget describes three types of **schemes**. Using a phrase, characterize each and indicate what age child uses those types of schemes predominantly. (p. 238-239)

SENSORIMOTOR SCHEMES:

SYMBOLIC SCHEMES:

OPERATIONAL SCHEMES:

6.   According to Piaget intelligent behavior is behavior that is adaptive. **Adaptation occurs as a result of two complementary activities,** assimilation and accommodation. Define **assimilation of accommodation** and give an example of each. (p. 240)

ASSIMILATION:

ACCOMMODATION:

7.   What is the **structure** called **that undergoes modification when accommodation occurs?** (p. 240)

PIAGET'S STAGES

8.   Piaget argued that **intellectual development occurs in stages** or an invariant developmental sequence. **He attributes the fixedness in order to what?** (p. 240-241)

(a)

(b)

9.   Did Piaget view the **age** at which a child reaches any given stage of intellectual development with the same invariance that he attributed to the sequencing of stages? Explain. (p. 241)

PIAGET'S STAGES: SENSORIMOTOR

10. **Important advances occur during the sensorimotor period** (birth to 2 yr.) in three main areas. Summarize by specifying the nature of the gains in each area. *Underline the key words that indicate what is gained. The first one is answered for you.* (p. 241-245, Table 7-1)

PROBLEM-SOLVING SKILLS: goes from responding with a limited set of reflexes <u>to</u> repeating behaviors that produce interesting consequences (circular reactions) <u>to</u> intentionally coordinating unrelated behaviors as a means-to-an-end <u>to</u> overt trial and error problem solving <u>to</u> internal, symbolic problem solving.

IMITATIVE ABILITIES:

OBJECT CONCEPT:

11. Box 7-1 presents an update on **object permanence** research. **Piaget** inferred that young infants do not search for a vanished object because they no longer remember its existence once it has disappeared. Research by **Baillargeon and Graber** (1988) and **Diamond** (1985, 1988) indicates that infants **may remember** that the object is there **but lack the ability to** _____ . (p. 246-247, Box 7-1)

PIAGET'S STAGES: PREOPERATIONAL

12. What kinds of **new cognitive activities are possible** for the **preconceptual child because of the appearance of symbolic thought**, i.e., the ability to use words and images to represent experiences? (p. 246-247)

According to Piaget _____ (cognitive, language) **development promotes** _____ (cognitive, language) **development**, not vice versa. That is, language is a manifestation of symbolic ability, not its "cause." (p. 246-247)

What positive contributions or **functions** is **pretend play** believed to make to a child's social, emotional, and intellectual development? (p. 248-249, Box 7-2)

13. **Piaget's** experiments with preschoolers led him to describe the **preconceptual child** as **animistic** and **precausal**. Characterize each type of thinking (p. 249-250). Then indicate what more recent studies have found. Finally, indicate what conclusion the text suggests is warranted about animism and causality at this time. (p. 254)

ANIMISM:

Recent Findings/Conclusions:

PRECAUSAL THINKING:

Recent Findings/Conclusions:

14. According to **Piaget**, the most striking deficiency in children's **preoperational reasoning** is its **egocentrism**. What does Piaget mean by egocentrism. (p. 249-250) What have more recent studies found? What conclusion is warranted according to the text? (p. 253-254)

EGOCENTRISM:

Recent Research:

Conclusion:

15. One manifestation of the young child's egocentric focus is difficulty attributing true identity when something looks different from what it really is (e.g., an eraser that looks like a Hershey bar; reality is an eraser but appearance is a Hershey bar). **Under what two conditions have Flavell and his colleagues found that 3-year-olds can distinguish reality from appearance?** (p. 250-251)

(a)

(b)

16. During the **intuitive period** (ages 4-7), how does **Piaget** describe/explain the **difficulties** children have with classification and conservation? (p. 251-252)

CLASSIFICATION:

CONSERVATION: (give three deficits)

17. Figure 7-4 presents examples of five conservation tasks. In each conservation task **a change occurs in how the materials** _____ rather than in actual amount, area, volume, etc. (p. 251-253 & Fig. 7-4)

18. Recent research on **conservation** indicates that **Piaget underestimated the preoperational child's cognitive abilities.** What training strategy has been found to be effective? What conclusion can be drawn? (p. 254-255)

TRAINING STRATEGY:

Conclusion:

Piaget's research may have **underestimated the preoperational child's cognitive capabilities because:** (p. 255)

(a)

(b)

19.   **Information-processing theorists** attribute young children's difficulties on complex, multidimensional tasks such as **conservation** and **class inclusion** to what? (p. 255)

PIAGET'S STAGES: CONCRETE OPERATIONS

20.   Describe what "concrete" and "operational" refer to in the **concrete-operational stage** designation. (p. 256)

CONCRETE:

OPERATIONAL:

21.   **Class inclusion** and **conservation** are both **concrete-operational acquisitions. Characterize** the two additional acquisitions listed below. Note whether **recent research** indicates some capability to perform these tasks by preschoolers. Also note any **limitations** concrete-operational children may have. (p. 256-257)

CONSTRUCTING COGNITIVE MAPS:

RELATIONAL LOGIC:

22.   **Horizontal decalage** refers to the fact that acquisitions of a given type, e.g., conservation tasks in Fig. 7-4, _____ (are, are not) attained simultaneously. (p. 252, 257) What **explanation** of horizontal decalage did Piaget offer? (p. 257)

23.   What did **Case** (1985) and **Kuhn** (1988) find about **sequencing of tasks** that **challenges Piaget's assumption** that some operational schemas are prerequisites for other, more complex ones? (p. 258)

24.   What type of **educational strategy** does **Piaget** suggest would be most effective in actually promoting real understanding of concepts? (p. 258)

25.   **Piaget emphasized self-initiated discovery** as leading to cognitive growth, the Russian developmentalist Lev **Vygotsky** stressed _____ _____. (p. 258-259)

26.   What evidence have **Freund** (1990) and **Radziszewska and Rogoff** (1988) found to support Vygotsky's emphasis? (p. 259)

PIAGET'S STAGES: FORMAL OPERATIONS

27.   Your text author uses three words in his summary of adolescent thought to characterize it. He says **formal thought** is _____, _____, and _____. (p. 261)

28.   Using the four beaker task or one of your choosing, **contrast** how the **formal-operational child** and the **concrete-operational child** would approach the task. (p. 260-261)

29.   We often think of young children as being more creative than older ones but the results of Box 7-3 suggest otherwise. What **formal-operational acquisition is believed to lie behind the older children's greater variety and creativity** in responding to the task of drawing where a third eye might go? (p. 261, Box 7-3)

30.   Achieving **formal-operational thought** is believed to open the way for **changes in other areas**, some positive, some less so. Characterize the nature of **positive and negative changes made possible by formal-operational thought.** (p. 262)

POSITIVE:

NEGATIVE:

31.   Piaget maintained that with the acquisition of formal thought comes a temporary period of increased egocentrism. Elkind has identified two forms of adolescent egocentrism. Describe each. (p. 262-263)

IMAGINARY AUDIENCE:

PERSONAL FABLE:

More recently Lapsley et al. has suggested that the imaginary audience and personal fable phenomena are not forms of egocentrism but instead reflect the growth of what new social-perspective-taking ability? (p. 263)

32.   What factors influence whether an individual reaches formal operational thought and influence the content areas in which an individual will show formal reasoning? (p. 263-264)

33.   What answer have researchers given to the question "Are there higher levels of intellectual development than formal thought"? (p. 264)

LANGUAGE AND THOUGHT

34.   Piaget claimed that self-talk was a sign of immature, egocentric communication attempts. In contrast Vygotsky claimed that self-talk (private speech) can facilitate a child's problem solving and is a precursor to internalized inner speech. The text concludes that Vygotsky's view has received more support. List three **types of evidence that support Vygotsky's view of private speech.** (p. 266)

(a)

(b)

(c)

AN EVALUATION OF PIAGET'S THEORY

35.   **Piaget's theory** has drawn four major **criticisms**. Specify the issue for each.
(p. 267-269)

TIMING:

COMPETENCY/PERFORMANCE:

STAGES:

EXPLAINING COGNITIVE CHANGE:

ACTIVITY 7-1

CONSERVATION OF NUMBER

INTRODUCTION: The purpose of this activity is to gain first-hand observations of how children of different ages respond to Piagetian tasks. This experience can demonstrate quite graphically how children at different developmental levels approach the same situation. It also makes very clear that we cannot always assume that a child will get the same information or use the same information that we do from a situation.

This activity relates to material in Chapter 7 (p. 251-254). Read the author's coverage of conservation and also look at the Piagetian conservation tasks illustrated in Figure 7-4 (p. 252). Note that common to all of the tasks is a transformation in shape, location, container, etc., a transformation that changes the appearance of one of the initially identical materials. In all cases, except number conservation, there is no way to know that the transformed substance is still the same amount (or area or volume) unless you actually observed the transformation and used that as your basis for making a judgment regarding sameness, rather than using how the transformed substance looked. It is a tendency to rely on how things look that is believed to lie behind the non-conservation responses that young children give.

Mastery of the **conservation of number task** is believed by some educators and developmental psychologists to be a prerequisite to understanding arithmetic since it requires the ability to establish a 1:1 correspondence between two sets of objects and to understand that those sets do not change in number unless something is added or taken away. It would be difficult to truly understand addition and subtraction if you believed sets could lose their equality just by rearranging positions of the objects within a set.

There is considerable controversy in the literature about what constitutes a conservation response, leading to inconsistencies in conclusions about children's capabilities. For the purposes of this project a child will be considered a "conserver" if she (a) asserts that there are still the same number of candies even when they have been rearranged and (b) gives an explanation that falls in at least one of the following categories:

(1) reversibility, e.g., "could just put the candies back the way they were, and there would still be the same number"

(2) compensation, e.g., "this row has gotten longer/shorter, but there's more/less space between the candies"

(3) addition/subtraction, e.g., "haven't added any candies or taken any away so must still be the same number"

(4) identity, e.g., "they are still the same candies, so must still be the same number"

A child will be considered "transitional" if she is inconsistent across subtasks or answers "yes, there are the same number" but does not give a convincing reason such as one of the four above. A child will be considered to be a "nonconserver" if she gives a "no, they are not the same any more" answer and/or gives a perceptually-based reason or an idiosyncratic response (e.g., "I just know" or "my mom told me").

INSTRUCTIONS:

Children. Locate two children, one 3-5 years of age and the second 6-9 years. Ask parental permission to do some tasks with their child as homework for your developmental class.

Materials. Small bag of M & Ms or other small, uniformally sized candies.

Procedure. Before actually working with a child, go through the procedure by yourself or with a friend playing the child. Practice placing the candies and going through the procedure. When you feel comfortable with the task presentation, then you are ready to meet with your first child.

1. Lay out a row of 5 candies, e.g.,   0 0 0 0 0

2.. Lay out a second row of 5 candies   0 0 0 0 0

Say: "I'm going to make a second row that has just the same number of candies."

Ask: "Do both rows still have the same number of candies? How do you know that?"

Response: (younger child)

Response: (older child)

3. Next, move the candies in the second row close together so there is no space between them, e.g., **00000**

Say: "Now I'm going to move this row of candies close together like this."

Ask: "Are there still the same number of candies in both rows?   How do you know that?" (Write down child's verbatim response)

Response: (younger child)

Response: (older child)

Ask: "What if we were going to eat the candies and I took this row (longer) and you took this one (shorter). Would it be fair? Would we both have the same amount of candy to eat?"

Response: (younger child)

Response: (older child)

4. Space the short row out now so that it is much longer than the first row, e.g.,   0   0   0   0   0

Ask: "Are there still the same number of candies in each row now? How do you know that?"

Response: (younger child)

Response: (older child)

5. Try any variations you want in (a) presentation of the materials or (b) way the questions are asked. Be sure to write down exactly what you did and said and exactly how each child responded. Also write about what effect you thought your variation might have and why, and then indicate whether your expectation was confirmed or disconfirmed.

6. Thank the child for participating and allow the child to eat one row of the candies. Note which row the child actually chooses, the longer row or the shorter, and what the child says.

Questions for you to answer

1. Based on your limited sample of children, what tentative conclusions would you draw about conservation of number for the two ages you assessed?

2. Do your findings support Piaget's view that preschoolers have no understanding of conservation of number, or do they support the view that even preschool children show some evidence of understanding of conservation?

3. What factors do you think might affect whether or not a young child shows conservation of number (or substance, or weight or liquid, etc.)?

RELATED REFERENCES

Your Shaffer text, p. 251-253, 254-255.

Gelman, R., & Baillargeon, R. (1983). A review of some Piagetian concepts, p. 181-184. In P.H. Mussen (ed.) *Handbook of Child Development, Vol. III*, New York: John Wiley & Sons.

Gelman, R., & Gallistel, C.R. (1986). *The child's understanding of number.* Harvard University Press.

Rothenberg, B.B. (1969). Conservation of number among four- and five-year-old children: Some methodolocial considerations. *Child Development, 40*, 383-406.

Sophian, C. (1988). Early developments in children's understanding of number: Inferences about numerosity and one-to-one correspondence. *Child Development, 59*, 1397-1414.

Winer, G.A., Hemphill, J., & Craig, R.K. (1988). The effect of misleading questions in promoting nonconservation responses in children and adults. *Developmental Psychology, 24*, 197-202.

ACTIVITY 7-2

ANIMISM AND ANTHROPOMORPHISM

INTRODUCTION: In a discussion of causal thinking, your text (p. 254) noted that Piaget's research had led him to conclude that preoperational children are animistic thinkers, i.e., they tend to attribute life and, sometimes, human qualities to inanimate objects. Although there is little question that animistic responses are produced by children (and by adults in some cultures), there is considerable controversy about whether it is appropriate to characterize the preschooler's thought as pervasively animistic. It is possible that animistic responses simply reflect ignorance about the qualities of a particular object. Some have suggested that the decrease with age in animistic responses to various objects reflects an increase in familiarity and knowledge of the defining properties of objects rather than a decline in the pervasiveness of animistic thought.

Whether because of a pervasive animistic quality of thought or because of uncertainty of attributes or some other reason, children seem to be particularly fascinated by stories about trucks that have personalities and can talk, about animals with human qualities, about stuffed animals who come alive such as the timid, weak Piglet or the pessimistic Eeyore in Winnie The Pooh, with cartoons that feature animals with human characteristics, with dolls or stuffed animals that have built-in tapes, animal puppets, etc. There is little question that younger children are particularly fascinated with such toys, books, and cartoons. The question is "Why?" Does their fascination reflect a pervasive tendency to attribute life to everything as Piaget maintained or does their fascination perhaps reflect that they are less certain than adults about the boundaries between alive and not-alive, human and not-human? Could the young child's fascination with talking animals also reflect a lack of constancy regarding identity?

The purpose of this activity is to provide you with an opportunity to gain first-hand interaction with children and to explore ways of assessing their understanding of the distinctions between alive/not-alive and human/not-human.

INSTRUCTIONS:

Part A

Visit the children's department of your local public library. Ask where the books for preschoolers are located. Sample several books. Briefly describe those books that feature animals with human qualities (talk, have feelings, engage in human activities, etc.) or feature inanimate objects as characters in the book with personalities and other human qualities.

Part B

Children. Locate two children, one 3-5 years old and another 6-9 years old. Get parental permission to ask their child some questions about how she knows something is living or human (or neither) as homework for your developmental psychology class.

Materials. Cut out pictures of several objects from magazines and catalogues to use for this project. Possible pictures to include are: real animals, stuffed toy animals, dolls, real children, wind-up toys, real cars, toy cars, a mountain, a rock, a waterfall, a swing, etc. The pictures should include some things that are in real-life alive, some that are human, some that are alive but not human, and some that are not alive. Include a maximum of three examples of each of those four categories.

Develop a set of questions to ask the child about each picture. The questions will concern attributes that distinguish living from nonliving and human from non-human, e.g.,

1. Do _____ eat?
2. Do _____ ever get sick or die?
3. Do _____ grow from babies to adults?
4. Do _____ talk like we do or just make sounds or nothing at all?
5. Do _____ have happy feelings and sad feelings and angry feelings like we do?
6. Do _____ think about things the way we do?
7. Are _____ alive/living? (choice of word "alive" or "living" may elicit somewhat different responses)

Be sure that you prepare a response-recording sheet ahead of time that includes the age of the child at the top, the name of each object presented; and, under each object, the number of the question that goes with each response; e.g.,

Child _____ years _____ months

DOLL
   Q1: (child's response)
   Q2:   "
   Q3:   "

.
.
.
.

Procedure. Present the pictures one by one in random order. Each time a picture is presented ask the child each of the questions that you developed. Record the child's responses. Also record any questions the child asks you.

The literature on animism has produced very inconsistent results in part because there are apparently many factors that affect how a child will respond. The particular objects presented or wording of the questions can affect the child's response. You may want to see whether you get a different response by changing the wording. (Be sure to record exactly what you asked as well as the child's response.)

WRITE-UP: Write a summary of your children's books survey and a summary of the data collected from the two children you questioned. Be sure to include a copy of the questions that you asked and a list of the pictures you presented. Note whether the children showed inconsistency in response over objects of the same type. Indicate what factors you think might affect how a child responds and why. If you made systematic variations in wording when questioning children, include the results. What conclusion would you draw based on the material presented in the text and your limited questioning of two children regarding the pervasiveness of animism and anthropomorphism in the thinking of young children?

RELATED REFERENCES

Your Shaffer text, p. 254.

Behrend, K.G., & Dolgrin, D.A. (1984). Children's knowledge about animates and inanimates. *Child Development, 55,* 1646-1650.

Bullock, M. (1985). Animism in childhood thinking: A new look at an old question. *Developmental Psychology, 21,* 217-225.

Loft, W.R., & Bartz, W.H. (1969). Animism revisited. *Psychological Bulletin, 71,* 1-19.

ACTIVITY 7-3

CHILDREN'S USE OF IMAGINED SPATIAL COORDINATES IN DRAWING CHIMNEYS, TREES, AND WATER LEVEL

INTRODUCTION: This activity relates to material presented in Chapter 7 and Chapter 8, specifically to children's concept development and the nature of memory. It involves the administration of a Piagetian task not discusssed in the text and the collection of two types of drawings from children. It is recommended because these tasks are a good catalyst for interaction with children as well as providing interesting data. The three tasks are drawing of a house with a chimney, drawing of a hill with trees, and a Piagetian water-level task.

Although children get many exposures to what a house with a chimney looks like or what trees look like growing out of the side of a hill, many preschool and early grade school children err in the orientation of chimneys on pitched roofs and trees on hillsides. They draw them perpendicular to the roofline or hillside rather than perpendicular to the less salient (but imaginable) "ground line." What is striking is that the nature of the error made is common across children of about the same age and developmental level--it is not random, suggesting that the error may reflect some incorrect, oversimplified assumption about reality. Also striking is the fact that many children will persist with the error in their drawing even when a correct drawing is in view and even when they can distinguish between a correctly drawn chimney and one drawn perpendicular to the roofline. Errors in placement of trees and chimneys is also quite independent of drawing ability. Some children will draw beautifully detailed pictures with the chimney at a cock-eyed angle. It strikes older children and adults as odd, just the way it strikes adults as odd when a child miscontrues an explanation that we have given them (perhaps about conception, electricity, the tides, etc.).

Even once their drawings of chimneys and trees are more in keeping with reality, many children still exhibit difficulty on another task that also involves using imagined coordinates: the Piagetian water-level task.

The water-level task involves the child indicating the water level in jars that are tipped in various orientations. Even by 11 years of age only about 50% of children respond correctly. Some individuals have difficulty into adulthood (even some college students!) despite the fact that they have undoubtedly seen liquid in tipped containers hundreds of times.

Some researchers have suggested that these errors reflect the fact that human memory is reconstructive. They further suggest that a similar type of error may occur across individuals if these individuals have all arrived at an oversimplified, erroneous notion. In the case of the chimney and tree drawing tasks, that oversimplified notion may be one about spatial relations. Young children may equate "on a surface" with perpendicular. In the case of the tipped bottles, erroneous responders may be assuming that the contents of a container move with the container or that the contents are always at the bottom.

CHILDREN: Locate two (or more) children between ages 4 and 12. Ask parental permission for the children to do some drawings for you as part of your homework for a class project. (Children will typically beam and be eager to cooperate if you also tell them that they are helping you with your college homework.)

MATERIALS: You will need paper, colored pens or crayons, and the water-level task (provided in this manual), and, for some children, prepared pictures of houses and hills for follow-up assessment (also provided in this manual). You may need a protractor to measure the deviation from correct orientation.

INSTRUCTIONS:

  Part A (**Drawing Tasks**)--After you have become acquainted with the child, ask the child to draw a house with a chimney. Tell the child you would like the kind with a steep roof (show what you mean using your index fingers to make an upside down V). Then ask for a mountain with trees on it. Praise the child's work and thank the child for making pictures for you. Explain that you would like to take the pictures to show your teacher.

Possible complications that you may run into include a child drawing a flat roof, putting the tree between two mountains, or drawing the chimney or trees on the face of the roof or hillside. Encourage the child to draw a sloped roof or draw one for the child if child is young. If you are unable to obtain a sloped roof, let it go but recognize that the drawing is "unscoreable" for this assignment.

Part A-1 (Memory Task)--If a child's chimney or trees were not drawn correctly, i.e., not drawn perpendicular to the imaginary ground line, show the child a picture of a house/mountain and say: **"Here is a picture of a house/tree. Notice that it has a chimney/tree."** Now show the child the half of the page that has the chimney/tree missing and say: **"Here is another house/mountain. The chimney/tree is missing. Would you put it on, please?"** Be sure to have the child draw from memory, without being able to see the correct drawing (fold the half of the page with the correct drawing underneath).

Part A-2 (Copying Task)--If a child's drawing of the chimney or tree still is not correct even after being shown the correct drawing (Part A-1), then leave the correct models in view and ask the child to add the chimney/tree to the pictures missing a chimney and tree.

Part A-3 (Recognition Task)--If a child fails to "match" the model chimney and tree orientations, then show the child the pair of drawings, one with the correct chimney/tree orientation and one incorrect. Ask the child to choose the drawing that shows how chimneys on houses really look and the one that shows how trees on mountains really look. Record the child's choice.

Part B (Water-Level Task)--Inform the child that you have one more thing you would like help with. Put out the sheet that has jars tipped in various orientations. Explain that the bottles all have caps so that no juice can run out no matter how they are tipped. Then ask the child to pretend that each bottle is about half-full and to color in the juice to show where it would be. You may demonstrate what you mean by coloring in the untipped jar. (Make a distinct line showing the level of the juice and then fill in the juice.)

WRITE-UP: Prepare a summary of your project that includes

1. Age of each child.

2. Description of each child's drawings, particularly the orientation of the chimney and tree (correct, perpendicular to roof or hill, or number of degrees of deviation from true vertical).

3. Whether accuracy was the same or different for the two drawings (accuracy on the chimney orientation often precedes correct orientation for trees).

4. Comparison of the two children's drawings (note if accuracy was related to age as is typical or if not).

5. For the children who erred in their chimney/tree orientations, note whether there was improvement when drawing from memory (Part A-1), when drawing with a visible model (Part A-2), or not until the recognition task (Part A-3) (most children can recognize the correct orientation irrespective of how deviant the orientation is in their own drawing).

6. Description of the water-level results indicating the number of jars in which the "top" of the juice was parallel with the bottom of the paper, i.e., correct; description of the nature of incorrect responses, e.g., level parallel with side of jar, level parallel with bottom of jar no matter what the orientation, water in correct end of the bottle but level not parallel with the bottom of the paper (or imagined horizontal coordinate), etc. (Place a letter beside each jar to refer to in your write-up description of each child's task performance if it varied from jar to jar.)

7. Comparison of the water-level results for the two children.

8. Attach the children's drawings and water-level sheets.

COMPARISONS WITH CLASSMATES' RESULTS: It is useful to be able to look over drawings brought in by classmates. You will see a clear developmental trend in the maturity of the chimney/tree orientations and water level results, but you will also see considerable individual variability. An occasional 10-year-old will draw a chimney or tree at quite a deviant angle. Some 6-year-olds' orientations of chimneys and trees will be very deviant from the vertical, whereas others will be perfectly vertical. You will see a lack of relationship between "artistic ability" and accuracy of orientation. You will see some surprising errors in children's representations of water level and you will find most children are not accurate. You will find yourself generating hypotheses about why children may have erred on the water-level task and have interesting ideas about alternate ways of tapping their understanding of water level.

RELATED REFERENCES

Beilin, H., Kagan, J., & Rabinowitz, R. (1966). Effects of verbal and perceptual training on water-level representations. *Child Development, 37,* 317-328.

Bjorklund, D. (1989). *Children's thinking: Developmental function and individual differences.* Pacific Grove, CA.: Brooks/Cole Publishing Co., p. 158-160.

Cowan, P.A. (1978) *Piaget: With feeling.* New York: Holt, Rinehart and Winston, p. 156-157. (See Fig. 10 for drawings of the stages in the development of chimney, tree and water-level orientation.)

Liben, L.S. (1981). Copying and reproducing pictures in relation to subjects' operative levels. *Developmental Psychology, 17,* 357-365.

Madden, J. (1986). The effects of schemes on children's drawings of the results of transformations. *Child Development, 57,* 924-933.

Perner, J., Kohlmann, R., & Wimmer, H. (1984). Young children's recognition and use of the vertical and horizontal in drawings. *Child Development, 55,* 1637-1645. (Good discussion of possible interpretations.)

Memory
A-1

Copying
A-2

Recognition A-3

TOP

age _____

TOP

age ____

ACTIVITY 7-4

EXAMPLES OF THREE FORMAL-OPERATIONAL ACQUISITIONS

INTRODUCTION: This activity focuses on the formal-operational stage of Piaget's theory of cognitive development. (See Chapter 7, p. 260-264, of the text for an overview.) Piaget maintained that adolescents develop formal thought operations that finally give them the tools to think logically, systematically, and hypothetically. There are more than a dozen different thought operations that Piaget identified as emerging during adolescence. Based on his original work, Piaget assumed that nearly everyone of normal intelligence would develop formal thought operations. Piaget subsequently modified that assumption as he and others found that by the end of adolescence (or even in adulthood) not everyone acquires facility with all of the formal thought operations that Piaget had identified, nor is everyone facile in utilizing the ones they do acquire with unfamiliar content. Education, experience, and utility for daily living are factors influencing whether an individual will develop a particular thought operation.

This activity provides three examples of types of formal thought operations. The purpose of the activity is to help you understand that a formal operation provides for the knower a tool or strategy for solving logical problems that might be encountered, a strategy for understanding some aspect of reality.

INSTRUCTIONS: Try all three problems. Do the best you can and realize that some may be easier than others for you, depending, in part, on your major, interests, and previous education. Show your work. This activity is intended to serve as the basis for discussion of formal thought or as an accompaniment to your reading in the text. Getting the answer "right" is incidental to the activity, although it is important to find out how to find the answer so that you can better appreciate the particular thought operation utilized in the solution.

Problem 1--Proportional Reasoning

What weight child sitting at a distance of 9 feet from the fulcrum of a teeter-totter would balance a 150-pound man sitting at a distance of 3 feet?

Answer: _____-pound child

(Show the "formula" for computing the answer; note that the "formula" provides a content-free strategy for arriving at a solution, i.e., it is an example of what Piaget meant by a thought operation.)

Problem 2--Combinatorial Logic

If your art teacher gave you four jars of paints and told you to combine the colors in all the possible ways, what would be all the logical possibilities (whether or not it would be a good resulting color is not important)? The four colors were:
  (W) white   (R) red   (B) blue   (Y) yellow

e.g., 1. WR

2.

3.
.
.
.

Problem 3--Separation of Variables

The coaches of a basketball team are in disagreement about the best diet for their players before games. One read that a high-carbohydrate diet is best and the other read that a high-protein diet is preferable. Let's assume that you have worked out a good way of measuring endurance and plan to assess each player after each quarter of the next two games. How could you set up a "fair" (unconfounded) test of the effects of diet on endurance? What factors would you have to control?

CHAPTER 7 ANSWERS TO STUDY QUESTIONS

1. (236)   Acquired, elaborated, stored, retrieved, used in problem solving

PIAGET'S BASIC IDEAS ABOUT COGNITION

2. (237)   Existing knowledge, external environment

3. (237-238) Children gain understanding by direct interaction with objects and events. Also, this view maintains that children interpret objects and events using the knowledge available at that time.

4. (238)   Schemes

5. (238-239) SENSORIMOTOR SCHEMES: patterns of action used to adapt to or deal with different objects, from birth to 2 years of age.
SYMBOLIC SCHEMES: satisfying objectives through problem solving and thinking about objects and events without taking action. Symbolic schemes are first used by children during the latter half of the second year.
   (239)   OPERATIONAL SCHEMES: internal mental processes performed on objects of thought to reach logical conclusions, beginning around age 7.

6. (240)   ASSIMILATION: the process of interpreting new experiences by incorporating them into existing schemes. Example: a child is given a new size of ball, much larger than others she has played with; she immediately plays with it as she has other balls.
ACCOMMODATION: the process of modifying existing schemes in order to incorporate or adapt to new experiences. Example: because of the larger size of the ball, the child must spread her fingers wider to accomodate her grasp to the ball. She also modifies her internal ball scheme to include this larger size object.

7. (240)   Scheme

PIAGET'S STAGES

8. (240)   a) biological maturation
             b) stages are <u>successive</u>, each building on the accomplishments of all previous stages; none can be skipped or achieved out of sequence

9. (241)   No, he recognized that there is tremendous variation in the ages children emerge from a particular stage. Cultural and environmental influences may accelerate or retard intellectual growth.

PIAGET'S STAGES: SENSORIMOTOR

10. (243)   IMITATIVE ABILITIES: a highly adaptive activity where <u>many new skills are added</u> to behavioral repertoire. Imitative schemes begin imprecisely and develop during the second year to allow more complex reenactment of behavioral sequences.
OBJECT CONCEPT: first signs emerge between 8-12 months; by 18-24 months infants are capable of <u>mentally representing invisible displacements</u> and using mental inference to search for objects that have disappeared.

11. (246-247)   Inhibit the response to A (when object is really at B)
    (Box 7-1)

PIAGET'S STAGES: PREOPERATIONAL

12. (246)   Thinking about things in past, objects and events not present, language, pretend play

    (246-247)   Cognitive, language

    (248-249)   Fosters creative thinking, gives practice in different strategies of resolving conflict,
    (Box 7-2)   gives practice in role taking

13. (248)   ANIMISM: attribution of life or lifelike qualities to inanimate objects.
<u>Recent Findings/Conclusion:</u> research indicates that young children <u>do not routinely</u> attribute life or lifelike qualities to inanimate objects. Rather, they are likely to presume that <u>unfamiliar</u> objects that appear to move on their own are alive. They show more animistic thinking than older children, but it is inaccurate to characterize preschool thought as animistic.

PRECAUSAL THINKING: reasoning from the particular to the particular. When any two events occur together the child is likely to assume that one has caused the other.
    (254)   <u>Recent Findings/Conclusion:</u> research indicates children are not truly "precausal" beings. They have some understanding of causality and will not always resort to transductive reasoning.

14. (249-250)   EGOCENTRISM: a tendency to view the world from one's own perspective and to have difficulty recognizing another person's viewpoint.
<u>Recent Findings:</u> results of several experiments indicate that Piaget underestimated the ability of preschool children to recognize and appreciate another person's point of view.
<u>Conclusion:</u> although children are not as egocentric as Piaget thought, he was correct in that children often rely on their own perspectives and thus fail to make accurate judgments about other people's motives, desires, and intentions. They also assume that others have the same knowledge they do.

15. (250-251)   a) 3-year-olds have less confusion over tactile incongruities, such as knowing an ice cube is cold even if it does not feel cold through a glove.
    b) Pretend/real distinctions (e.g., a candle that looks like an apple) are seldom confused for the real thing if the child has pretended the object was real previously.

16. (251)   CLASSIFICATION: During this period children have difficulty with class inclusion. There is an inability to simultaneously relate a whole class to its component parts. CONSERVATION: failure to reverse, tendency to center, and lack of recognition of compensation.

17. (251-252)   Look
    (Fig 7-4)

18. (253)   TRAINING STRATEGY: identity training; recognizing that the transformed object or substance is still the same regardless of its appearance

    (254-255)   Conclusion: contrary to Piaget's viewpoint, preoperational children can learn to conserve

    (255)   a) problems he presented were often complex and unfamiliar
     b) Piaget required verbal justifications to receive credit

19. (255)   Memory deficiencies that prevent children from gathering, storing, and simultaneously comparing the many pieces of information needed to arrive at the correct answer, rather than Piaget's explanation of "centered" thinking

PIAGET'S STAGES: CONCRETE OPERATIONS

20. (256)   CONCRETE: objects and situations that are real or imaginable as opposed to abstract or hypothetical
OPERATIONAL: internal mental schemes that enable a child to modify and reorganize images and symbols to reach a logical conclusion

21. (256)   CONSTRUCTIVE COGNITIVE MAPS: the ability to construct accurate mental representations of a complex series of actions. Recent research confirms Piaget's findings. Preschool children do tend to rely on few discrete landmarks. Concrete-operational children pay more attention to route information (patterning left and right turns).

    (257)   RELATIONAL LOGIC: understanding of relations and relational logic such as seriation and transitivity. Preoperational children are not able to perform seriation or transitivity tasks. Most 7- to 11-year-olds cannot yet apply relational logic to abstract signifiers such as algebraic variables.

22. (257)   Are not; because tasks differ in complexity, with some involving coordination of the results of two conservation tasks (e.g., must conserve both liquids and mass to conserve volume)

23. (258)   Sequencing of different concrete-operational skills is highly variable.

24. (258)   Piaget recommends "discovery based" education, where children learn by doing in a self-initiated way while working with concrete materials.

25. (258)   The role of social contributions to cognitive growth

26. (259)   Children do not always learn more when working as isolated explorers; conceptual understanding is more likely to be enhanced by the child's interactions with other people.

PIAGET'S STAGES: FORMAL OPERATIONS

27. (261)   Rational, systematic, abstract

28. (260)   Concrete-operational children <u>imitate</u> what they have seen as an example by the experimenter. They <u>proceed unsystematically</u>. Formal-operational children begin the same way, but continue to <u>systematically test</u> every possible combination.

29. (261)   Ability to generate logical and creative responses to hypothetical propositions

30. (262)   POSITIVE: may pave the way for thinking about what is possible in one's life, forming stable identity, and achieving a richer understanding of other people's psychological perspectives and causes of behavior.
NEGATIVE: the more logical inconsistencies and other flaws that adolescents detect in the real world, the more confused they become and the more inclined they are to become frustrated with or even rebelliously angry toward agents such as parents or the government.

31. (262)   IMAGINARY AUDIENCE: phenomena referring to adolescents' feeling that they are constantly "on stage"--the focus of everyone's attention
PERSONAL FABLE: belief in uniqueness of oneself and one's thinking

An awareness of how other people <u>might</u> perceive them or react to their conduct

32. (263)   Exposure to education that stresses logic, math, and science; achieving some miminal IQ level; content area requiring formal operations is of interest or importance to one's life

33. (264)   Dialectical and systematic reasoning have been proposed as possible forms of post-formal thought; however, only a few adults seem to achieve this level.

LANGUAGE AND THOUGHT

34. (266)   a) children rely on private speech more when facing difficult rather than easy tasks and when deciding how to proceed without errors
b) performance often improves after turning to self-instruction
c) higher-IQ preschool children use more self talk, suggesting that its emergence is a sign of cognitive competence not immaturity

AN EVALUATION OF PIAGET'S THEORY

35. (267)   TIMING: children do not always display various intellectual skills or enter a particular stage of development when Piaget contended they should.
COMPETENCE/PERFORMANCE: Piaget perhaps falsely assumed children who failed one of his problems lacked the underlying concepts or thought structures necessary. Later researchers have argued that there are a number of factors that may affect a child's performance on Piaget's tests.
(268)   STAGES: today many cognitive theorists believe that intellectual development is a complex, multifaceted process in which children are gradually acquiring skills in many different content areas rather than going through a series of discontinuous stages.
(269)   EXPLAINING COGNITIVE CHANGE: Piaget's vague explanation of cognitive growth raises more questions than it answers.

CHAPTER 8

LEARNING AND INFORMATION PROCESSING

STUDY CHECKLIST

_____ Read Chapter Outline and Summary (Study guide)

_____ Read Chapter (Text)

_____ Completed Vocabulary Fill-Ins (Study guide)

_____ Re-Read Outline and Summary (Study guide)

_____ Reviewed Lecture Notes and Integrated with Text

_____ Reviewed Vocabulary, Study Questions, and Text Chapter

CHAPTER 8 OUTLINE AND SUMMARY

I. **What is learning?**
II. **Habituation: Early evidence of information processing**
    A.   Developmental trends
    B.   Habituation and later development

Learning, a relatively permanent change in behavior resulting from experience, is the process by which we acquire new information, attitudes, and many of our habits and abilities. The simplest form of learning is habituation, a process in which infants come to recognize and cease responding to stimuli that are presented over and over. Although habituation may be possible even before birth, this early form of learning improves dramatically over the first few months of life.

III. **Classical conditioning**
    A.   The classical conditioning of emotions and attitudes
    B.   Can neonates be classically conditioned?

In classical conditioning, an initially neutral, or conditioned, stimulus (for example, a bell) is repeatedly paired with a nonneutral, or unconditioned, stimulus (for example, food) that always elicits an unconditioned response (salivation). After several such pairings, the conditioned stimulus alone will acquire the capacity to evoke what is now called a "conditioned" response (in this case, salivation). Although neonates can be classically conditioned, they process information very slowly and are less susceptible to this kind of learning than older infants are. It is important to understand classical conditioning because many of our fears, attitudes, and prejudices may be acquired in this way.

IV. **Operant conditioning**
    A.   Reinforcement and punishment
    B.   Operant conditioning in infancy
    C.   Shaping of complex behaviors
    D.   Why reinforcers reinforce: An informational perspective

In operant conditioning, the subject first emits a response and then associates this action with a particular outcome. Reinforcers are outcomes that increase the probability that a response will be repeated; punishments are outcomes that suppress an act and decrease the likelihood that it will be repeated. Even very young infants are susceptible to operant conditioning and will recall what they have learned for a period of weeks if subtly reminded of the consequences of their actions. Complex responses may be acquired through a process called shaping, in which a subject is reinforced for emitting successively closer approximations of the desired behavior. Among the factors that determine the strength or effectiveness of operant conditioning are the timing, the scheduling, and the informational value of the stimulus offered as a reinforcer.

V. Punishment: The aversive control of behavior
    A.   How does punishment suppress a response?
    B.   When does punishment suppress a response?
        1.   Punish immediately rather than later
        2.   Punish with intensity (but not too much)
        3.   Punish consistently
        4.   Be otherwise warm and accepting
        5.   Give explanations
    C.   Some possible side effects of punishment
        1.   May avoid punisher
        2.   May become more aggressive
        3.   Punisher is reinforced
        4.   May misbehave as a means of getting attention
    D.   Removing positive stimuli: The "other side" of punishment

Punishment, properly applied, can be an effective means of suppressing undesirable conduct. The social information-processing view maintains that it is the child's interpretating of punishment that determines its effectiveness. Factors that influence the effectiveness of punishment include its timing, intensity, consistency, and underlying rationale, as well as the relationship between the subject and the punitive agent. When applied improperly, punishment may produce a number of undesirable side effects that limit its usefulness. Undesirable side effects are less likely if adults choose to punish by withholding something desirable rather than administering aversive stimuli. Two such techniques are the response-cost technique and the time-out technique.

VI. Observational learning
    A.   How do we "learn" by observation?
        1.   An example of "no trial" learning without reinforcement
        2.   The learning/performance distinction
        3.   What do children acquire in observational learning?
    B.   Developmental trends in imitation and observational learning

Much of what children learn is acquired by observing the behavior of social models. This "observational learning" occurs as the child attends to the model and constructs symbolic representations of the model's behavior. These symbolic codes are then stored in memory and may be retrieved at a later date to guide the child's attempts to imitate the behavior he or she has witnessed. Reinforcement is not necessary for observational learning. What reinforcement does is to increase the likelihood that children will perform that which they have already learned by observing a model. By the end of the first year, children are beginning to imitate social models, and their capacity for observational learning continues to improve throughout childhood.

VII. Learning and development reconsidered
A. Learning is a fundamental developmental process
B. Human learning is an active, cognitive process

Although learning is clearly an important developmental process, the behaviorists of yesteryear were incorrect in assuming that children are passive pawns of environmental influence. Our review of the literature suggested that learning is an active process that occurs at a cognitive level. As learning theorists gradually became more interested in the cognitive aspects of learning and problem solving, many began to study the growth of children's cognitive-processing skills, thereby contributing to a new, information-processing theory of intellectual development.

VIII. Cognitive development: An information-processing viewpoint
A. A model of human information processing
B. Attentional processes: getting information into the system
    1. The growth of attentional strategies
    2. What do children know about attention?
C. Memory processes: Retaining and retrieving what one has experienced
    1. Do basic capacities change?
    2. Development of memory strategies
    3. Development of metamemory
    4. Does the growth of general knowledge contribute to improvements in memory?
D. Problem solving: Making use of information one has retained
E. Current status of the information-processing approach

Information-processing theorists approach the topic of intellectual growth by charting the development of cognitive-processing skills such as attention, memory, and problem solving. Many analogies are drawn between human information processing and the functioning of computers. The human "system" is said to consist of a sensory register to detect or "log in" input; short-term memory, where information is stored temporarily until we can operate on it; long-term memory, where input that we operate on will remain until we retrieve it to solve problems; and executive control processes by which we play, monitor, and control all phases of information processing.

In order to understand something or to solve a problem, one must first pay attention to the right kinds of information. Between the preschool period and adolescence, children become better able to sustain attention for longer periods, more planful and systematic in their search for information, and more knowledgeable about and practiced in using strategies that permit them to focus selectively on task-relevant information and ignore sources of distraction.

Memory also improves over the course of childhood. Four explanations for these improvements that have received some support are (1) older children process information faster (or more automatically) than younger children, thus leaving more space in short-term memory for storing task-relevant information; (2) older children use more effective strategies (rehearsal, organization, and elaboration) for transferring information to long-term memory and retrieving this input; (3) older children know more about memory processes (metamemory), which helps them to select appropriate memory strategies and to monitor their performance; and (4) older children have larger knowledge bases than younger children, which improves their ability to learn and remember.

Like Piaget, information-processing theorists have sought to explain how developing children generate hypotheses and solve problems. As children mature, they encode more and more task-relevant information and formulate increasingly sophisticated problem-solving strategies, or rules, that are based largely on the information they are encoding. Cognitive-processing theorists can agree with Piaget that children progress through a series of "alternative understandings" before mastering certain concepts, but they argue that their rule-assessment approach is better able than Piaget's theory to specify why children of different ages approach problems in different ways.

CHAPTER 8 VOCABULARY FILL-INS
(Definitions below are in order of appearance in text margins)

MATCH VOCABULARY WORD/PHRASE TO ITS DEFINITION.
THEN COVER YOUR ANSWERS TO TEST YOUR MASTERY.

dishabituation   **habituation**
encoding   **learning**

1. _____ A relatively permanent change in behavior (or behavioral potential) that results from one's experiences or practice.

2. _____ A simple form of learning in which an organism eventually stops responding to a stimulus that is repeated over and over.

3. _____ The first step in learning (or remembering). It is the process of entering information into the mental system and organizing it in a form suitable for storing.

4. _____ Recovery of a response to a previously habituated stimulus.

classical conditioning
conditioned response (CR)
conditioned stimulus (CS)
discrimination
extinction

stimulus generalization
unconditioned response
(UCR)
unconditioned stimulus
(UCS)

5. _____ A type of learning in which an initially neutral stimulus is repeatedly paired with a meaningful stimulus so that the neutral stimulus comes to elicit the response originally made only to the meaningful stimulus.

6. _____ A stimulus that elicits a particular response without any prior learning.

7. _____ The unlearned response elicited by an unconditioned stimulus.

8. _____ A learned response to a stimulus that was not originally capable of producing the response.

9. _____ An initially neutral stimulus that comes to elicit a particular response after being paired with a UCS that always elicits the response.

10. _____ The fact that one stimulus can be substituted for another and produce the same response that the former stimulus did.

11. _____ The process of differentiating and responding differently to stimuli that vary on one or more dimensions.

12. _____ Gradual weakening and disappearance of a learned response that occurs because the CS is no longer paired with the UCS (in classical conditioning) or the response is no longer reinforced (in operant conditioning).

continuous reinforcement
operant conditioning
negative reinforcer
partial reinforcement
partial reinforcement effect

positive reinforcer
punishment
reinforcer
shaping

13. _____ A form of learning in which freely emitted acts (or operants) become either more or less probable depending on the consequences they produce.

14. _____ Any consequence of an act that increases the probability that the act will recur.

15. _____ Any stimulus whose presentation, as the consequence of an act, increases the probability that the act will recur.

16. _____ Any stimulus whose removal or termination, as the consequence of an act, increases the probability that the act will recur.

17. _____ Any consequence of an act that suppresses the response and decreases the probability that it will recur.

18. _____ A method of teaching complex patterns of behavior by reinforcing successively closer approximations of these responses.

19. _____ A schedule of reinforcement in which every occurrence of an act is reinforced.

20. _____ A schedule of reinforcement in which only some of the occurrences of an act are reinforced.

21. _____ The finding that behaviors that have been partially reinforced are more resistant to extinction than those that have been reinforced on a continuous schedule.

---

incompatible-response technique
learned helplessness
observational learning
response-cost technique

self-instructional technique
time-out technique

22. _____ The failure to learn how to respond appropriately in a situation because of previous exposures to uncontrollable events in the same or a similar situation.

23. _____ A form of punishment in which the punitive agent removes or withholds a valuable commodity from the transgressor.

24. _____ A strategy in which the disciplinary agent "punishes" a child by disrupting or preventing the prohibited activity that the child seems to enjoy.

25. _____ A nonpunitive method of behavior modification in which adults ignore undesirable conduct while reinforcing acts that are incompatible with these responses.

26. _____ A nonpunitive method of self-control in which children learn to verbalize the rationale for inhibiting an act whenever they feel the urge to perform it.

27. _____ Learning that results from observing the behavior of others.

---

executive control processes   recognition memory
long-term memory (LTM)   sensory store
memory   short-term memory
recall memory   (STM)

28. _____ First information processing unit, in which stimuli are noticed and are briefly available for further processing.

29. _____ Second information processing unit, in which stimuli are retained for several seconds and operated upon (also called working memory).

30. _____ Third information processing unit, in which information that has been examined and interpreted is permanently stored for future use.

31. _____ The processes involved in regulating attention and in determining what to do with information just gathered or retrieved from long-term memory.

32. _____ The processes by which people retain information and later retrieve it for use.

33. _____ Realizing that an object or event that one experiences has been experienced before.

34. _____ Recollecting objects, events, and experiences when examples of these bits of information are not available for comparative purposes.

---

counting span
elaboration
M-space
memory span

production deficiency
rehearsal
semantic organization

35. _____ Mental space; number of separate schemes or concepts that a child can manipulate simultaneously.

36. _____ A measure of the amount of information that can be held in short-term memory.

37. _____ A measure of M-space that requires individuals to operate on the information they have in short-term memory.

38. _____ A strategy for remembering that involves repeating the items one is trying to retain.

39. _____ A failure to spontaneously generate and use known strategies that could improve learning and memory.

40. _____ A strategy for remembering that involves grouping or classifying stimuli into meaningful (or manageable) clusters that are easier to retain.

41. _____ A strategy for remembering that involves adding something to (or creating meaningful links between) the bits of information one is trying to retain.

knowledge base
metacognition

metamemory
rule assessment

42. _____ One's knowledge about cognition and about the regulation of cognitive activities.

43. _____ One's knowledge about memory and memory processes.

44. _____ One's existing information about a topic or content area; significant for its influence on how well one can learn and remember.

45. _____ A method of assessing a child's level of cognitive functioning (or problem solving) by noting the information that he encodes and the principle, or rule, he uses to operate on this information and draw conclusions.

CHAPTER 8 STUDY QUESTIONS

WHAT IS LEARNING?

1. **Domjan and Burkhard** define **learning as a change in behavior meeting three requirements:** (p. 274-275)

    (a) Thinking, perceiving or reacting to environment in a _____ way.

    (b) Change is attributable to one's _____ (rather than to heredity, maturation or physiological damage).

    (c) The change is _____ _____.

2. What four **types of learning** are described in the text? (p. 275)

    (a)

    (b)

    (c)

    (d)

HABITUATION: EARLY EVIDENCE OF INFORMATION PROCESSING

3.   **How can habituation be distinguished from fatigue** of the sensory receptors? (p. 275)

4.   **How early** in development has **habituation** been demonstrated? (p. 275)

5.   **How does the rate of habituation differ** for infants **0-3 months old** and infants **4-12 months** of age? (p. 275)

How is the difference explained? (p. 275)

6.   If the parents of a **7-month-old** claimed that their infant **recognized a toy** she had played with at a relative's house during a single visit a month earlier, could they possibly be correct or does research evidence show that their claim must be false? (p. 275)

7.   What **relationship** between **rate of habituation** during early infancy and later indices of **intelligence** has been found? (p. 276)

8.   **What link does Fagan claim** exists between rate of habituation in infancy and later intellectual performance? (p. 276)

CLASSICAL CONDITIONING

9.   If a child is provided positive experiences by a particular aunt -- e.g., being picked up and cuddled, being given positive attention, being given special treats -- in time just seeing a **picture of that aunt** can come to elicit those positive feelings again.   In this case the picture of the aunt would be called the _____ _____. The **positive feelings elicited by the picture** would be _____ _____.   The **attention and treats** would be the _____ _____. (p. 276-277)

10.   **Emotions** and **attitudes** are often the product of what kind of conditioning? (p. 277-278)

11.   Emergency room personnel at hospitals often give suckers to young patients. They tell the child it is a reward for their bravery and cooperation, but it is also intended as means of _____; i.e., **replacing negative associations with** the hospital with **the pleasurable one** of the taste of the sucker. (p. 278)

12.   One text heading asks, **"Can neonates be classically conditioned?"** What answer does research to date warrant? (p. 278)

Are any qualifications to the answer necessary? (p. 278)

OPERANT CONDITIONING

13.   Your text author describes **classical conditioning as learned responses that are elicited** by a conditioned stimulus. In **operant conditioning** there is a **change in the frequency of a behavior emitted** by the learner **because of the** _____ it produces, either pleasant or unpleasant. (p. 278)

14. What are the **two ways of increasing the frequency of a behavior** described in the text. Give examples. (p. 280)

    (a) _____ reinforcement, e.g.,

    (b) _____ reinforcement, e.g.,

15. What are the **two ways of suppressing/punishing** a response, i.e., decreasing the frequency? (p. 280)

    (a)

    (b)

16. **To promote desirable behavior,** which procedure has been found **most effective**--punishing undesirable behavior or reinforcing desired behavior? Why? (p. 280-281)

17. How do **newborns, 3-month-olds,** and **5-month-olds** compare in their **susceptibility to operant conditioning?** (p. 281)

18. **Rovee-Collier** and colleagues have studied **whether infants can remember** and **how long they can remember** a previously learned response such as kicking to get a mobile to move. What did their results show? (p. 281-282)

How did Rovee-Collier find that the infant's retrieval could be facilitated?

19.   What **if a child does not already have the behavior in his/her repertoire** that we would like learned, e.g., a complex skill such as shoelace tying or basketball? **What operant conditioning procedure could be used?** Describe the procedure. (p. 282-283)

20.   What type of **reinforcement schedule** produces persistent responding (both good and bad) even when there is no one around to reinforce each response? (p. 283-284)

21.   What **operant conditioning principle** might account for the high level of nagging, whining, and tantrum throwing some children show in the grocery store? (p. 284)

22.   **Sometimes rewarding children seems to backfire** and reduce rather than maintain or increase their frequency of a behavior they already enjoy, such as reading. What is believed to undermine the child's intrinsic interest? (p. 286, Box 8-1)

Under what conditions can reinforcement of an intrinsically-interesting activity enhance enjoyment and performance?

23.   In a similar vein as above, research has shown that **infants' pleasure in making a mobile move** comes not so much from the pretty sight and sounds that result but **their _____ over the mobile.** (p. 285)

24.   **Five factors** are listed in the text that have been shown to **influence how effective a particular punisher will be** in suppressing the punished behavior. Specify each. (p. 287-289)

(a)

(b)

(c)

(d)

(e)

25.   What is one **reason** that giving **rationales** is believed to **increase the effectiveness (achieve long-term inhibition) of punishment?** (p. 288-289)

Characterize the difference in the explanations offered by social information-processing theorists and conditioning theorists for the suppressive effects of punishment. (p. 289)

26.   What **negative side-effects** are associated with the use of **punishment involving aversive controls?** (p. 289)

(a)

(b)

(c)

27.   What **alternative forms of punishment** have fewer negative side-effects than the aversive types of punishment? (p. 289-290)

   (a)

   (b)

OBSERVATIONAL LEARNING

28.   **Bandura** describes two **advantages of observational learning** over other forms of learning. These are (p. 290)

   (a)

   (b)

29.   What **role** has **reinforcement** been shown to **play in observational learning?** (p. 291)

30.   **Bandura** and his associates found that children who counted out loud while watching a model, later produced fewer of the model's behavior. In contrast **Coates and Hartup** found that children who were instructed to verbalize what they saw the model do, produced about twice as many of the model's responses as did uninstructed children. **These studies together suggest that _____ plays an important role in observational learning.** (p. 292)

31.   **Kuczynski** and his associates found that younger infants imitated different types of behavior than older toddlers imitated. Indicate which **type of behaviors predominated in the children's imitation.** (p. 293)

   16-month-olds:

   29-month-olds:

32. What **conclusion** does the text suggest is warranted about the **child's role in learning**? (p. 294-295)

COGNITIVE DEVELOPMENT: AN INFORMATION-PROCESSING VIEWPOINT

33. The **information-processing viewpoint attributes executive processes** to the human, something a computer lacks. **What tasks are subsumed under executive processes**? (p. 298)

(a)

(b)

(c)

34. **Contrast** the kind of reasons that the **information-processing model** might give **with Piaget's reasons for a child's failure to solve a problem** correctly. (p. 298)

35. How do young children (preschool) compare with older children and adults in the amount of information they can hold in their **sensory store**? (p. 298-299)

36. What two major gains do children make during the grade-school years in their **attentional strategies**? (p. 299-300)

(Miller & Harris, 1988; Vliestra, 1982):

(Miller & Weiss, 1981):

37. How do **DeMarie-Dreblow and Miller** explain that **children know what attention strategies would be helpful at an earlier age than they regularly employ them**? (p. 300-301)

38. How good are the **recognition** and **recall** memories of infants during the **first year**? (p. 301-302)

RECOGNITION:

RECALL:

39. **One possible explanation** for the dramatic improvements in recall between ages 3 and 12 is that there is an **increase in basic processing capacity with age**, specifically, the capacity of _____-_____ memory. What evidence supports or refutes each of the two hypotheses for what actually changes with age? *Circle the hypothesis that is best supported by evidence.*
(p. 303-304 & Fig. 8-9)

PHYSICAL CAPACITY HYPOTHESIS (Pascual-Leone):

OPERATING EFFICIENCY HYPOTHESIS (Case):

What **relationship** do **Case** and **Brainerd** suggest **memory capacity has to logical reasoning**? (p. 304-305)

40. A **second possible explanation for improvement in recall memory** with age is that older children have acquired and consistently use **effective strategies for storage and retrieval of information.** List three storage strategies and summarize evidence indicating that memory improvement with age could be due, in part, to increased use of such strategies. (p. 305-307)

(a)

(b)

(c)

Best and Ornstein and **Carr et al.** studied the effect of **adult-directed training on the use of organizational strategies.** What conclusion does the text author draw regarding the effectiveness of such training with 9-year-olds? (p. 306-307)

Pressley and Levin and **Kee and Bell** have found that younger children may recall less than older children even when they have used organization or elaboration strategy at the time of storage. **What accounts for the younger children's poorer retrieval?** (p. 308)

41. A **third possible reason for improvement in recall with age** is that older children know more about memory and memory processes, or **metamemory.** What evidence is there that the dramatic increase in memory between ages 4 and 12 accounts for improvements in memory? (p. 308-310)

What determines whether knowledge of a memory strategy will improve recall (e.g., Fabricius & Cavalier, 1989)? (p. 309)

42.   A **fourth possible reason for improvement in recall with age** is that older children have a **broader knowledge base** and are therefore more familiar with information to be retained. What have **Chi, Lindberg,** and **Schneider et al. (1989)** found happens to the recall of younger or less intelligent children when they recall highly familiar material? (p. 310-311 & Fig. 8-11)

43.   What overall **conclusion** does the text make **regarding the role of memory capacity/efficiency, memory strategies, metamemory, and knowledge base in accounting for the improvement in memory** between ages 4 and 12? (p. 311)

44.   Describe in what way **Siegler's rule-assessment** results agree with **Piaget's views** on intellectual development and how they extend Piaget's theory. (p. 311-313)

AGREE WITH PIAGET ON:

EXTEND PIAGET BY:

45. **Information-processing theorists** agree with Piaget that children are active learners who must construct knowledge from experiences. They differ, however, in **advocating a directive role of the teacher** and recommend the following **six guidelines for structuring learning** for children: (p. 314-315, Box 8-3)

(a)

(b)

(c)

(d)

(e)

(f)

46. Your text author discusses the current **status of the information-processing approach**. What shortcomings does it display? What conclusion is drawn with respect to whether it supercedes, extends, and/or complements Piagetian theory? (p. 315-316)

SHORTCOMINGS:

(a)

(b)

CONCLUSION:

ACTIVITY 8-1

VERBAL COMMENTS AS CONSEQUENCES AFFECTING BEHAVIOR

INTRODUCTION: Chapter 8 (p. 274-295) introduces learning as an important contributor to development. Through learning, children add new responses to their repertoire and either increase or decrease the frequency of exisiting behaviors depending on the consequences of those behaviors. As was discussed in the text section on operant learning, a response is strengthened and more likely to occur in the future if it is followed by pleasant consequences (or results in the removal of aversive consequences). Similarly, a response will be weakened and less likely to occur if it is followed by unpleasant consequences. We often think of reinforcers and punishers as something concrete such as food, money, a spanking, etc. Not all reinforcers and punishers are concrete, however. A smile, a pat, a kind word as responses to our behavior may increase the likelihood of those responses being repeated again. Likewise, a frown, a slap, an unkind word may decrease the likelihood of responses they follow being repeated. One of the implications for us as adults is that what we say to children can affect them markedly by encouraging or discouraging behaviors. The purpose of this activity is to increase your awareness of the impact verbal comments can have on behavior and attitudes by having you recall some of your own reactions to the comments of others.

This activity also relates to a theme that runs through several chapters: what others say to us can affect the internal self-talk we engage in and affect our self-attributions (e.g., Chapter. 14, p. 544, 567-569, Box 14-4). Self-talk and self-attributions may promote self-control, altruism, mature moral reasoning, etc.--or may promote negative outcomes when a child engages in behaviors consistent with self-talk derived from other-talk, such as, "I'm clumsy," I'm so dumb," "I'm the black sheep of this family," "I can't do anything right," etc.

INSTRUCTIONS:

Part A

Write down as many examples as you can recall of comments people close to you have made that
   a. made you feel good
   b. made you want to try even harder
   c. made you angry or made you feel down on yourself
   d. made you not want to try at all

It would be optimal to do this activity over a few days because it may take some time for various previous experiences and the comments made to you to come to mind. For each comment indicate who made it, how it made you feel, and how it impacted your behavior. Think of how your parents, siblings, teachers, and others responded to you verbally when you shared, when you were helpful, when you were successful, when you were mean, when you were forgetful, when you were unsuccessful, etc.

Part B

Over a 2-5 day period, make a special effort to provide positive verbal statements to someone you know. Keep daily records describing the context, your positive verbal statement, and both the immediate- and longer-term effect on the other person's behavior and effect.

Before beginning Part B, it would be useful to spend some time "brain-storming" with a classmate some possible positive statements to use.

ACTIVITY 8-2

PIAGET'S SECONDARY CIRCULAR REACTIONS: EVIDENCE FOR OPERANT CONDITIONING AND MEMORY IN YOUNG INFANTS

INTRODUCTION: The text author describes three major cognitive acquisitions during the first two years of life: the development of (a) object permanence, (b) problem solving skills, and (c) deferred imitation (Chapter 7, p. 241-245, Table 7-1). Piaget called this period the sensorimotor stage of cognitive development because during infancy, coordination of sensory input and motor responses is the major cognitive task. The acquisitions are monumental when you realize that (a) the infant comes to be able to search appropriately for an object that has undergone a succession of invisibile displacements, meaning that the infant must be able to imagine possible locations; (b) the infant becomes capable of engaging in both overt and covert trial and error, meaning the infant is able to imagine possible solutions (and consequences) without having to necessarily carry them all out--a capability important to many areas of development (and to keeping out of trouble!); and (c) the infant can rapidly increase her behavior repertoire when she becomes capable of systematic imitation, and even gains more when she is capable of systematic deferred imitation, meaning that she can imagine the previously observed response and that image can mediate her responding at another place and time. These capabilities, all acquired during the sensorimotor period, bring the infant a long way from the newborn's limited repertoire of inborn reflexes.

This activity focuses on one subperiod of the sensorimotor stage: the secondary circular reaction substage. During this substage infants begin to repeat actions that lead to interesting external stimulation. According to Piaget this substage is a forerunner of intentionality in problem solving (see Table 7-1, p. 245).

Beginning around 4 months of age, Piaget observed that infants would repeat an action that produced sensory input--sounds (e.g., rattle, squeeze toy) or movement (e.g., mobile). Piaget maintained that these responses, which he called secondary circular reactions, represented an important advance over the primary circular reactions found in younger infants.

Primary circular reactions also involve repetition of actions that produce interesting consequences, but the consequences always center around the infant's own body (e.g., actions such as sucking, cooing, blowing bubbles, etc.). Although secondary circular reactions represent an advance, Piaget viewed them as still lacking in true intentionality. They are important, though, because they indicate that the infant can take advantage of an accidental happening, and systematically repeat an action that produces interesting consequences.

The purpose of this activity is to allow you to watch first-hand an infant's fascination with the discovery that she can make interesting things happen to external objects--a cognitive advance that undoubtedly plays a role in the development of competence and sense of self. This activity will also provide you an example of a special case of operant conditioning, a type of learning described in Chapter 8 (p. 281-282). It is a special case because not only is the reinforcement (movement of an external stimulus) contingent upon the infant's responses, but the intensity of the reinforcing stimulus is directly in the infant's control. This activity also relates to material on infant memory discussed in Chapter 8 (p. 301). Rovee-Collier and colleagues have shown that a 2-month-old infant will show retention of the kicking response to a mobile for as long as 18 days if given a brief "reminder" exposure to the mobile moving 24 hours before the retention test. These ingenious experiments have shown that infant memory is not as fleeting as once believed. (Note--Rovee-Collier has also shown that secondary circular reactions occur in infants long before the 4 months that Piaget observed.)

INSTRUCTIONS:

Children. Ask the parents of an infant 2 to 6 months of age if they can help you with your homework for a class project. Tell the parents that you would like to see how babies react when they can make a mobile shake by moving their arm, instead of having an adult move it or turn on a motor.

Materials. Use a mobile the parents already have for the infant or create your own. If you construct your own, be sure to think about how you will suspend it. Consider including a small bell on your homemade mobile or adding one to the infant's for some auditory stimulation.

Procedure. Attach one end of a ribbon, piece of yarn, or string to the mobile. Place the child in an infant seat facing the mobile and tie the second end to the infant's wrist or foot. Sit back and watch the infant discover that she is in control of the movement of the mobile. Take notes on the infant's facial expressions and vocalizations, indicating the end of each 5 minute block of time. (Be prepared to stay a while; some 4-month-olds can keep the mobile going for 40 minutes the first time they are attached.)

If you can arrange for it, return a day or two later. Set the child in the infant seat in front of the mobile. Observe carefully the infant's facial expressions and movement of the arm or leg that was attached during original learning. Make notes. Then attach the infant again and record her behavior, again indicating the end of each 5 minute block of time. You should observe evidence of memory for the kicking response when the infant sees the mobile. If the infant shows no evidence of remembering, set it in motion for a moment. You should see good evidence of recognition then, followed by energetic kicking or hand movements. Because the infant does recognize the mobile, habituation will occur more rapidly the second day and the mobile will lose its reinforcing power sooner--meaning you probably will not have to wait 40 minutes for the infant to get bored!

Note--Students often wonder if the infant's arm or leg movements are simply reactions to the movement of the mobile. Check this out if you wish. Before starting the project, move the mobile by pulling on the ribbon. Observe and write down the infant's reaction. Compare the infant's behavior when your movement versus her own movement produced the consequences. Her behavior should differ markedly in both quality and quantity.

Write-up. Prepare a write-up that includes (a) the infant's age in months, (b) the number of minutes the infant moved the mobile, (c) a description of the infant's reaction when she first discovered the link between her movements and the mobile's movement, (d) the infant's facial expressions and vocalizations throughout the duration of her attachment to the mobile, and finally (e) a description of how the infant acted as interest waned and the arm or leg movements decreased in frequency.

If you are able to do the memory test a day or two later, also describe the infant's reactions and behavior during that session.

RELATED REFERENCES

Davis, J.M., & Rovee-Collier, C.K. (1983). Alleviated forgetting of a learned contingency in 8-week-old infants. *Developmental Psychology, 19,* 353-365.

Hayne, H., Rovee-Collier, C., & Perris, E.E. (1987). Categorization and memory retrieval by three-month-olds. *Child Development, 58,* 750-767.

Rovee-Collier, C. (1987). Learning and memory in infancy. In J. D. Osofsky (Ed.), *Handbook of child psychology: Vol. 4 Socialization, personality and social development.* New York: Wiley.

Shields, P.J., & Rovee-Collier, C. (1992). Long-term memory for context-specific category information at six months. *Child Development, 63,* 245-259.

CHAPTER 8 ANSWERS TO STUDY QUESTIONS

WHAT IS LEARNING?

1. (274-275) a) new
b) experiences
c) relatively permanent

2. (275) a) habituation
b) classical conditioning
c) operant conditioning
d) observational learning

HABITUATION: EARLY EVIDENCE OF INFORMATION PROCESSING

3. (275) When a baby has habituated to one stimulus, he will often attend to or even react vigorously to the presentation of a slightly different stimulus. This indicates that the sensory receptors are not fatigued and that there is discrimination between the familiar and the unfamiliar.

4. (275) As early as the last trimester of pregnancy.

5. (275) Infants less than 4 months may require <u>many exposures to stimulus before they habituate</u> and will soon dishabituate. Infants 4 to 12 months old show <u>rapid habituation</u>, are slow to dishabituate, and are more likely to explore novel rather than familiar stimuli.

The difference is explained as due to maturation.

6. (275) Yes; 5- to 12-month-olds may recognize something as familiar after only one or two brief exposures, and they are likely to retain that "knowledge" for weeks or even months (Fagan, 1984; Rose, 1981).

7. (276) Early competence in habituation has been linked to higher scores on infant intelligence tests and more rapid understanding and usage of language in the second year.

8. (276) Habituation may be the fundamental intellectual process.

CLASSICAL CONDITIONING

9. (276) Aunt (picture): conditioned stimulus
Positive feelings: conditioned response
Attention, treats: unconditioned stimuli

10. (277) Classical

11. (278) Counterconditioning

12. (278)   Although it is extremely difficult, neonates can be classically conditioned.

Only a small number of responses (mostly biologically programmed reflexes such as blinking, sucking, breathing) can be classically conditioned during the first few weeks of life, and the infant must be alert and attentive for the conditioning to have any chance of success.

OPERANT CONDITIONING

13. (278)   Consequences

14. (280)   a) <u>positive</u> reinforcement, e.g., presentation of candy or a pat on the head
b) <u>negative</u> reinforcement, e.g., removal of an irritating noise or aversive scolding

15. (280)   a) presentation of an aversive stimulus in response to an undesired behavior
b) removal of something desirable in response to an inappropriate behavior

16. (280-281)   <u>Reinforcement</u> is generally more effective than punishment in producing desired changes in behavior <u>because</u> punishment merely suppresses ongoing or established responses without really teaching anything new.

17. (281)   Newborns can be operantly conditioned, but older infants learn much faster with fewer trials.

18. (282)   Two-month-olds remember how to make the mobile move for up to three days from the original learning. Three-month-olds can recall for more than a week.

Subtle <u>reminders</u> (e.g., a brief exposure to a moving mobile previously controlled by the infant's kicks) help infants retrieve stored information; very young infants are capable of retaining information for weeks, if not longer, when given a brief reminder prior to the retrieval situation.

19. (283)   SHAPING: reinforcement is given for production of successively closer approximations of the desired behavior.

20. (283)   Partial reinforcement

21. (284)   Partial reinforcement

22. (286)   The <u>belief</u> that they are engaging in the activity <u>in order to obtain a reward</u>. It is not the reward itself that undermines intrinsic interest.

Extrinsic reward can sustain and increase intrinsic interest in an activity if the reinforcer is given only for <u>successful</u> task performance. A rewarded success informs the child he is in control of his own fate through the quality of his efforts.

23. (285)   Control

24. (287-288)   a) punish immediately rather than later
b) punish with intensity (but not too much intensity)
c) punish consistently
d) be otherwise warm and accepting
e) provide rationales

25. (288)   Rationales provide the child with information specifying why the punished act is wrong and why there should be a guilty or shameful feeling if the behavior is repeated.

    (289)   Conditioning theorists attribute suppression to <u>anxiety</u> whereas social information-processing theorists stress the <u>informational value</u> of punishment.

26. (289)
    a) children may resent and avoid punitive adults
    b) children may become quite aggressive and difficult to control
    c) immediate effectiveness of the punishment may reinforce the punitive agent and increase use of this form of discipline.

27. (289,290)
    a) response-cost technique: removal of a tangible reinforcer that the child already has
    b) time-out technique: preventing a prohibited activity that the child seems to enjoy, often by sending the child to her room or setting her in a chair as a "time out"

OBSERVATIONAL LEARNING

28. (290)
    a) Learning through observation may spare the learner needless errors; more efficient.
    b) Permits the young child to acquire many new responses in a large number of settings where her "models" are simply pursuing their own interests and not attempting to teach.

29. (291)   Not necessary for learning, but reinforcement increases the likelihood that the child will perform what he or she has already learned through observation.

30. (292)   Symbolic coding (imagery, verbalization)

31. (293)   16-month-olds: tend to imitate <u>affective displays</u> such as laughing, cheering, and jumping.
29-month-olds: tend to imitate <u>instrumental behaviors</u> such as household tasks and self-care routines.

32. (295)   They are active information processors whose interpretations of the environment and its contingencies are what determine the impact of these events on their conduct and their eventual development.

COGNITIVE DEVELOPMENT: AN INFORMATION-PROCESSING VIEWPOINT

33. (298)
    a) deciding what to attend to
    b) selection of strategies
    c) choosing problems

34. (298)   The information-processing model proposes that <u>deficiencies in processing</u> rather than a lack of necessary logic (or cognitive structures according to Piaget) might account for a person's failure to solve a problem. For example, the person <u>might not be paying attention to the most relevant information or using an appropriate strategy</u>.

35. (298)   Same; research indicates that preschool children can hold just as much information in their sensory store as older children and adults do. (Bjorklund, 1989; House, 1982)

36. (299-300)
   a) Miller & Harris, 1988; Vliestra, 1982: improved planful, adaptive information gathering.
   b) Miller & Weiss, 1981: improved concentration on relevant information and filtering out of extraneous input that may interfere with task performance.

37. (300-301)   <u>Not routinized enough</u> to really help them. That is, when children first acquire an appropriate attentional strategy, they go through a transitional phase in which they employ the strategy sporadically. The cognitive effort required in accessing and implementing a new, unpracticed strategy may so tax the limited capacity of working memory that the transitional child has little capacity to encode the information she is supposed to retain. The child gradually comes to rely on these strategies as they become more routinized and effective.

38. (301)   RECOGNITION: the ability to recognize the familiar is <u>apparently inborn</u>, for neonates who habituate to the repeated administration of a stimulus are indicating that they recognize this object or event as something they have experienced before. Recognition memory improves dramatically over the first year.
RECALL: research by Rovee-Collier demonstrated <u>recall in infants 2-3 months old</u>. During the latter half of the first year, babies are <u>actively</u> retrieving things from memory, even when cues to remind them of these experiences are not physically present.

39. (303-304)   Short-term

(Fig. 8-9)   PHYSICAL CAPACITY HYPOTHESIS: has received little support; cannot account for the finding that young children's recall of familiar children's items is better than adults' recall of the same items.
OPERATING EFFICIENCY HYPOTHESIS: is <u>better supported</u>. Children who identify and operate on items quickly have longer memory spans than less efficient processors. Accounts for the better recall of child experts than adult novices.

(304-305)   Maintain that increasing automization of information processing makes <u>possible</u> (but does not guarantee) logical thinking. Studies have shown that when the memory demands are reduced, young children often show more advanced reasoning.

40. (305-307)
   a) REHEARSAL: use of rehearsal and effectiveness of rehearsal strategy improves with age (3- to 4-year-olds rarely rehearse; 5- to 10-year-olds do so increasingly; by age 12 children are more likely to rehearse clusters even when earlier items are not visually displayed.
   b) SEMANTIC ORGANIZATION: children tend not to spontaneously use possible organization categories until age 9-10. Best and Ornstein (1986) have shown that 9-year-olds were responsive to training in categorization and were more likely to organize subsequent lists that were difficult to categorize.
   c) ELABORATION: creation of an image that helps associate two or more things to be remembered is <u>rarely used spontaneously before adolescence</u> (Pressley, 1982). When used, elaboration improves recall. Elaboration may be a late developing strategy because of younger children's limited working memory or their more limited knowledge.

(306-307)   The recall of 9-year-olds benefited from training in sorting easily categorized items and they later utilized the categorizing strategy on a more difficult list to facilitate their recall.

(308)   Younger children tend to fail to utilize the categories or elaborative images used to aid storage at the time of recall.

41. (308-310)   Good metamemory was not found to be required for good recall (Bjorklund & Zeman, 1982) or to guarantee good recall (Salatas & Flavell, 1976). Understanding why a strategy works was found to improve recall (e.g., Fabricius & Cavalier, 1989; Paris & Oka, 1986).

(309)   Training research has shown understanding why and when to use a strategy improved recall.

42. (310-311)   If younger or less intelligent children are more knowledgeable in an area, they
(Fig. 8-11)   will recall more than will older or more-intelligent-but-less-knowledgeable children or adults.

43. (311)   The text author concludes that children change in all four areas and that those changes interact with one another and underlie the improvement found in memory with age.

44. (313)   AGREES WITH PIAGET ON: children progress through a series of "alternative understandings" before mastering various concepts.
EXTENDS PIAGET BY: the rule-assessment approach allows the investigator to specify exactly how children are processing (or failing to process) relevant information and thus to indicate why they fail to solve a particular problem or set of related problems.

45. (314-315)   a)   Analyze the requirements of the problems and tasks that you present to your pupils.
b)   Reduce short-term memory demands to a bare minimum.
c)   Treat the child's incorrect answers as opportunities to promote new learning.
d)   Encourage children to "have fun" using their memories.
e)   Provide opportunities to learn effective memory strategies.
f)   Structure lessons so that children are likely to acquire metacognitive knowledge and to understand why they should plan, monitor, and control their cognitive activities.

46. (315-316)   SHORTCOMINGS:
a)   underestimates the richness of human cognitive activity (computer analogy is too simplistic)
b)   suffers from vagueness in its explanation of developmental change (as does Piaget's theory)
(316)   CONCLUSION: author concludes that the information-processing approach complements but does not replace Piaget's theoretical framework.

CHAPTER 9

INTELLIGENCE: MEASURING MENTAL PERFORMANCE

STUDY CHECKLIST

_____ Read Chapter Outline and Summary (Study guide)

_____ Read Chapter (Text)

_____ Completed Vocabulary Fill-Ins (Study guide)

_____ Re-Read Outline and Summary (Study guide)

_____ Reviewed Lecture Notes and Integrated with Text

_____ Reviewed Vocabulary, Study Questions, and Text Chapter

CHAPTER 9 OUTLINE AND SUMMARY

I. **What is intelligence?**
   A. The psychometric view of intelligence
      1. Nature/nurture and stability of intelligence
      2. Is intelligence a single attribute or many attributes?
   B. Early factor-analytic studies of intelligence
   C. A modern information-processing viewpoint

   The psychometric, or testing, approach defines intelligence as a trait (or set of traits) that allows some people to think and solve problems more effectively than others. Relying on the factor-analytic procedure, theorists such as Spearman, Thurstone, and Guilford have disagreed about the nature, or structure, of intellect, although almost everyone agrees that intelligence is not merely a singular attribute that determines how well people perform on all cognitive tasks. Robert Sternberg's recent triarchic theory criticizes psychometric theories of intelligence for their failure to consider the contexts in which intelligent acts are displayed, the test taker's experience with test items, and the information-processing strategies on which people rely when thinking or solving problems.

II. **How is intelligence measured?**
   A. Alfred Binet and the Stanford-Binet Test
   B. The Wechsler Scales
   C. Distribution of IQ scores
   D. Group tests of mental performance
   E. Some new approaches to Intelligence Testing
   F. Assessing infant intelligence
   G. Is IQ a stable attribute?

   The first intelligence tests were designed to predict children's academic performance and to identify slow learners who might profit from special education. Today there are literally hundreds of intelligence tests, and instruments such as the Stanford-Binet and the Wechsler scales are widely respected and heavily used. Intelligence tests differ considerably in format and content, but most of them present the examinee with a variety of cognitive tasks and then evaluate his or her performance by comparing it with the average performance of agemates. An examinee whose performance equals that of the average agemate is assigned an intelligence quotient (IQ) of 100. An IQ greater than 100 indicates that the child's performance is superior to that of other children her age; an IQ less than 100 means that the child's intellectual performance is below that of a typical agemate.

IQ is a relatively stable attribute for some individuals. However, many others will show wide variations in their IQ scores over the course of childhood. The fact that IQ can wander upward or downward over time suggests that IQ tests are measuring intellectual performance rather than an inborn capacity for thinking and problem solving.

III. What do intelligence tests predict?
   A. IQ as a predictor of scholastic achievement
   B. IQ as a predictor of occupational success
   C. IQ as a predictor of health, adjustment, and life satisfaction

When we consider trends for the population as a whole, IQ scores seem to predict important outcomes such as future academic accomplishments, occupations status, and even health and happiness. However, a closer examination of individual profiles suggests that an IQ score is not always a reliable indicator of one's future health, happiness, or success. Many people with very high IQs are not very prosperous or well adjusted, whereas other people of average or below-average intelligence are happy, healthy, and highly successful. So a high IQ, by itself, does not guarantee success. Other factors such as one's work habits and motivation to succeed are also important contributors.

IV. Factors that influence IQ scores
   A. The evidence for heredity
   B. The evidence for environment

Both hereditary and environmental forces contribute heavily to intellectual performance. The evidence from family studies and studies of adopted children indicates that about half the variation among individuals in IQ is attributable to hereditary factors. But regardless of one's genetic predispositions, barren intellectual environments clearly inhibit cognitive growth, whereas enriched, intellectually stimulating environments can have the opposite effect.

V. Sociocultural correlates of intellectual performance
   A. Home environment and IQ
   B. Birth order, family configuration, and IQ
   C. Social-class, racial, and ethnic differences in IQ
   D. Why do groups differ in intellectual performance?
      1. The test bias hypothesis
      2. The genetic hypothesis
      3. The environmental hypothesis

Parents who provide a stimulating home environment by becoming involved in their child's learning activities, carefully explaining new concepts, furnishing age-appropriate toys, and consistently encouraging the child to achieve are likely to have children who score high on IQ tests. Two other family characteristics that affect intellectual performance are family size and birth order: first-borns and children from smaller families tend to obtain slightly higher IQs than later-borns and children from large families.

On average, children from lower-class and minority backgrounds score lower on IQ tests than White children and other members of the middle class. Apparently these group differences in IQ are not solely an artifact of our tests and testing procedures. Nor is there any conclusive evidence that they result from genetic differences among the various social-class, racial, or ethnic groups. Perhaps the best explanation for group differences in IQ is the environmental hypothesis: many poor people and minority-group members score lower on IQ tests because they grow up in impoverished environments that are much less conducive to intellectual development than those of their middle-class agemates.

VI. **Improving intellectual performance through compensatory education**
   A.   Long-term follow-ups
   B.   The importance of parental involvement
   C.   Limitations of compensatory education and implications for the future

Several enrichment programs for disadvantaged preschoolers have now been evaluated. Although these early interventions do not produce dramatic long-term gains in IQ, they do improve children's chances of succeeding in the classroom, and they help to prevent the progressive decline in intellectual performance so often observed among students from disadvantaged backgrounds.

VII. **Creativity and special talents**
   A.   What is creativity?
   B.   How does creativity develop?

Creativity, the ability to produce novel and socially valued ideas and solutions, is a distinct talent that requires divergent rather than convergent thinking. Creativity is largely independent of IQ, although a minimum level of intelligence is necessary for one to be very creative. Interestingly, neither tests of general intelligence nor tests of general creativity are very accurate for forecasting exceptional accomplishments in a specific field. The development of special talent and abilities seems to require a special motivation to develop one's skills and special environment--namely, the encouragement of close companions and prolonged training in one's area of interest under the supervision of experts.

CHAPTER 9 VOCABULARY FILL-INS

(Definitions below are in order of appearance in text margins)

MATCH VOCABULARY WORD/PHRASE TO ITS DEFINITION.
THEN COVER YOUR ANSWERS TO TEST YOUR MASTERY.

---

crystallized intelligence (g_c)
factor analysis
fluid intelligence (g_f)
g
psychometric approach

s
"structure of intellect"
    model
triarchic theory

1. _____ A theoretical perspective that portrays intelligence as a trait (or set of traits) on which individuals differ; psychometric theorists are responsible for the development of standardized intelligence tests.

2. _____ A statistical procedure for identifying clusters of tests or test items (called factors) that are highly correlated with one another and unrelated to other test items.

3. _____ Spearman's abbreviation for *neogenesis*, which, roughly translated, means one's ability to understand relations (or general mental ability).

4. _____ Spearman's term for mental abilities that are specific to particular tests.

5. _____ Guilford's factor-analytic model of intelligence, which proposes that there are 180 distinct mental abilities.

6. _____ The ability to perceive relations and solve relational problems of the type that are relatively free of cultural influences.

7. _____ The ability to understand relations or solve problems that depend on knowledge acquired from schooling and other cultural influences.

8. _____ A recent information-processing theory of intelligence that emphasizes three aspects of intelligent behavior not normally tapped by IQ tests: the context of the action; the person's experience with the task (or situation); and the information-processing strategies the person applies to the task (or situation).

---

developmental quotient (DQ)
deviation IQ
intelligence quotient (IQ)

mental age (MA)
normal distribution
test norms

9. _____ A measure of intellectual development that reflects the level of age-graded problems a child is able to solve.

10. _____ A numerical measure of a person's performance on an intelligence test relative to the performance of other examinees.

11. _____ Standards of normal performance on psychometric instruments that are based on the average scores and the range of scores obtained by a large, representative sample of test takers.

12. _____ An IQ score based on the extent to which a child's test performance deviates from the average performance of agemates.

13. _____ A symmetrical, bell-shaped curve that describes the variability of certain characteristics within a population; most people fall at or near the average score.

14. _____ A numerical measure of an infant's performance on a developmental schedule relative to the performance of other infants of the same age.

confluence hypothesis
cultural bias
"culture-fair" IQ tests

cumulative-deficit hypothesis
HOME inventory
"test bias" hypothesis

15. _____ The notion that impoverished environments inhibit intellectual growth and that these inhibiting effects accumulate over time.

16. _____ A measure of the amount and type of intellectual stimulation provided by a child's home environment.

17. _____ Zajonc's notion that a child's intellectual development depends on the average intellectual level of all family members.

18. _____ The notion that IQ tests have a built-in, middle-class bias that explains the substandard performance of children from lower-class and minority subcultures.

19. _____ Intelligence tests constructed to minimize any irrelevant cultural biases that could influence test performance.

20. _____ The situation that arises when one cultural or subcultural group is more familiar with test items than another group and therefore has an unfair advantage.

---

genetic hypothesis　　　　　　　　　　**Level II abilities**
Level I abilities

21. _____ The notion that group differences in IQ are hereditary.

22. _____ Jensen's term for lower-level intellectual abilities (such as attention and short-term memory) that are important for simple association learning.

23. _____ Jensen's term for higher-level cognitive skills that are involved in abstract reasoning and problem solving.

---

compensatory interventions　　　　　　**Head Start**
environmental hypothesis　　　　　　　**home-based interventions**

24. _____ The notion that groups differ in IQ because the environments in which they are raised are not equally conducive to intellectual growth.

25. _____ Special educational programs designed to further the cognitive growth and scholastic achievements of disadvantaged children.

26. _____ A large-scale preschool educational program designed to provide children from low-income families with a variety of social and intellectual experiences that might better prepare them for school.

27. _____ Compensatory interventions that take place in the home and involve one or more family members in the child's learning experiences.

---

convergent thinking	giftedness
creativity	ideational fluency
divergent thinking	

28. _____ The possession of unusually high intellectual potential or of other special talents.

29. _____ The ability to generate novel ideas or works that are valued by others.

30. _____ Thinking that requires a variety of ideas or solutions to a problem when there is no one correct answer.

31. _____ The most common measure of creativity; the sheer number of different ideas or solutions one can generate.

32. _____ Thinking that requires one to come up with a single correct answer to a problem; what IQ tests measure.

CHAPTER 9 STUDY QUESTIONS

WHAT IS INTELLIGENCE?

1.   Psychometricians have proposed that there are as few as two main factors that compose intelligence, *g* and *s* (Spearman), or as may as 180 factors (Guilford). What conclusion does your text suggest is warranted regarding the **number of factors contributing to intelligence** (based on the factor analytic studies)? (p. 321-323)

2.	Indicate the **number of factors** each of the following **psychometricians believed make up intelligence.** (p. 321-323)

SPEARMAN:	_____

THURSTONE:	_____

GUILFORD:	_____

3.	How does the more recent psychometric view of intelligence proposed by **Cattell and Horn** differ from the views of Spearman and Thurstone? (p. 324)

4.	What criticism **of psychometric views** of intelligence has been recurringly leveled? (p. 324)

5.	Characterize each component of **Sternberg's triarchic theory of intelligence.** (p. 324-326)

CONTEXT:

EXPERIENCE:

INFORMATION-PROCESSING SKILLS:

HOW IS INTELLIGENCE MEASURED?

6.	How did **Binet and Simon** go about selecting items for the **first intelligence test?** (p. 326)

7.   For what **purpose** was the **first intelligence test** developed? (p. 326)

8.   The notion of mental age has been abandoned in favor of the **deviation IQ.** How does this newer scoring procedure arrive at the IQ score? (p. 328)

9.   What change (from the Stanford-Binet) did **Wechsler** make when he constructed his own intelligence scales? (p. 328)

10.   What IQ test score is considered to be **average,** i.e., the score above and below which 50% of the population score? (p. 329 & Fig. 9-2)

What percentage of people fall **within 15 points of average?**   **30 points of average?**   (p. 329, Table 9-2 & Fig. 9-2)

11.   The **Kaufman Assessment Battery for Children** (K-ABC) differs from the Stanford-Binet and the Wechsler scales in its emphasis on what aspect of intelligence? (p. 330)

12.   **Feuerstein** and **Sternberg** argue that **intelligence should assess** _____ rather than what a person already knows. (p. 330-331)

ASSESSING INFANT INTELLIGENCE

13.   **Infant intelligence** has typically been assessed using the **rate at which infants reach various milestones.** These tests have been found to be **poor predictors of later IQ** test performance for what **major reason?** (p. 331)

14.   What **two attributes of infant information processing** have been found to be **correlated with childhood IQ?** (p. 332)

   (a)

   (b)

15.   Starting at age _____ IQ scores show meaningful **predictability** to later IQ. (p. 333)

16.   The text points out that, even though there is some predictability of IQ scores across ages, when individual profiles are studied there is considerable fluctuation in some individuals. **McCall** and associates found that half of a sample of 140 children showed fluctuations in IQ over time and that the **average fluctuation** was _____ IQ points. (p. 333)

How can the finding that some individuals show considerable stability whereas others show marked fluctuation in IQ scores be explained? (p. 333)

WHAT DO INTELLIGENCE TESTS PREDICT?

17.   What answer can be given to the question: Does IQ **predict academic achievement?** (p. 333-334)

18.   Minton and Schneider found that IQ is **not** the best **predictor** of future grades; _____ **are.** (p. 334)

19.   What do individuals with an **impulsive cognitive style** do that is **not conducive to successful performance** on many academic tasks? (p. 334, Box 9-1)

In what way have impulsive children been shown to be less cognitively competent than reflective children? (Box 9-1)

20.   How did the text author answer the question of the **relationship between IQ and occupational success?** (p. 335-336)

What other factors predict occupational success?

21.   Does research indicate that a **high IQ** is a guarantee of **happiness and health?** Elaborate, indicating what other factors have been found to **co-determine positive outcomes.** (p. 336-337)

22.   Does research on the adult lives of mildly and moderately **retarded individuals** support the common assumption that they will necessarily be unhappy and unsuccessful in life? Elaborate. (p. 338-339, Box 9-2)

FACTORS THAT INFLUENCE IQ SCORES

23.   Evidence for a **role of heredity** on intellectual performance comes from what two main sources? Summarize briefly the findings for each. (p. 338)

   (a)

   (b)

24.   According to **Scarr and McCartney,** what might account for the finding that **identical twins often show remarkable resemblance** in behavior even when reared in different homes or after not seeing each other for years? (p. 338-339)

25.   Children who live in impoverished environments tend to score lower on IQ tests than children in more favorable circumstances. In addition, the **IQs of the impoverished children** _____ over time if they remain in the disadvantaged environment, a finding in keeping with the _____-_____ hypothesis. (p. 340)

26.   If living in an impoverished environment results in lower IQ scores, IQ scores should improve if the environments of disadvantaged children are **enriched.** Is there any evidence for this proposition? Cite the findings of one or more studies. (p. 340-341)

27.   Which aspects of **home environment** did **Gottfried** find best **predicted later IQ scores?** (p. 341-342)

(a)

(b)

(c)

28.   How do we know that the **quality of home environment** has an **effect independent of genetics** (could it be that high IQ parents just provide more stimulating environments)? (p. 343)

(a)

(b)

How do the **Yeates et al. findings** bear on **McCall's argument** that environmental (e.g., home) **factors become more important to intellectual development after infancy?**

29.   How strong have **birth-order** and **family-size effects on IQ** been found to be? (p. 343-345)

What two **explanations** for the effects have been offered?

(a)

(b)

30.   To what extent do the distributions of IQ scores for Blacks and Whites **overlap**? (p. 345-346, Fig. 9-4)

31.   Write a summary statement of the evidence for and against each of the following **four hypotheses** that have been **proposed to account for racial, ethnic, and social-class differences in IQ.** (p. 346-351 & Box 9-3)

TEST BIAS:

ZIGLER'S MOTIVATIONAL HYPOTHESIS:

GENETIC HYPOTHESIS:

ENVIRONMENTAL HYPOTHESIS:

What argument can be made against Jensen's claim that the IQ difference between Black and White children reflects genetic differences? How, instead, can between-group variation be explained? (Box 9-3)

32. Patterson and associates found that _____ is a **better predictor of the academic competencies** of Black and White children than is race per se. (p. 350-351)

33. In a recent adoption study, **Moore** (1986) found that compared with Black mothers, **White mothers** provided _____ _____ while supervising their children's problem-solving activities, **a difference that suggests that there may be differences in the two racial groups' parenting styles** that account for the racial differences in IQ test performance when they are found. (p. 351)

IMPROVING INTELLECTUAL PERFORMANCE THROUGH COMPENSATORY EDUCATION

34. Have **follow-up studies of Head Start** found any **lasting benefits of participation?** If any, describe. (p. 352-353)

35. **What factor** has been found to be common to the most **successful early intervention** programs, e.g., Levenstein's or Sprigle and Schaefer's? (p. 353-354)

36. Compensatory education programs "graduate" children who score better than controls on IQ tests, but they still score 5-15 points below the national average on IQ tests. Apparently more intense programs are necessary. The **Carolina Abecedarian Project** represents one such attempt. What kind of interventions did they try? How successful was the program in bringing children up to the national norms on IQ test scores? (p. 354-355 & Fig. 9-6)

CREATIVITY AND SPECIAL TALENTS

37.   What **relationship** has been found between **IQ** and **creativity**? (p. 356)

38.   What factors have been identified as most related to the **development of special talent** in areas such as music, gymnastics, or art? (p. 357-358)

    (a)

    (b)

    (c)

WAYS IN WHICH HOME ENVIRONMENT SUPPORTS
INTELLECTUAL DEVELOPMENT

INTRODUCTION: This activity relates to material in Chapter 12 (p. 341-343) on the relationship between home environment and intellectual performance. Gottfried (1984) found that of six home environment variables assessed, the three that best predicted children's later IQ were parental involvement with the child, provision of age-appropriate play materials, and opportunities for variety in daily stimulation. Other researchers (Crockenberg, 1983; Estrada, et al., 1987) added that the warmth and responsiveness of the parents is as important as the amount of involvement and stimulation.

INSTRUCTIONS:

Part A

For this activity give specific examples of how your parents supported your intellectual development in each of the ways listed below. Also, give examples of things they did that were not as supportive of intellectual development as they might have been (nobody's parents are perfect!) and examples of things you wish they had done to promote intellectual development. (If you have children, you could give examples of ways you are supporting the intellectual development of your children and examples of additional ways that you might do so.)

1. **Parental involvement with the child.**
2. **Age-appropriate play materials.**
3. **Opportunities for variety in daily stimulation.**
4. **Warm, responsive interaction.**

Part B

Continuously-present aspects of home environment represent only one possible type of environmental contributor to intellectual performance. What other people, experiences outside of your family, or short-term, one-time experiences within the family (e.g., a move, a health problem, a special trip) do you think made significant contributions (positive or negative) to your intellectual development? Describe briefly.

WHAT IS INTELLIGENCE?

1. (323)   Based on factor-analytic studies, it is clear that intelligence is not merely a singular attribute; however, how many components there are is unknown. Most studies suggest that there are fewer basic mental abilities than Guilford's figure of 180.

2. (322)   Spearman: 2
             Thurstone: 7
             Guilford: 180

3. (324)   Cattell and Horn propose a theory more developmental in nature that subdivides Spearman's and Thurstone's primary mental abilities into two major dimensions: fluid intelligence and crystallized intelligence. Crystallized intelligence increases over the lifespan since it reflects one's cumulative learning. Fluid intelligence increases gradually through childhood and adolescence as the nervous system matures.

4. (324)   Psychometric views are very narrow, focusing primarily on intellectual content.

5. (324)   CONTEXT: successful adaptation to the environment or successful shaping of the environment to better suit needs--in everyday language, practical wisdom or "street smarts."

   (325)   EXPERIENCE: it is a sign of intelligence if a person is able to generate new ideas or fresh insights in response to a novel problem/situation. It is also a sign of intelligence if experience results in automization, (i.e., increasing efficiency with practice) leaving more processing space for other processing activities.
             INFORMATION-PROCESSING SKILLS: the cognitive processes by which we size up the requirements of problems, formulate strategies to solve them, and then monitor our cognitive activities until we have accomplished our goals.

HOW IS INTELLIGENCE MEASURED?

6. (326)   Binet and Simon began by constructing a large battery of cognitive tasks that measured skills presumed necessary for classroom learning: attention, perception, memory, reasoning, and verbal comprehension. Items that did not discriminate between dull and normal children were eliminated.

7. (326)   Binet and Simon were commissioned by the French government to devise a test that would identify "dull" children who might benefit from remedial instruction.

8. (328)   A child's test performance is now compared with that of other children his own age. A child is considered bright, average, or dull depending on the deviation from the average score of children the same age.

9. (328) Wechsler subdivided his test into <u>performance</u> (nonverbal) and <u>verbal subtests</u> to avoid total emphasis on verbal abilities of the Stanford Binet. He maintained that many intellectual skills are primarily nonverbal. He argued that nonverbal subtests are less likely to discriminate against those who have English as a second language or those with reading or hearing difficulties. Another possible advantage would be the possibility of detecting inconsistencies between verbal and nonverbal subscales that might signal brain damage or a learning disability.

10. (329) 100

68%, 95%

11. (330) Focuses on measurement of what Cattell and Horn call <u>fluid intelligence</u>. Test items are primarily nonverbal and assess basic information-processing skills. Several features have been incorporated in an attempt to reduce cultural bias and make the K-ABC fairer than other tests to minority, low-income, and handicapped youngsters.

12. (330) What <u>can</u> be learned

ASSESSING INFANT INTELLIGENCE

13. (331) Infant tests and IQ tests <u>tap very different types of abilities</u> (sensory, motor, social <u>versus</u> memory, problem solving, verbal reasoning).

14. (332) a) <u>rate infants habituate</u> to repetitive stimuli
b) <u>extent to which infants prefer novel stimuli</u> to familiar ones are two infant attention attributes that correlate .46 with IQ in childhood.

15. (332) 4 years

16. (333) 28.5 IQ points

Home environment was unstable for the children who fluctuated

WHAT DO INTELLIGENCE TESTS PREDICT?

17. (333) Yes, moderately; the average correlation between IQ scores and children's current grades in school is about .50. Children with high IQs tend to do better in school and stay there longer.

18. (334) <u>Past grades</u> are a better predictor than IQ of future grades

19. (334) Children classified as impulsives tend to answer very quickly and inaccurately, often picking the first alternative that seems correct without carefully examining all possibilities.

Impulsive children tend to know less about memory processes and how to plan and monitor their cognitive activities.

20. (335-336)   Most prestigious jobs are filled by people with high IQs, but not all people with high IQs have prestigious jobs.

Bright people tend to out-perform less gifted colleagues; however, there are reasons to look beyond IQ for job performance. Variables such as workers' prior job performance and motivation to succeed may be better predictors of performance.

21. (336-337)   No, but there is a relationship. Terman found that children that with IQs of 140 or higher were rated by teachers as better adjusted emotionally, morally mature, physically healthier than average, and quicker to take charge and assume leadership. As adults fewer than 5% were rated seriously maladjusted and the incidence of ill-health, psychiatric disturbance, alcoholism, and delinquent behavior was a fraction of what is normally observed in the general population. High IQ helps, but does not guarantee happiness and good adjustment. Family environment has been found to be an important co-determinant.

22. (339)   Although research reports seem dismal at first glance, there are many reasons for optimism. 80% of retarded males are gainfully employed. Most mentally retarded individuals marry and express satisfaction with their accomplishments.

FACTORS THAT INFLUENCE IQ SCORES

23. (338)   a) FAMILY STUDIES: the intellectual resemblance of pairs of individuals living in the same home increases as a function of their kinship.
b) ADOPTION STUDIES: adopted children's IQs are more highly correlated with the IQs of their biological parents than their adoptive parents.

24. (339)   People seek out environments that are compatible with their genetic predispositions, so identical twins (who share identical genes) will seek out similar environments, thereby enhancing the effects of heredity.

25. (340)   Decrease, cumulative-deficit hypothesis

26. (340)   Enriched environment improves IQ. Two studies of isolated mountain children (Wheeler, 1932, 1942), studies conducted in Hawaii and the American Midwest (Finch, 1946; Smith, 1942), and studies of adopted children leaving disadvantaged family backgrounds for educated, successful adoptive-parent placements (Scarr & Weinberg, 1977, 1983; Skodak & Skeels, 1949) support this statement. In each study children reared in more favorable environments outscored children reared in disadvantaged environments.

SOCIOCULTURAL CORRELATES OF INTELLECTUAL PERFORMANCE

27. (341-342)   a) parental involvement with the child
b) provision of age-appropriate play materials
c) opportunities for variety in daily stimulation

28. (343)   a)   adopted children in stimulating home environments attain higher IQs than adoptees in less stimulating homes.

           b)   in Yeates's longitudinal study of mothers and their 2- to 4-year-old children, quality of home environment not only predicted IQ scores, it was a better predictor than the mother's IQ by age 4.

Yeates's findings are consistent with McCall's assertion that early intellectual development is more canalized and under stronger maturational forces than later intellectual development. However, Yeates's findings are also consistent with the interpretation that the full impact of home environment may accumulate over time, becoming apparent by 4 years of age.

29. (345)   Birth-order and family-size effects tend to be quite small and are observed only when large numbers of families are compared.

      (344)   a)   first-borns and children from small families may receive more intellectual stimulation from their parents than later-borns.

                 b)   a child's intellectual development depends on the average intellectual level of all family members.

30. (346)   Approximately 15-20% of the Black population score higher than half of the White population (Shuey, 1966).

31. (346)   **TEST BIAS:** claims that group differences in IQ are an artifact of our testing
(Box 9-3)   procedures. There is little question that predominately verbal tests are biased; yet, some group differences persist even with more "culture-fair" IQ tests. Also IQ and various aptitude tests predict future academic success for Black and other minorities as well as for Whites.

    (347-348)   **ZIGLER'S MOTIVATIONAL HYPOTHESIS:** claims social-class and ethnic differences in IQ are due largely to motivational factors. Flexible administration procedures (as in the K-ABC) allow the examiner to minimize children's wariness and maximize motivation. As a result of the more flexible procedures, the typical IQ discrepancy between Blacks and Whites has been cut in half.

      (348)   **GENETIC HYPOTHESIS:** claims members of various social-class, ethnic, and racial groups intra-marry resulting in a restriction in the gene flow between subgroups. Jensen cites as evidence the fact that White children outperform Black children on subtests assessing ability to reason abstractly and to manipulate words and symbols to form concepts and solve problems. However, data based on mixed-race children provide little support for the genetic hypothesis.

    (350-351)   **ENVIRONMENTAL HYPOTHESIS:** claims that environment plays a major part in IQ. Scarr and Weinberg's adoption studies show clear evidence that home evironment is an important factor behind group differences in IQ performance. Black children adopted into White, middle-class homes scored 20 points above comparable children reared in the Black community. Moore's research suggests that socioeconomic status only accounts for part of the home-environment effects in the Scarr and Weinberg research. Subcultural differences in parenting style also play a role.

(Box 9-3)   Heritability estimates apply only to understanding within-group variability. Even though the heritability estimate for IQ may be high, it says nothing about between-group differences. Between-group differences more likely reflect differences in experiences related to doing well on IQ tests rather than in inherited capacity.

32. (350)   Income

33. (351)   A great deal of positive encouragement

34. (352-353)   Yes, there are immediate gains on IQ test performance and other indicators of cognitive development that may last for 3 or 4 years after the program is ended. More lasting benefits have been found on other measures, e.g., program participants are less likely to require special education or to be retained in grade, and both children's and mother's attitudes about achievement tend to be more positive several years after Head Start has ended.

35. (353)   Parental involvement

36. (354-355)   Starting early (6-12 weeks of age) and attending full-days until 5 years of age.

(Fig. 9-6)   From age 3 the children were slightly above national norms in IQ test performance.

37. (356)   Among people with above average IQs, scores on creativity tests are not highly correlated with scores on IQ test, suggesting that creativity and general intelligence are independent attributes.

38. (357)   a) exceptional motivation
b) supportive environment
c) intense tutoring or coaching by experts

CHAPTER 10

DEVELOPMENT OF LANGUAGE AND COMMUNICATION SKILLS

STUDY CHECKLIST

_____ Read Chapter Outline and Summary (Study guide)

_____ Read Chapter (Text)

_____ Completed Vocabulary Fill-Ins (Study guide)

_____ Re-Read Outline and Summary (Study guide)

_____ Reviewed Lecture Notes and Integrated with Text

_____ Reviewed Vocabulary, Study Questions, and Text Chapter

CHAPTER 10 OUTLINE AND SUMMARY

I. **Four components of language**
   A. Phonology
   B. Semantics
   C. Syntax
   D. Pragmatics

Students of language development have tried to answer two basic questions. The first is the "what" question: What is the normal course of language development, and just what are children acquiring that enables them to become language users? The four aspects of language that children acquire are phonology, a knowledge of the phonemes used in producing language; semantics, an understanding of the meaning of words and sentences; syntax, the rules that specify how words are combined to produce sentences; and pragmatics, the principles governing how language is to be used in different social situations. The second basic question is the "how" question: How do young children acquire a working knowledge of a highly abstract symbol system such as language? Empiricists have argued that children learn language as they imitate others' speech and are reinforced for grammatical statements. However, nativists contend that children are biologically programmed to acquire language and do not have to be reinforced for grammatical speech.

II. **Before language: The prelinguistic period**
   A. The infant's reactions to language
   B. Producing sounds: The infant's prelinguistic vocalizations
   C. What do prelinguistic infants know about language?

Although babies respond to speech at birth, they will not utter their first meaningful words for about a year. During this prelinguistic phase, infants vocalize by crying, cooing, and babbling. As infants continue to babble, they begin to match the intonation of their babbles to the tonal qualities of the language they hear, and will eventually use sounds to represent objects and experiences, producing their own unique words, or "vocables." Although babies less than 1 year of age rarely if ever understand the meaning of individual words, they have already learned that people take turns when vocalizing to each other and they know a speaker's tone of voice can be an important communicative prompt.

At about 1 year of age, infants produce their first recognizable words and enter the holophrastic phase of language development. For the next several months, children talk in one-word utterances and will expand their vocabularies one word at a time. They talk most about those things that interest them--objects that move, make noise, or can be manipulated. Young children infer the meaning of words in a variety of ways including fast mapping, analyzing the semantic features (perceptual characteristics) of their referents, and forming hypotheses about probable meanings from the word's position in a sentence (form contrast) and from its assumed contractive relation with the meaning of other words (lexical contrast). These strategies permit young toddlers to rapidly acquire impressive vocabularies, although their use may also contribute to semantic errors, such as overextension and underextension. Some psycholinguists believe that a child's single words are often intended as holophrases--one-word messages that represent an entire sentence's worth of meaning.

At about 18-24 months of age, children enter the telegraphic phase of language development as they begin to combine words into simple sentences. These utterances are called "telegraphic" because they typically include only nouns, verbs, and occasionally adjectives, omitting prepositions, auxiliary verbs, articles, conjunctions, and other grammatical markers. Although telegraphic sentences are not grammatical by adult standards, they represent far more than random word combinations. Not only do all children follow the same rules of word order when combining words, but they also express the same categories of meaning (semantic relations) in their earliest sentences. So telegraphic speech is not merely a shortened version of adult speech; it is a universal "child language" that has a grammar of its own.

During the preschool period (ages 2 1/2 to 5) the child's language becomes much more similar to an adult's. As children produce longer utterances, they begin to add grammatical morphemes such as the -s for plurality, the -ed for past tense, the -ing for present progressive, articles, prepositions, and auxiliary verbs. Although individual children acquire grammatical markers at different rates, there is a striking uniformity in the order in which these morphemes appear. The preschool period is also the time when a child learns basic transformational rules that will enable him or her to change declarative statements into questions, negations, imperatives, relative clauses, and compound sentences. By the time they enter school, children have mastered most of the syntactical rules of their native language and can produce a variety of sophisticated, adultlike messages. Another reason language becomes increasingly complex during the preschool years is that youngsters are beginning to appreciate semantic and relational contrasts such as big/little, wide/narrow, more/less, and before/after. Preschool children are also communicating more effectively as they begin to detect at least some of the uninformative messages they receive and to ask for clarification. Moreover, they have learned another important pragmatic lesson: if you hope to be understood, you must tailor your message to the listener's level of understanding.

Middle childhood and early adolescence (ages 6-14) is a period of linguistic refinement: children learn subtle exceptions to grammatical rules and begin to understand even the most complex syntactical structures of their native language. Vocabulary continues to grow, and children are rapidly developing metalinguistic awareness--an ability to think about language and to comment on its properties. School-age children are also becoming much better communicators as they attend more carefully to literal meanings of ambiguous utterances and are more likely to clarify the uninformative messages they send and receive.

VII. **Theories of language development**
  A. The learning (empiricist) perspective
      1. Skinner's reinforcement model
      2. Imitation as a basis for language learning
      3. How do the child's companions promote language learning?
  B. The nativist perspective
      1. The evidence for nativism
      2. Problems with the nativist approach
  C. The interactionist perspective

There are three major theories of language acquisition: learning theory, nativism, and the interactionist approach. Learning theorists believe that language is acquired as children imitate the speech of their companions and are reinforced for their grammatically correct imitations. However, careful analyses of conversations between parents and their young children reveal that children do not mimic the sentences they hear, nor do adults selectively reinforce their children's grammatical statements. Yet the child's companions do promote language learning by conversing successfully with him or her and thereby introducing new linguistic principles in sentences that are carefully tailored to the child's level of understanding.

Nativists argue that human beings are innately endowed with linguistic processing capabilities (that is, a language acquisition device or language-making capacity) that function most efficiently prior to puberty. Presumably, children require nothing other than speech to analyze in order to learn any and all languages to which they are exposed. The identification of linguistic universals is consistent with the nativist viewpoint, as are the recent observations that deaf children of hearing parents and other children exposed to ungrammatical pidgins may create formal languages of their own. However, there is little support for the nativist assumption that language learning is easiest prior to puberty. And, unfortunately, nativists are not very clear about how children sift through verbal input and make the crucial discoveries that will further their linguistic competencies.

Proponents of the interactionist position acknowledge that children are biologically prepared to acquire language. However, they suggest that what may be innate is not any specialized linguistic processor but, rather, a nervous system that gradually matures and predisposes children to develop similar ideas at about the same age. Thus, biological maturation is said to affect cognitive development, which in turn influences language development. However, interactionists stress that the environment plays a crucial role in language learning, for children will not acquire the linguistic concepts that promote language development unless they have ample opportunities to converse with responsive companions who tailor their own speech to the children's levels of understanding.

CHAPTER 10 VOCABULARY FILL-INS
(Definitions below are in order of appearance in text margins)

MATCH VOCABULARY WORD/PHRASE TO ITS DEFINITION.
THEN COVER YOUR ANSWERS TO TEST YOUR MASTERY.

communication
language
morphemes
phonemes
phonology

pragmatics
psycholinguists
semantics
syntax

1. _____ A small number of individually meaningless signals (sounds, letters, gestures) that can be combined according to agreed-on rules to produce an infinite number of messages.

2. _____ The process by which one organism transmits information to and influences another.

3. _____ Those who study the structure and development of children's language.

4. _____ The sound system of a language and the rules for combining these sounds to produce meaningful units of speech.

5. _____ The basic units of sound that are used in a spoken language.

6. _____ The smallest meaningful units of language; these include words and grammatical markers such as prefixes, suffixes, and verb-tense modifiers (for example, -ed, -ing).

7. _____ The expressed meaning of words and sentences.

8. _____ The structure of a language; the rules specifying how words and grammatical markers are to be combined to produce meaningful sentences.

9. _____ Principles that underlie the effective and appropriate use of language in social contexts.

---

babbles	prelinguistic stage
coos	productive language
fake cries	receptive language
formats	vocables

10. _____ The period before children utter their first meaningful words.

11. _____ Low-pitched moans that young infants make when seeking attention or experimenting with sounds.

12. _____ Vowel-like sounds that young infants repeat over and over during periods of contentment.

13. _____ Vowel/consonant combinations that infants begin to produce at about 3 to 4 months of age.

14. _____ Unique patterns of sound that a prelinguistic infant uses to represent objects, actions, or events.

15. _____ Interactions in which a young child and an older companion assume separate but reversible (reciprocal) roles.

16. _____ That which the individual comprehends when listening to others' speech.

17. _____ That which the individual is capable of expressing (producing) in his or her own speech.

**fast mapping
form class hypothesis
holophrase
holophrastic period**

**lexical contrast theory
overextension
underextension**

18. _____ The period when the child's speech consists of one-word utterances.

19. _____ Process of linking a word with an underlying concept after hearing the word a time or two.

20. _____ The young child's tendency to use relatively specific words to refer to a broader set of objects, actions, or events than adults do (for example, using the word <u>car</u> to refer to all motor vehicles).

21. _____ The young child's tendency to use general words to refer to a smaller set of objects, actions, or events than adults do (for example, using <u>candy</u> to refer only to mints).

22. _____ Notion that young children make inferences about the meaning of words by analyzing the way words are used in sentences and inferring whether they refer to objects (nouns), actions (verbs), or attributes (adjectives).

23. _____ Notion that young children make inferences about word meanings by contrasting new words with words they already know.

24. _____ A single-word utterance that represents an entire sentence's worth of meaning.

**grammatical morphemes
mean length of utterance (MLU)
overregularization**

**semantic grammar
telegraphic speech
transformational
        grammar**

25. _____ Early sentences that consist solely of content words and omit the less meaningful parts of speech, such as articles, prepositions, pronouns, and auxiliary verbs.

26. _____ An analysis of the semantic relations (meanings) that children express in their earliest sentences.

27. _____ The average number of meaningful units (morphemes) in a child's utterances.

28. _____ Prefixes, suffixes, prepositions, and auxiliary verbs that modify the meaning of words and sentences.

29. _____ The overgeneralization of grammatical rules to irregular cases where the rules do not apply (for example, saying "mouses" rather than "mice").

30. _____ Rules of syntax that allow one to transform declarative statements into questions, negatives, imperatives, and other kinds of sentences.

**communication pressure
hypothesis**

**metalinguistic awareness
referential
communication**

31. _____ A knowledge of language and its properties; an understanding that language can be used for purposes other than communicating.

32. _____ Communication that makes reference to objects or events that the listener is not currently experiencing.

33. _____ The idea that children learn to speak clearly and grammatically because clear, grammatical statements will effectively communicate their needs and desires.

**expansions
motherese**

recasts

34. _____ The short, simple, high-pitched (and often repetitive) sentences that adults use when talking with young children.

35. _____ Responding to a child's ungrammatical utterance with a grammatically improved form of that statement.

36. _____ Responding to a child's ungrammatical utterance with a nonrepetitive statement that is grammatically correct.

---

aphasia
interactionist theory
critical-period hypothesis
language acquisition device (LAD)

language-making
    capacity (LMC)
linguistic universal

37. _____ Chomsky's term for the innate knowledge of grammar that humans were said to possess--knowledge that might enable young children to infer the rules governing others' speech and to use these rules to produce language.

38. _____ A hypothesized set of specialized linguistic processing skills that enable children to analyze speech and to detect phonological, semantic, and syntactical relationships.

39. _____ Loss of one or more language functions due to an injury to the brain.

40. _____ The notion that human beings are most proficient at language learning before they reach puberty.

41. _____ An aspect of language development that all children share.

42. _____ The notion that biological factors and environmental influences combine to determine the course of language development.

CHAPTER 10 STUDY QUESTIONS

FOUR COMPONENTS OF LANGUAGE

1.   One question researchers have attempted to answer is **What do children learn about language?** The answer is complex because there are four types of knowledge a child acquires. Give a phrase to characterize each of the four **types of linguistic knowledge.** (p. 362-364)

PHONOLOGY:

SEMANTICS:

SYNTAX:

PRAGMATICS:

2.   In answer to the question of **how children acquire language,** there are two opposing views. **Learning theorists** argue that children learn by _____ adult language and by being _____ by adults for producing successive approximations of adult language. In contrast, **nativists** argue that humans are born with _____ that enable them to detect and apply the rules of language they hear. (p. 364)

3.   In a phrase indicate the type of evidence each of the researchers below has found that demonstrates infants are remarkably **sensitive to language right from birth.** (p. 365)

Rheingold & Adams:

DeCasper & Fifer:

Molfese:

Butterfield & Siperstein:

Clarkson & Berg:

4.   At what age does the **babbling** of infants begin to **sound like the language of their parents?** (p. 365)

5.   **What aspect of babbling were Bates, O'Connell,** and **Shore** referring to when they said that babies are **"learning the tune before the words"?** (p. 366)

Based on the results of research by **Stern** and associates and other research groups, several theorists have concluded that a young infant's successful interpretation of _____ may provide the first evidence that speech conveys meaning. (p. 367)

6.   One aspect of the pragmatics of language is taking turns when communicating with language. Give an example of a kind of **vocal turntaking** that occurs during infant-parent interactions. (p. 366)

7.   Parents will sometimes claim that their infant seems to understand a few words by 8-10 months of age. A study by **Thomas** et al. found that not until 13 months of age do children show evidence of comprehending **words**. What **basis** does the text suggest the younger infants are using when their behavior looks as if they understand? (p. 367-368)

8.   During the second year which aspect of language tends to be ahead or precede the other, **production** or **comprehension**? (p. 368)

THE HOLOPHRASTIC PERIOD

9.   **Nelson** found that about **half of infants' first words** were names of objects **(nominals)**. What special characteristics did these early-labeled objects have? (p. 368, Table 10-1)

10.   What kind of evidence has been found to support each of the hypotheses below about **semantic development**? (p. 370)

FORM CLASS HYPOTHESIS:

LEXICAL CONTRAST THEORY:

11.   Young children have been found to often **overextend** words, e.g., a child may call a horse, "doggie." **Ingram** suggests that such overextensions probably _____ (do/do not) indicate that the child actually thinks the horse is a dog. (p. 371)

12.   At the **holophrastic** (one-word) phase of language acquisition, children seem to be using single words to express an entire idea. What has lead researchers to infer multiple meanings from children's repeated uses of the same word? (p. 371)

THE TELEGRAPHIC PERIOD

13.   What **characteristics** of early two-word utterances have led **Brown** and others to describe this speech as **telegraphic**? (p. 372-373)

Does evidence (Petretic & Tweney, 1977; Gerken et al., 1990) suggest the omitted words are totally ignored by 2-year-olds? Justify your answer. (p. 372-373)

14.   Like holophrases, **two-word utterances often convey an entire idea** and the same two words may have different meanings depending on the context. What are **two** (or more) **possible meanings for an utterance such as "daddy bike"**? (p. 373-374)

15.   The **acquisition** of **spoken language** and **American Sign Language** has been **compared** and found to proceed _____ (very similarly, very differently). Give examples that illustrate your answer. (p. 375, Box 10-1)

LANGUAGE LEARNING DURING THE PRESCHOOL PERIOD

16.   **Brown** found that children add in **grammatical morphemes** such as *-ing, -s, -ed, -'s*, etc. in a **fixed order**. He attributed the invariant order to what? (p. 377)

17.   How does the text **interpret the tendency for children to overregularize** irregular plural nouns and irregular verbs (as an error, or as a developmental milestone)? Why? (p. 378)

18.   **"What daddy eat"** and **"No daddy eat"** represent a phase that toddlers go through in the production of both **questions** and **negatives**. **How are these productions similar?** (p. 378-379)

19.   Even though preschoolers seem to understand that concepts such as big and little are relative (i.e., an object may be big when compared to a smaller one and very small when compared to a huge one), there is still a **tendency among 4- and 5-year-olds to interpret "big"** as meaning what? (p. 380, Fig. 10-2)

20.   The **pragmatics** of language includes such things as making adjustments in speech to fit the audience, recognizing when a message is ambiguous, etc. What conclusion does recent research suggest regarding **preschoolers' pragmatic skills**? (p. 381-382)

REFINEMENT OF LANGUAGE SKILLS

21.   Give two examples of **grammatical refinements** made during **middle childhood.** (p. 382)

(a)

(b)

22.   Two **semantic advances** during the **grade school years** are growth in the ability to draw inferences and in the ability to detect hidden meanings. Give an example of each. (p. 383)

INFERENCES:

HIDDEN MEANING:

23. The text cites research suggesting that some degree of **metalinguistic awareness** may be a **better predictor of reading achievement** than amount parents read to the child or traditional tests of reading readiness. What is metalinguistic awareness? (p. 383)

24. Fig. 10-3 presents the mean errors of K, 1st-, 3rd-, and 5th-grade children on a communication task described in the text. What does the graphed data reveal about the **developmental trend of communication effectiveness?** (p. 384-385 & Fig. 10-3)

What is it about the errors preschoolers make when talking about unfamiliar designs that makes their messages uncommunicative or ambiguous? (p. 384 & Table 10-6)

25. **Effective communication** requires generation of informative messages and active listening skills. Give examples of specific acquisitions for both of these requirements. (p. 385)

INFORMATIVE MESSAGES:

ACTIVE LISTENING:

THEORIES OF LANGUAGE DEVELOPMENT

26.   Although there is no definitive answer to the question of **how children acquire language**, the text indicates that there are some factors that have not been confirmed as playing an important role, some factors that have been supported as facilitative if not essential to language acquisition, and some minimal conditions that seems to be essential for language acquisition.

For each of the **environmental** factors listed below, indicate with an **X what role** (little, facilitative, or essential) it has been found to play in vocabulary/semantic and in syntactic development. *Use a ? if the text did not explicitly discuss roles or you are unsure.* (p. 386-390)

	LITTLE/NO ROLE		FACILITATIVE		ESSENTIAL	
	VOC	SYN	VOC	SYN	VOC	SYN
REINFORCEMENT/ SHAPING	__	__	__	__	__	__
IMITATION	__	__	__	__	__	__
TALK ABOUT OBJECTS JOINTLY	__	__	__	__	__	__
MOTHERESE	__	__	__	__	__	__
EXPANSIONS/ RECASTS	__	__	__	__	__	__
TELEVISION	__	__	__	__	__	__
1:1 CONVERSATIONS (WITH CHILD)	__	__	__	__	__	__

27.   What are 4 **characteristics of motherese?** (p. 388)

(a)

(b)

(c)

(d)

28.   Give an example of an **expansion** and a **recast** of the utterance, "more milk." (p. 389)

EXPANSION OF "MORE MILK":

RECAST OF "MORE MILK":

Is there any evidence that children learn from adult expansions and recasts of the children's own utterances? (p. 389)

29.   The **nativist** view of language acquisition suggests that humans are biologically programmed to acquire language. **Chomsky** has proposed that children come equipped with a **language acquisition device (LAD)** whereas **Slobin** suggests children come equipped with a **set of** _____ _____ _____ _____. (p. 390) Cite **three types of evidence** for this view. (p. 390-394)

(a)

(b)

(c)

30. The text discusses some of the problems with a strong version of the nativist view. **What data conflict with** each of the following **nativist views?** (p. 395)

   CRITICAL PERIOD:

   (a)

   (b)

   (c)

   What **conclusion** is warranted?

   ABILITY TO DISCRIMINATE PHONEMES 1ST FEW DAYS:

   LAD OR LMC EXPLAINS ACQUISITION:

31. The text suggests that an **interactionist view of language acquisition is best supported.** Describe this view. (p. 397-398) How does this view account for the apparent universals in children's early language? (p. 397-398)

ACTIVITY 10-1

CHILDREN'S UNDERSTANDING OF NONLITERAL LANGUAGE

INTRODUCTION: As your text author made very clear in Chapter 10, children make tremendous gains in language during the preschool years. They are very sophisticated language producers and comprehenders by the time they go to school--so much so that parents, older siblings, and teachers sometimes wish children came with "off" buttons for both their mouths and their ears. Language acquisition is not totally complete by the time a child begins school, however. Children still make gains in understanding of concepts such as kinship terms, comprehension and production of passives, metalinguistic awareness, pragmatics, comprehension of nonliteral language, etc. Much of the language arts curriculum during the elementary grades attempts to increase a child's knowledge about language in all of these areas and more. Language arts workbooks contain lessons on using idioms; use of language to create headlines, subtitles, pictures in the minds; using descriptive words; placement of phrases close to the word being described; etc. All of these activities provide practice with the subtleties of the language and increase children's awareness of the characterisitics of language, i.e., their metalinguisitic awareness.

The purpose of this activity is to give you a chance to explore children's understanding (or lack of understanding) of some types of nonliteral language. Because comprehension of metaphors, similes, idioms, and other forms of non-literal language is so automatic, we sometimes fail to appreciate how confusing these forms can be for children and adolescents or for non-native speakers. The research literature on children's understanding of similes, metaphors, proverbs, and other types of nonliteral language indicates that there are many factors influencing children's accuracy of interpretation such as mode of response (verbal explanation, choosing from alternatives, enacting meaning with toy), abstractness of the expression, availability of contextual cues, and familiarity with underlying concepts.

It was once believed that young children simply were not capable of comprehending metaphoric language, but more recent studies have found that even 2- and 3-years-olds spontaneously produce some metaphor-like expressions and understand some of the perceptually-based metaphors by age 4 (Vosniadou, 1987). This evidence suggests that even though we may find that the preschool and elementary child have difficulty with some of the examples of nonliteral language presented to them, we need to be cautious about assuming total lack of competence if a child fails to comprehend the particular metaphoric examples we present.

INSTRUCTIONS:

<u>Children.</u> Locate three children, one 4-7, another 8-11, and another 12-14 years of age. Ask parental permission to have the child help you with your homework for a class project. Tell the parents you are studying about children's language development.

<u>Procedure</u>. Spend a few minutes getting acquainted with the child. Then tell her you have some sentences you would like to read to her to get her ideas on what they might mean. Read each saying to the child and ask her to tell you what she thinks the person who said it meant. Write down the child's reaction (laughs, looks puzzled, etc.) and the child's interpretation.

1. Tree bark is like skin.
2. A cloud is like a marshmallow.
3. Anger ate him up.
4. He had a pickle for a nose.
5. The grass is always greener on the other side.
6. He "beat around the bush."
7. He "got wind" of it.
8. (a saying, idiom, or metaphor of your choice; specify)

<u>Questions.</u> Include the following in your write-up:
1. Describe each child's performance on the sayings, giving the child's reaction (laughter, confusion, etc.), giving the number correct, and a qualitative description of the nature of the child's errors (e.g., did the child only think of the concrete, literal interpretion of the words?).

2. How did children of different ages differ in the number correct and in the nature of of the errors they made?

RELATED REFERENCES

Billow, R.M. (1975). A cognitive developmental study of metaphor comprehension. *Developmental Psychology, 11,* 415-423.

Gentner, D. (1988). Metaphor as structure mapping: The relational shift. *Child Development, 59,* 47-59.

Marks, L., Hammeal, R., Bornstein, M. (1987). Perceiving similarity and metaphor comprehension. *Monographs of the Society for Research in Child Development, Serial No. 215.*

Vosniadous, S. (1987). Children and metaphors. *Child Development, 58,* 870-885.

ACTIVITY 10-2

"WHERE BALL?", "NO WET," "GHETTI," AND OTHER EARLY UTTERANCES

INTRODUCTION: Chapter 10 of the text reviews the course of language acquisition from cooing and babbling to the production of sophisticated passives and questions. This activity focuses on the periods of acquisition between single-word utterances and simple three- and four-word negatives and questions. The purpose is to provide you a chance to listen to examples of the early forms of language discussed in Chapter 10, specifically, holophrastic language, telegraphic language, overgeneralizations of plurals and past tense, and early negative sentences and questions.

INSTRUCTIONS:

Children. Obtain permission to visit a day-care facility that has children 18 months to 3 years of age or obtain permission from parents you know who have children in that age range to spend some time at their home. Explain that you are studying children's language development and want an opportunity to listen to young children as they play. Obtain language examples from at least two children.

Procedure. You may be an unobtrusive observer or interact with the child.

1. Write down (or tape for later transcription) examples of the children's language that fit the categories below. See the text pages listed after each category for category definition and for examples.

      a.   **HOLOPHRASTIC LANGUAGE** (See text, p. 368-371)

      b.   **TELEGRAPHIC LANGUAGE** (See text, p. 371-374)

      c.   **OVERGENERALIZATION OF RULES FOR PLURALS AND PAST TENSE VERBS** (See text, p. 377-378)

      d.   **PREPOSING OF NEGATIVE OR QUESTION, e.g., "No" + "he go" or "Who" + "he is?"** (See text, p. 378-379)

2. For the holophrastic and telegraphic examples include a brief description of likely meaning of the utterance (base your inference of meaning on contextual cues).

3. Be sure to include age in months on each child's record sheet.

CHAPTER 10 ANSWERS TO STUDY QUESTIONS

FOUR COMPONENTS OF LANGUAGE

1. (363)   PHONOLOGY: basic units of sound and the rules for combining these to make words and sentences
SEMANTICS: expressed meaning of words and sentences
SYNTAX: form or structure of a language
   (364)   PRAGMATICS: principles specifying how language is to be used in different contexts and situations

2. (364)   Imitating, being reinforced (learning theorists)

Specialized language-making capabilities (nativists)

BEFORE LANGUAGE: THE PRELINGUISTIC PERIOD

3. (365)   a) Rheingold & Adams: visual contact and vocalization
b) DeCasper & Fifer: preference for mother's voice
c) Molfese: cerebral hemisphere differentiation
d) Butterfield & Siperstein: discrimination between speech and music or other rhythmic patterns
e) Clarkson & Berg: discrimination between vowels and consonants

4. (365)   4-6 months

5. (366)   Advanced babblers matching the intonation of their babbles to the tonal qualities of the language they hear.

   (367)   Intonational cues

6. (366)   Parents may talk to the baby and then wait for a response before talking again.

7. (368)   Correct interpretation of nonverbal gestures and other contextual cues

8. (368)   Comprehension

THE HOLOPHRASTIC PERIOD

9. (368)   Things that move, make noise, or can be acted on

10. (370)   FORM CLASS HYPOTHESIS: use of a word "zav" used either as a noun and verb was comprehended by 2-year-olds indicating ability to use syntactic information to infer meaning.
LEXICAL CONTRAST THEORY: two-year-olds taught a new noun for "dog" made an assumption that that new word must signify a subclass; assume each word must have a unique referent.

11. (371)   Do not

12. (371)   Single-word utterances are often accompanied by actions such as pointing or
               signaling, and intonational cues that provide evidence of use of the same holophrase
               to "stand for" different meanings, (e.g., a child may use "ghetti" when asking for
               confirmation of identity of a food, when requesting spaghetti, and when declaring
               that, indeed, the food in the pot was spaghetti).

THE TELEGRAPHIC PERIOD

13. (373)   Children omit the function words and other low-information words just as is done
               in telegrams.

               Evidence indicates 2-year-olds do not ignore function words in speech they hear.
               They give more appropriate responses to sentences containing function words thaN
               to those that do not.

14. (373-374) That is daddy's bike.
               Daddy, get my bike.
               Daddy, is this a bike?
               etc....

15. (375)   Very similarly (e.g., there is a distinct sign for each morpheme, some signs
    (Box 10-1) represent entire words, each sign is constructed from a limited set of gestural
               components, etc.)

LANGUAGE LEARNING DURING THE PRESCHOOL PERIOD

16. (377)   Semantic and syntactic complexity (not frequency of mention), the less complex
               morphemes being acquired earlier.

17. (378)   As a developmental milestone; overregularization is a manifestation of the
               application of newly discovered linguistic principles in a creative way.

18. (378-379) Interrogatives consist of "wh-" words placed at the beginning of an affirmative
               utterance. Negatives are formed similarly by placing a negative marker at the
               beginning of an affirmative sentence.

19. (380)   Tall

20. (381-382) Preschoolers are not as likely to detect ambiguities in meaning or detect missing
               information from messages as are older children. However, they are not totally
               incapable of doing so and are often successful in deducing meaning from
               nonlinguistic contextual cues.

REFINEMENT OF LANGUAGE SKILLS

21. (382)   a) refined use of personal pronouns
               b) occasional production of complex passive sentences
               c) tag questions, e.g., "you like candy, don't you?"

22. (383) INFERENCES: "John did not see the rock; the rock was in the path; John fell." (Inference: John tripped)
HIDDEN MEANING: "My, but you're quiet today." (Hidden meaning: sarcastic declaration that the child is very noisy)

23. (383) An ability to think about language and to comment on its properties

24. (384) Communication effectiveness improves markedly over grades.

25. (385)
   a) INFORMATIVE MESSAGES: older children are better than younger ones at anticipating what different listeners may need to know and in tailoring their messages accordingly. 6-to 10-year-olds provide longer messages to "unfamiliar" than to "familiar" listeners. 9- to 10-year-olds develop further, adjusting the content of their communication to the listener's needs by providing richer differentiating information to an unfamiliar listener.
   b) ACTIVE LISTENING: 6- to 7-year-olds often overlook problematic messages because they have at least a vague idea of what the speaker means and will assume that his intentions are clearly stated, particularly if the speaker is an adult. 8- to 10-year-olds are more likely to monitor the "literal" meaning of the message they hear, to detect its ambiguity, and to request that it be clarified.

THEORIES OF LANGUAGE DEVELOPMENT

26. (386-390)

	Little/No Role		Facilitative		Essential	
	VOC	SYN	VOC	SYN	VOC	SYN
Reinforcement/ Shaping		X	X		?	
Imitation		X	X			
Talk about objects jointly			X	?	?	
Motherese			?	?		
Expansions/ Recasts			?	X		
Television	X	X				
1:1 Conversations (with child)					X	X

27. (388)
   a) spoken slowly
   b) high pitched voice is used
   c) short, simple sentences (but slightly above child's length and complexity)
   d) frequent use of questions or simple imperatives that may be paraphrased several times.

28. (389)   EXPANSION: "Here is some more milk?"
              RECAST: "Do you want more milk?" or "The milk is almost gone."

              Yes; young children imitate expansions and recasts more than other kinds of adult utterances. Also, children who hear more expansions and recasts show earlier acquisition of syntactic principles.

29. (390)   Cognitive and perceptual abilities

   (393-394) a)   all children in all cultures show a similar pattern of early phonological development.
              b)   all normal children acquire and use the basic syntax of their native language by the time they enter school.
              c)   Down syndrome, severely retarded, and deaf children all develop language--though at a slower pace (for deaf children, non-verbal sign language).

30. (395)   CRITICAL PERIOD:
              a) prepubescent children are not more likely to recover from traumatic aphasia than adults are.
              b) second language-learning is by no means impossible for adults and at times accelerated.
              c) children who reach puberty without opportunities to converse with anyone learn language skills rapidly when placed in an enriched environment.

              Conclusion: The period between 2 years and puberty seems to be a sensitive period for first-language learning, rather than an absolutely critical period.

              ABILITY TO DISCRIMINATE PHONEMES 1ST FEW DAYS: Rhesus monkeys and chimpanzees show similar powers of auditory discrimination without complex language function.

              LAD OR LMC EXPLAINS ACQUISITION: Fails to explain how and why of language acquisition by failing to identify underlying variables. The large human brain may simply be capable of detecting a wide variety of rules and creating many codes rather than being uniquely specialized to process and interpret language.

31. (397-398) The interactionist view is both a synthesis and an extension of the learning and nativist theories. Interactionists agree with the nativists that children are biologically prepared for language learning but stress the interactive role of biological maturation with cognitive development and the linguistic environment to account for the universals seen in child language. Interactionists agree with learning theorists that environmental factors are important but stress the interactive role of biological maturation, cognitive development, and a particular aspect of the environment--the role of conversations with companions as a means of introducing new semantic and syntactic input--rather than stressing imitation or reinforcement.

CHAPTER 11

EARLY EMOTIONAL GROWTH AND THE ESTABLISHMENT OF INTIMATE RELATIONS

STUDY CHECKLIST

_____ Read Chapter Outline and Summary (Study guide)

_____ Read Chapter (Text)

_____ Completed Vocabulary Fill-Ins (Study guide)

_____ Re-Read Outline and Summary (Study guide)

_____ Reviewed Lecture Notes and Integrated with Text

_____ Reviewed Vocabulary, Study Questions, and Text Chapter

CHAPTER 11 OUTLINE AND SUMMARY

I. **Are babies emotional creatures?**
    A. Displaying (and controlling) emotions
    B. Recognizing emotions: Can babies "read" faces and voices?
    C. Emotions and early social development

Infants are clearly emotional creatures. At birth, babies are capable of expressing interest, distress, disgust, and pleasure (as indexed by their facial expressions). Anger, sadness, fear, and surprise appear by 6 months of age, followed later in the second year by complex emotions such as embarrassment, pride, guilt, and shame, which emerge after children achieve such cognitive milestones as self-recognition. Although mothers are training infants to control emotions according to culturally defined display rules, not until the elementary school years will children become truly skilled at regulating their emotional displays.

The infant's ability to recognize and interpret emotions improves dramatically over the first year of life. During the first six months, infants begin to discriminate and respond appropriately to their mother's naturalistic displays of emotion, and by age 8-12 months they are actively seeking emotional information from their companions. Emotions play at least two important roles in an infant's social development. The child's own emotional expressions are adaptive in that they promote social contact with others and assist caregivers in adjusting their behavior to the infant's needs and goals. At the same time the infant's ability to recognize and interpret the emotions of other people serves an important social-referencing function by helping the child to infer how he or she should be feeling, thinking, or behaving in a wide variety of situations.

II. **What are emotional attachments?**
III. **The caregiver's attachment to the infant**
    A. Early emotional bonding
        1. Why might early contact matter?
        2. Is early contact necessary for optimal development?
    B. How infants promote attachments
        1. Oh, baby face: The kewpie-doll syndrome
        2. Innate responses as sociable gestures
        3. Interactional synchrony
    C. Problems in establishing caregiver-to-infant attachments
        1. Some babies may be hard to love
        2. Some caregivers are hard to reach
        3. Some ecological constraints on attachment

Infants begin to form affectional ties to their close companions during the first year of life. These "bonds of love," or attachments, serve many purposes and are important contributors to social and emotional development. Attachments are usually reciprocal relationships, for parents and other intimate companions will often become attached to the infant.

Parents may become emotionally involved with an infant during the first few hours if they have close contact with their baby during this period. An initial bond may then be strengthened as the infant begins to emit social signals (smiles, vocalizations) that attract the attention of caregivers and make them feel that the baby enjoys their company. Eventually the infant and a close companion will establish highly synchronized interactive routines that are satisfying to both parties and are likely to blossom into a reciprocal attachment. However, some parents may have a difficult time becoming attached to their infant if the child is irritable, unresponsive, or unwanted, or if they are clinically depressed, are unhappily married, or have other problems that prevent them from being sensitive and responsive to the baby.

IV. **The infant's attachment to caregivers**
   A. Development of primary social attachments
   B. Theories of attachment
      1. Psychoanalytic theory: I love you because you feed me
      2. Learning theory: Rewardingness leads to love
      3. Cognitive-developmental theory: To love you, I must know you
      4. Ethological theory: Perhaps I was born to love
      5. Comparing the four theoretical approaches

Most infants have formed their primary attachment to a close companion by 6-8 months of age, and within weeks they are establishing these affectional ties with other regular companions. Many theories have been proposed to explain how and why infants form attachments. Among the most influential theories of attachment are the psychoanalytic, the learning-theory, the cognitive-developmental, and the ethological viewpoints. Although these theories make different assumptions about the roles that infants and caregivers play in the formation of attachments, each viewpoint has contributed to our understanding of early social and emotional development.

V. **Two common fears of infancy**
   A. Stranger anxiety
   B. Separation anxiety
   C. Why do infants fear separations and strangers?

At about the time infants are becoming attached to a close companion, they often begin to display two negative emotions, or "fears." The first, stranger anxiety, is the child's wariness of unfamiliar people. It is by no means a universal reaction and is most likely to occur in response to an intrusive stranger who appears in an unfamiliar setting where loved ones are unavailable. The second, separation anxiety, is the discomfort infants may feel when separated from the person or persons to whom they are attached. As infants develop intellectually and begin to move away from attachments objects to explore the environment, they will become increasingly familiar with strangers and better able to account for the absence of familiar companions. As a result, both stranger anxiety and separation anxiety will decline in intensity toward the end of the second year.

VI. Individual differences in the quality of attachments
    A. How do infants become securely or insecurely attached?
    B. Long-term correlates of secure and insecure attachments
    C. Working mothers, alternative care, and children's emotional development

Children differ in the security of their attachments to caregivers. A securely attached infant is one who derives comfort from close companions and can use them as safe bases for exploration. Insecurely attached infants do not venture far from their attachment objects even though they derive very little comfort or security from their contacts with them. A secure attachment is fostered by caregivers who are very responsive and affectionate toward their babies. The quality of the infant's attachments may affect his or her later behavior, and it is advantageous for the child to be attached to the father and other close companions as well as to the mother. Children who are securely attached are generally more curious than insecurely attached infants and more interested in learning, more cooperative, and friendlier toward adults and peers. Moreover, these differences persist throughout the preschool period and possibly much longer. It was once feared that regular separations from attachment objects would undermine a child's emotional security. However, there is little evidence that a mother's employment outside the home or alternative caregiving will have such an effect, provided that the day care is of good quality and parents are sensitive and responsive caregivers when they are at home.

VII. The unattached infant
    A. Harlow's studies of socially deprived monkeys
    B. Social deprivation in humans: The institutionalized child
    C. Why is early deprivation harmful?
    D. Can children recover from early deprivation effects?

Some infants have had very limited contacts with caregivers during the first year or two of life; as a result, they do not become attached to anyone. Both monkeys and children who experience little social contact during infancy are likely to be withdrawn, apathetic, and (in humans) intellectually deficient. The longer infants suffer from social and sensory deprivation, the more disturbed they become. However, both monkeys and humans have a strong capacity for recovery and may overcome many of their initial handicaps if placed in settings where they will receive ample amounts of individualized attention from responsive companions. "Therapy" with younger normal peers has been found to help remediate social behavior of monkey isolates and socially withdrawn children.

CHAPTER 11 VOCABULARY FILL-INS
(Definitions below are in order of appearance in text margins)

MATCH VOCABULARY WORD/PHRASE TO ITS DEFINITION.
THEN COVER YOUR ANSWERS TO TEST YOUR MASTERY.

attachment	primary emotions
attachment object	sensitive-period
complex emotions	hypothesis
emotional display rules	social referencing
kewpie-doll effect	synchronized routines

1. _____ The set of emotions present at birth or emerging early in the first year that some theorists believe to be biologically programmed.

2. _____ Self-conscious or self-evaluative emotions that emerge in the second year and are thought to be tied to cognitive development.

3. _____ Culturally defined rules specifying which emotions should or should not be expressed under which circumstances.

4. _____ The use of others' emotional expressions to infer the meaning of otherwise ambiguous situations.

5. _____ A close emotional relationship between two persons, characterized by mutual affection and a desire to maintain proximity.

6. _____ A close companion to whom one is attached.

7. _____ Klaus and Kennell's notion that mothers will develop the strongest possible affection for their babies if they have close contact with them within 6-12 hours after giving birth.

8. _____ The notion that infant-like facial features are perceived as cute and lovable and will elicit favorable responses from others.

9. _____ Generally harmonious interactions between two persons in which each participant adjusts his or her behavior in response to the partner's actions.

conditioned reinforcer
critical period

imprinting
preadapted characteristic

10. _____ An initially neutral stimulus that acquires reinforcement value by virtue of its repeated association with other reinforcing stimuli.

11. _____ An innate or instinctual form of learning in which the young of certain species will follow and become attached to moving objects (usually their mothers).

12. _____ A brief period in the development of an organism when it is particularly sensitive to certain environmental influences; outside this period, the same influences will have little if any effect.

13. _____ An innate attribute that is a product of evolution and serves some function that increases the chances of survival for the individual and the species.

early-experience hypothesis
secure-base phenomenon

separation anxiety
stranger anxiety

14. _____ A wary or fretful reaction that infants and toddlers often display when approached by an unfamiliar person.

15. _____ A wary or fretful reaction that infants and toddlers often display when separated from the person(s) to whom they are attached.

16. _____ The tendency of infants to venture away from a close companion to explore the environment.

17. _____ The notion that the social and emotional events of infancy are very influential in determining the course of one's future development.

anxious and avoidant attachment
anxious and resistant attachment
caregiving hypothesis
disorganized and disoriented
  attachment

secure attachment
strange-situations test
temperament hypothesis

18. _____ A series of eight mildly stressful situations to which infants are exposed in order to determine the quality of their attachments to one or more close companions.

19. _____ An infant/caregiver bond in which the child welcomes contact with a close companion and uses this person as a secure base from which to explore the environment.

20. _____ An insecure infant/caregiver bond, characterized by strong separation protest and a tendency of the child to resist contact initiated by the caregiver, particularly after a separation.

21. _____ An insecure infant/caregiver bond, characterized by little separation protest and a tendency of the child to avoid or ignore the caregiver.

22. _____ Ainsworth's notion that the type of attachment an infant develops with a particular caregiver depends primarily on the kind of caregiving he has received from that person.

23. _____ An insecure infant/caregiver bond, characterized by the infant's dazed appearance on reunion or a tendency to first seek and then abruptly avoid the caregiver.

24. _____ Kagan's view that the strange-situations test measures individual differences in infants' temperaments rather than the quality of their attachments.

---

learned helplessness

younger-peer therapy

25. _____ A method of rehabilitating emotionally withdrawn individuals by regularly exposing them to younger but socially responsive companions.

26. _____ The failure to learn how to respond appropriately in a situation because of previous exposures to uncontrollable events in the same or similar situations.

CHAPTER 11 STUDY QUESTIONS

ARE BABIES EMOTIONAL CREATURES?

1.   What answer does research by **Izard** and colleagues and by others indicate is warranted to the question: **Do babies display a range of emotions** such as fear, anger, surprise, etc.? (p. 406-407)

How did Izard and associates **assess** whether young infants display distinct emotions? (p. 406-407)

2.   Indicate the approximate **ages** at which each of the following groups of **emotions** have been found to **emerge.** (p. 406-407)

INTEREST, DISTRESS, DISGUST, CONTENTMENT: _____

ANGER, SURPRISE, FEAR, SADNESS: _____

EMBARRASSMENT, SHAME, GUILT, PRIDE: _____

3.   The various types of emotions emerge in a relatively fixed sequence in children. What three **factors** were mentioned in the text as causing or being linked to the **emergence of emotions?** Describe the link. (p. 407-408)

(a)

(b)

(c)

4.   **Lewis** and associates found that by age _____ there is clear evidence that children **can conceal and hence, control, emotions.** (p. 408)

However, **Saarni** (1984) found that many _____-year-olds are **still unable to conceal their disappointment over an uninteresting gift.** (p. 408-409 & Fig. 11-1)

5.   Infants as young as _____ months **discriminate and are reactive to adult emotions.** By 8-10 months they are clearly interpreting the emotional expressions of others and are social referencing. Provide an **example of social referencing.** (p. 409-410)

WHAT ARE EMOTIONAL ATTACHMENTS?

6.   Attachment refers to strong affectional ties. **According to Bowlby, how do infants manifest their attachments/ties?** (p. 410)

THE CAREGIVER'S ATTACHMENT TO THE INFANT

7.   **Klaus** and **Kennell** have argued that contact between the mother and baby are important during the **first 6-12 hours after birth,** a time they believe to be a _____ **for emotional bonding.** What **two hypotheses** have been offered to justify and explain the importance of the first 12 hours to bonding? Has either been supported? (p. 411-412)

(a)

(b)

8.   **Goldberg** thoroughly reviewed the bonding literature and reached what conclusion regarding the necessity of **early contact** (first 6-12 hours) **for emotional-bonding?** (p. 412-413)

9.   **Bowlby** and **Lorenz** argue that infants are sociable and are born with characteristics that elicit positive, loving responses from adults. What three **characteristics** does the text describe as **elicitors of adult contact and positive response?** (p. 413-415)

   (a)

   (b)

   (c)

10.   The text describes synchronized routines that involve interactive turntaking between the mother and infant and the mother's reading of the child's signals of readiness to interact. **How important do developmentalists (e.g., Tronick, 1989; Stern, 1977) believe these synchronous interactions are to the establishment of affectional ties/social attachments?** (p. 414-415)

11.   Babies differ in their ability to elicit positive responses and parents differ in their ability to respond positively. What infant variables and what caretaker-ecological variables have been found to be **associated with problems in development of social attachment?** (p. 416-418)

   INFANT CHARACTERISTICS:

   CAREGIVER CHARACTERISTICS:

   ECOLOGICAL CHARACTERISTICS:

12.   Characterize the **nature of infants' attachments** at each of the following ages as described by **Schaffer and Emerson.** (p. 418-419)

0-6 weeks:

6 weeks to 6-7 months:

7-9 months:

9+ months:

13.   What impact are **multiple attachments** believed to have on the child's attachments to the parents? (p. 419)

14.   Your text presents four different **possible explanations for the development of attachment.**   Describe the factors each hypothesizes to be important determinants of attachment.   Also summarize evidence for and against each hypothesis. (p. 419-423)

PSYCHOANALYTIC

Hypothesis:

Evidence:

LEARNING

Hypothesis:

Evidence:

COGNITIVE

Hypothesis:

Evidence:

ETHOLOGICAL

Hypothesis:

Evidence:

What **conclusion** does the text author reach regarding the usefulness of the four theories of attachment? (p. 423)

TWO COMMON FEARS OF INFANCY

15.   At what age have studies of North American children found **stranger anxiety** to peak? (p. 423-424)

16.   What four **strategies for reducing stranger anxiety** were presented in Box 11-1? (p. 424-425, Box 11-1)

    (a)

    (b)

    (c)

    (d)

17.   At what age has **stranger anxiety** been found to peak? (p. 424-425)

18.   Have children in all **cultures** been found to begin to show **separation protests** at about the same age?   How can any differences be accounted for? (p. 425)

19.   Several **explanations for separation and stranger anxiety** have been offered. How does each of the following theoretical viewpoints account for these phenomena? (p. 426-427)

CONDITIONED ANXIETY HYPOTHESIS:

ETHOLOGICAL VIEWPOINT (Bowlby; Ainsworth):

COGNITIVE-DEVELOPMENTAL VIEWPOINT (Kagan):

20.   How does the **ethological viewpoint** account for the **decline in stranger and separation anxiety** by the end of the second year? (p. 426-427)

INDIVIDUAL DIFFERENCES IN THE QUALITY OF ATTACHMENTS

21.   **Ainsworth** has identified **three types/qualities of attachment.** Indicate the characteristic response to the mother's departure and return for each. Also characterize the maternal behavior associated with each type of attachment. (p. 428-431)

SECURE
        SEPARATION:

        RETURN:

        MOTHER'S BEHAVIOR:

INSECURE (ANXIOUS AND RESISTANT)
        SEPARATION:

        RETURN:

        MOTHER'S BEHAVIOR

INSECURE (ANXIOUS AND AVOIDANT)
        SEPARATION:

        RETURN:

        MOTHER'S BEHAVIOR:

22.   **Main** has described an additional pattern of attachment that seems to be **common among abused and neglected children** called _____ attachment. Characterize this type of attachment. (p. 430-431)

23.   **Kagan** has proposed that infants differ in type/quality of attachment because of their temperament rather than because of caretaker behavior. What **three kinds of evidence contradict the temperament hypothesis?** (p. 431-432)

Sroufe:

Thompson & Lamb:

Goldberg et al.:

What is the most appropriate conclusion regarding the relative roles of caregiver behavior and infant temperament in determining quality of attachment? (p. 432)

24.   Box 11-2 presents a discussion of the influence of a child's attachment on the child's social responsiveness and emotional conflict when exposed to a friendly clown. **How did having a secure attachment with both parents influence social responsiveness and emotional conflict ratings?** How did children who had a secure attachment with the father and a nonsecure one with the mother score on the ratings compared with infants who had nonsecure attachments with both? (p. 432-433, Box 11-2)

    SOCIAL RESPONSIVENESS

        Secure with both:

        Secure with father only:

Secure with both:

Secure with father only:

What do these findings suggest about the **father's role** in a child's early emotional development?

25.   **Secure attachment** in infancy has been found to **correlate** with **what later behaviors/characteristics?** (p. 433-434)

26.   What answer has research evidence suggested is warranted to the question: **Can the quality of an attachment change during or after infancy** to an improved one or a poorer one? (p. 434)

27.   Generally **maternal employment** has not been found to be associated with insecure attachment. However, there are some **conditions** when maternal employment is more likely to be **associated with insecure attachment.** These are: (p. 435-436)

   (a)

   (b)

   (c)

28. What two **factors** have been found to **moderate the impact of maternal employment and day care on infant social, emotional, and cognitive development?** (p. 436-437)

(a)

(b)

29. What are the characteristics of a **high-quality day-care** facility? (p. 436)

(a)

(b)

(c)

(d)

THE UNATTACHED INFANT

30. **Harlow's** studies of monkeys reared in **social isolation** showed that six months or more of isolation results in very abnormal social behavior. **Suomi and Harlow** (1972) found they could **reverse the results with a special kind of therapy.** Describe what they found worked. (p. 438-439)

31. What kinds of outcomes are associated with **social deprivation** for children? (p. 439-440)

32.   Describe the two **hypotheses** that have been offered to account for the devastating **effects of early deprivation** and indicate whether each hypothesis has been supported or not. (p. 441-442).

MATERNAL-DEPRIVATION HYPOTHESIS:

SOCIAL-STIMULATION HYPOTHESIS:

33.   What is the **prognosis** (likelihood of recovery) for children who have suffered from severe early social deprivation? (p. 442-443)

What **factors improve** the **chance of recovery?** (p. 442-443)

34.   **Furman, Rahe, and Hartup** assessed the potential of **younger-peer therapy** as a remediation for social deprivation. The socially withdrawn preschool children who played with younger peers showed _____ in their sociability, a finding _____ with the results of younger-peer therapy for monkey isolates. (p. 442-443 & Fig. 11-6)

ACTIVITY 11-1

SYNCHRONOUS INTERACTION BETWEEN BABY AND ADULT

INTRODUCTION: This activity relates to material in Chapter 11 (p. 414-415) on interactional synchrony between infant and caretaker. These synchronous routines are exchanges that involve taking turns behaving in a social manner: baby coos--caretaker vocalizes back; baby clicks tongue--caretaker clicks tongue back or vocalizes; mother smiles--infant smiles and vocalizes, etc. Such moments of seemingly inconsequential interaction are believed by Stern and others to be important building blocks for successful social attachment and later relationships.

Truly synchronous interactions reflect a sensitivity of the caretaker to the infant's needs at that moment. The caretaker takes cues from the infant regarding what kind and how much stimulation to provide. The caretaker "reads" the infant's need for an occasional time-out from the interaction and the infant signals that she is ready to engage again. For the interaction to be synchronous it is important that the caretaker be sensitive to the child's needs and feelings at that moment. This activity will provide an opportunity for you to observe synchronous interactions and to see an example of what is meant by a caretaker responding "sensitively" to a child--an important aspect of parenting that is mentioned at several points throughout the text as being critical to effective parenting.

INSTRUCTIONS:

Infant. Contact parents you know who have an infant between 1-12 months (3-9 months is optimal). Ask if you can come over to spend some time observing their infant for a class project. Tell them you would like to take notes on the infant's behavior for this project. Arrange to visit during a time when the infant is likely to be awake, fed, and in a play mood (although you can also see many instances of synchronous interaction during routine caretaking if necessary). (Note--you will probably observe more infant-parent interaction if only one parent is present.)

Chapter 11

Data. Keep a running record of behaviors that the parent and child direct toward each other. Connect with a line (in the left margin) those pairs of behaviors that reflect a response of one to the other that would qualify as synchronous. Do not connect any behaviors initiated by one that are ignored by the other. Place an **X** beside any interactions that you judge to be nonsynchronous, i.e., the interaction is uncomfortable or conflictful (e.g., the mother is intrusive and pushes the infant to interact when the infant is signaling the need for a time-out, or the mother remains neutral in expression and does not return a vocalization).

Write-up. Summarize the interactions you observed. Give approximate percentage of interactions that were synchronous and percentage that were clearly nonsynchronous. Briefly describe your impressions of the affective quality of the interaction.

RELATED REFERENCES

Drotar, D., Woychik, J., Mantz-Clumpner, B., Negray, J., Wallace, M., & Malone, C. (1985). The family context of failure to thrive. In D. Drotar (Ed.), *Failure to thrive: Implications for research and practice.* New York: Plenum Press.

Stern, D. (1985). *The interpersonal world of the infant.* New York: Basic Books.

Thoman, E., & Browder, S. (1988). *Born dancing: How intuitive parents understand their baby's unspoken language and natural rhythms.* New York: Harper & Row.

ACTIVITY 11-2

WORKING MOTHERS AND DAY CARE

INTRODUCTION: Today the majority of mothers work, even those with preschool children. Day care of some sort is a fact of life for their children. Most parents worry about leaving their children. They worry about the child becoming more attached to the alternative caregiver than to the parents, they worry about whether the child will be insecure, etc. In the chapter on emotional development the text author includes a review of research on the relationship between maternal employment/day care and attachment (Chapter 14, p. 435-437). This activity asks you to make use of the material presented in the text to build an "advice column" to parents on the impact of day care on children.

INSTRUCTIONS: Assume that you were contacted by Ann Landers because you are knowledgeable about the research on the relationship between maternal employment/day care and emotional attachments in young children. You were asked to give a response to a question raised by a column reader: "I have to go back to work a few weeks after my baby is born. I'm worried that my baby will not know who its mother really is if I have to leave the baby every day with someone. Can you tell me if day care is always bad for infants and young children?"

Using the information presented in the text, construct a reply to the mother that will calm her fears but will also alert her to the factors that place an infant's attachment at risk. (Keep in mind that the research in this area uses the quasi/natural method, i.e., existing groups. Causal statements must be made with caution because there may be differences between the day-care and non-day-care children and families in addition to maternal employment and day care that could be contributing to the outcomes. See Chapter 1, p. 25-27, to review the limitations of this type of study.)

RELATED REFERENCES

Your Shaffer text (p. 435-437) and referenced articles.

Belsky, J. (1988). The "effects" of infant day care reconsidered. *Early Childhood Research Quarterly, 3,* 235-272.

Fox, N., & Fein, G.G. (1990). *Infant day care: The current debate.* Norwood, NJ: Ablex.

Hoffman, L. (1989). Effects of maternal employment in the two-parent family. *American Psychologist, 44,* 283-292.

CHAPTER 11 ANSWERS TO STUDY QUESTIONS

ARE BABIES EMOTIONAL CREATURES?

1. (406-407)   Yes, Izard's studies confirmed that different adult raters observing the same expression can detect the same emotion in the babies' faces.

Infants were videotaped responding to a variety of situations such as grasping an ice cube, having a toy taken away, or seeing their mother after a separation. Adults, unaware of the event that elicited the response, told what emotion the child was experiencing by the facial expression displayed.

2. (407)   INTEREST, DISTRESS, DISGUST, HAPPINESS: birth
ANGER, SURPRISE, FEAR: 2 1/2 to 6 months
EMBARRASSMENT, SHAME, GUILT, PRIDE: 2nd year

3. (407-408)   a) biological preprogramming; many basic emotions emerge at relatively fixed times
b) learning; surprise, anger and sadness emerge after certain expectancies are formed and when disconfirmed, will trigger these emotions
c) cognitive development; embarrassment, shame, guilt and pride emerge after the child can recognize himself in a mirror or picture and has a firm understanding of rules of conduct according to Lewis et al.

4. (408-409)   3 years, 7-9 years

5. (409-410)   3 months

Observing a sibling respond positively to the family dog allows the infant to learn that the dog is a friend and not to be feared.

WHAT ARE EMOTIONAL ATTACHMENTS?

6. (410)   Trying to maintain proximity to the caretaker

THE CAREGIVER'S ATTACHMENT TO THE INFANT

7. (411-412)   Sensitive period

a) hormones present at the time of delivery may help to focus the mother's attention on her baby.
b) intense emotional arousal of parents at time of birth is attributed to the baby's behavior.

Neither hypothesis has been supported. Hormonal mediation does not explain the bonding that frequently takes place between fathers and neonates or adoptive parents and adopted infants. Parents are able to establish positive relationships even without early contact.

8. (413)   Early contact is <u>neither crucial nor sufficient</u> for the development of strong parent-to-infant or infant-to-parent attachments, i.e., it is not essential but <u>may facilitate</u> parent-to-infant bonding.

9. (413-415)
    a)   "kewpie doll" appearance
    b)   reflexive behaviors such as smiling and grasping
    c)   interactional synchrony

10. (415)   Very important, as illustrated by the author's contrasting examples of a conflictual, nonsynchronous interaction and a very positive synchronous interaction

11. (416-418)   INFANT CHARACTERISTICS: unresponsive, physically unattractive, aversive cry, difficult temperament
CAREGIVER CHARACTERISTICS: clinically depressed, formerly mistreated, infant unplanned or unwanted
ECOLOGICAL CHARACTERISTICS: caregiver has several small children with little or no assistance, poor relationship with spouse

THE INFANT'S ATTACHMENT TO CAREGIVERS

12. (418-419)   0-6 weeks: asocial stage
6 weeks to 7 months: stage of discriminate attachments
7-9 months: stage of specific attachments
9+ months: stage of multiple attachments

13. (419)   Multiple attachments are not believed to dilute attachment to parents but be complementary.

14. (419-423)   PSYCHOANALYTIC
    <u>Hypothesis</u>: "I love you because you feed me." Oral satisfaction (through feeding) creates pleasure associated with the caretaker.
    <u>Evidence</u>: Responsiveness of the caregiver (rather than feeding) and total amount of stimulation provided by the caretaker have been found to be predictive of attachment.
    LEARNING
    <u>Hypothesis</u>: "Rewardingness leads to love." Rewards given by the caregiver elicit positive responses and provide comfort. Reinforcement is the mechanism responsible for social attachments.
    <u>Evidence</u>: Harlow's studies show that feeding is less important for attachment than contact comfort. Responsiveness of the caregiver and total amount of stimulation provided by the caregiver have been found to be predictive of attachment.
    COGNITIVE
    <u>Hypothesis</u>: "To love you, I must know you." The ability to form attachments depends, in part, on the infant's level of intellectual development.
    <u>Evidence</u>: Attachments first appear at the same time infants show clear evidence of acquiring object permanence.

ETHOLOGICAL

Hypothesis: "Perhaps I was born to love." All species, including human beings, are born with a number of innate behavioral tendencies that have in some way contributed to the survival of the species over the course of evolution. Many of these built-in behaviors are specifically designed to promote attachments between infants and caregivers. Ethological theory predicts that the more close physical contact a mother has with her baby in early infancy, the more responsive she should become to the baby and the more secure the baby should feel with her.

Evidence: Anisfeld and colleagues found that mothers who carried their infants in cloth carriers allowing close contact were more responsive to their infants at 3 months than mothers who had used plastic infant seats. Also, at 13 months the infants were more securely attached than those who had spent more time in plastic infants seats.

(423)   Conclusion: Each theory has contributed to our understanding of how infants become attached to their caretakers. Together, the theories have led us to understand the role the infant plays in the process and what aspects of parent behavior influence the quality of attachment.

TWO COMMON FEARS OF INFANCY

15. (424)   8-10 months

16. (425)   a) have parent nearby; provide positive social referencing feedback
             b) familiar setting
             c) be a less intrusive stranger; let child take initiative to approach
             d) have an approachable, familiar look (a look not too discrepant from the infant's expectation of hair, clothing, etc.)

17. (425)   14-20 months

18. (425)   No; children raised in some cultural settings where separation is a very unusual event protest separations from the mother at an earlier age than North American and European infants do.

19. (426)   CONDITIONED ANXIETY HYPOTHESIS: Infants may learn to fear separation because they associate discomfort (hunger, wet diapers, pain) with the absence of their caregiver. Stranger anxiety is an extension of separation anxiety where the child protests the intrusion of strangers because of fear of separation.
             ETHOLOGICAL VIEWPOINT (Bowlby; Ainsworth): Infants are biologically programmed to fear such events as strange people, strange settings, and separation. Infants become less wary of strangers and separations as they begin to use their attachment objects as secure bases.

(427)   COGNITIVE-DEVELOPMENTAL VIEWPOINT (Kagan): Six- to 8-month-olds have developed stable schemes for familiar faces. Infants also have developed schemes for a familiar person's probable whereabouts. Violations of these "familiar faces in familiar places" schemes are the primary cause for separation distress.

20. (426)   As attachment figures become secure bases of exploration, wariness wanes

21. (428)   SECURE
SEPARATION: infant actively explores while alone with the mother and is visibly upset by separation
RETURN: infant greets mother warmly and welcomes physical contact
MOTHER'S BEHAVIOR: enjoys close contact with her baby, highly sensitive to infant's social signals, emotionally expressive, encouraging of exploration
INSECURE (ANXIOUS AND RESISTANT)
SEPARATION: infant is unlikely to explore when the mother is present and becomes very distressed when the mother departs
RETURN: infant is ambivalent; may remain near mother but avoids contact initiated by the her
MOTHER'S BEHAVIOR: inconsistent in caregiving, moody
INSECURE (ANXIOUS AND AVOIDANT)
SEPARATION: infant is uninterested in exploring when alone with the mother; shows little distress over separation
RETURN: infants avoid contact with their mother
MOTHER'S BEHAVIOR: often impatient and unresponsive or overzealous, stimulating the infant during periods when the child prefers not to be stimulated

22. (431)   Disorganized/disoriented attachments: infants tend to show conflict over whether to approach or avoid the caretaker (or looked dazed) at reunion

23. (431)   a) Sroufe: infants can be securely attached to one close companion and insecurely attached to another.

            b) Thompson and Lamb: the quality of a child's attachment to a particular caregiver can change relatively quickly if the caregiver experiences life changes (divorce, a return to work) that alter interaction with the child.

            c) Goldberg et al.: the best predictor of an infant's later attachment classification was the style of caregiving their mother had used; neither infant social behavior nor infant temperamental characteristics reliably forecasted the quality of these attachments.

(432)   The author concluded that although evidence indicates that caregiver behavior is the primary determinant of quality of attachment, infant termperament is not unimportant. It is more difficult for caretakers to be consistently sensitive and responsive with difficult children.

24. (432-433)   SOCIAL RESPONSIVENESS
    (Box 11-2)   Secure with both: more socially responsive than children having secure
                 attachment only with mother
                 Secure with father only: more socially responsive than children with
                 nonsecure attachments to both parents
             EMOTIONAL CONFLICT
                 Secure with both: less emotional conflict than children having secure
                 attachment only with the mother
                 Secure with father only: less emotional conflict than children with
                 nonsecure attachments to both parents

             Findings suggest that infants benefit from a secure attachment to both parents
             and also that a secure attachment to the father can help protect a child from
             the results of an insecure attachment to the mother.

25. (433-434)   Being social leaders, initiating play activities, being sensitive to the needs and
             feelings of other children, being popular, curious, self-directed, eager to learn

26. (434)   Security of attachment can change; a secure relationship with another person,
             e.g., the father or grandparent, can off set an insecure attachment to the
             mother; a change in life experiences can undermine a secure attachment.

27. (435-436)   a) when families are economically disadvantaged
             b) when the working mother is a single parent
             c) when the mother returns to work during the latter half of the first year.

28. (436)   a) quality of alternative caregiving
    (437)   b) parental attitudes about work and parenting

29. (436)   a) a reasonable child-to-caregiver ratio
             b) warm, emotionally expressive, responsive caregivers
             c) little staff turnover
             d) curriculum made up of age-appropriate games and activities

THE UNATTACHED INFANT

30. (439)   Isolates were exposed to daily play sessions with younger monkeys. The
             younger monkeys were less aggressive and more passive than normal age-
             mates, allowing the isolated older monkey to be drawn out of his shell.

31. (439-440)   Tizard found that children who spent at least four years in an institution were
             more restless, more disobedient, more unpopular in elementary school, and
             more emotionally troubled and antisocial at age 16. Goldfarb found that
             children who had spent three years in an institution lagged in all aspects of
             development when assessed at 3, 6, 8, and 12 years of age.

32. (440)   MATERNAL-DEPRIVATION HYPOTHESIS: Infants will not develop normally unless they receive the warm, loving attention of a single mother figure to whom they can become attached. Studies of adequately staffed institutions in the Soviet Union, People's Republic of China, and Israel have not confirmed this hypothesis finding good adjustment among infants reared by multiple responsive caregivers.

SOCIAL-STIMULATION HYPOTHESIS: Isolate monkeys and institutionalized humans develop abnormally because they have very little exposure to anyone who responds to their social signals. <u>Research supports this hypothesis</u> and the conclusion that infants need sustained interaction with responsive companions in order to develop normally.

33. (442)   Socially deprived infants can recover from many of their handicaps when placed in an enriched environment.

(442)   The most successful recoveries occur when children are placed with highly educated, relatively affluent parents. The combination of a stimulating home environment and individualized attention from responsive caregivers have produced excellent results, even in the most severely disturbed children.

34. (443)   Improvement; consistent

CHAPTER 12

BECOMING AN INDIVIDUAL: THE SELF, SOCIABILITY, AND ACHIEVEMENT

STUDY CHECKLIST

_____ Read Chapter Outline and Summary (Study guide)

_____ Read Chapter (Text)

_____ Completed Vocabulary Fill-Ins (Study guide)

_____ Re-Read Outline and Summary (Study guide)

_____ Reviewed Lecture Notes and Integrated with Text

_____ Reviewed Vocabulary, Study Questions, and Text Chapter

CHAPTER 12 OUTLINE AND SUMMARY

I. **Development of the self-concept**
   A. The emerging self: Differentiation and self-recognition
   B. Who am I? Responses of preschool children
   C. Conceptions of self in middle childhood and adolescence
   D. Self-esteem: The evaluative component of self
   E. Who am I? Forming a stable identity

This chapter has traced the development of children's knowledge about the self and other people (that is, social cognition) and has focused on the growth of two personal attributes--sociability and instrumental competence (or achievement)--that are very important contributors to children's self-concepts.

Most developmentalists believe that infants are born without a sense of self and will gradually come to distinguish themselves from the external environment over the first 2-6 months of life. By 18-24 months of age toddlers have formed stable self-images and have begun to categorize themselves along socially significant dimensions such as age and sex. Although preschoolers are showing some awareness of a private "inner" self and know how they typically behave in many contexts, their self-descriptions are very concrete, focusing on their physical features, their possessions, and the activities they can perform. By about age 8 children begin to describe themselves in terms of their inner psychological attributes and begin to think of this inner self as a better reflection of their character than the external facade they present to others. Adolescents have an even more integrated and abstract conception of self that includes not only their dispositional qualities (that is, traits, beliefs, attitudes, and values) but a knowledge of how these characteristics might interact with one another and with situational influences to affect their behavior.

Grade-school children differ in their perceived self-worth, of self-esteem. Children are most likely to develop high self-esteem if (1) their parents are both loving and democratic in enforcing rules and (2) they fare well by comparison with peers in their cognitive and social competencies. Although some adolescents may experience a decline in self-esteem, most teenagers cope rather well with the changes they are experiencing, showing no change or even a modest increase in their perceived self-worth.

One of the more difficult challenges of adolescence is the task of forming a stable identity (or identities) with which to embrace the responsibilities of young adulthood. From the diffusion and foreclosure statuses, many college-age youth progress to the moratorium status and ultimately to identity achievement. Identity formation is an uneven process that often continues into adulthood and is fostered by such social experiences as interactions with loving parents who encourage individuality.

II. Knowing about others
A. Age trends in impression formation
B. Theories of social-cognitive development
1. Cognitive theories of social cognition
2. The social-experiential viewpoint

Children younger than 7 or 8 are likely to describe friends and acquaintances in the same concrete observable terms (physical attributes and activities) that they use to describe the self. But as they compare themselves and others on noteworthy behavioral dimensions, they become more attuned to regularities in their own and others' conduct and begin to rely on stable psychological constructs, or traits, to describe these patterns. As they approach adolescence, their impressions of others become more abstract as they begin to compare and contrast their friends and acquaintances on a number of psychological dimensions. And by age 14 to 16 adolescents are becoming sophisticated "personality theorists" who know that any number of situational influences can cause a person to act "out of character."

The growth of children's social-cognitive abilities is related to cognitive development in general and to the emergence of role-taking skills in particular: to truly "know" a person, one must be able to assume her perspective and understand her thoughts, feelings, motives, and intentions. However, equal-status contacts with friends and peers are crucial to social-cognitive development; they contribute indirectly by fostering the growth of role-taking skills and in a more direct way by providing the experiences children need to learn what others are like.

III. Sociability: Development of the social self
A. Sociability during the first two years
B. Horizons broaden: Sociability during the preschool period
C. Individual differences in sociability
1. The genetic hypothesis: Sociability as a heritable attribute
2. The security-of-attachment hypothesis
3. Who raises sociable children? The parental socialization hypothesis
D. Is sociability a stable attribute?

Sociability refers to the child's tendency to approach and interact with other people and to seek their attention or approval. Over the first two years infants become increasingly sociable with one another (and with strange adults), showing a major breakthrough at 18-24 months as they display truly coordinated interactions and begin to assume complementary roles. During the preschool period children take an even greater interest in one another's company and are becoming less inclined to seek the companionship of adults. Nursery-school attendance often accelerates this trend, although children initially low in sociability and lacking in social skills may become even more inhibited.

Several factors contribute to individual differences in sociability, and among the more important influences are the child's genotype, the security of the child's attachments, and the child-rearing practices that parents employ. Warm, supportive parents who require their children to display social etiquette and who are not overly directive or controlling tend to raise appropriately sociable youngsters who establish good relations with their peers. By contrast, permissive parents and those who are highly controlling tend to have children who establish nonharmonious peer relations. Because sociability is such a stable attribute from about age 2 onward, highly unsociable children may require therapeutic intervention to avoid the risk of poor peer relations and emotional difficulties later in life.

IV. **Achievement: Development of the competent self**
    A. What is achievement motivation?
    B. Home and family influences on mastery motivation and achievement
    C. Beyond the achievement motive: Cognitive determinants of achievement
        1. Can I achieve? The role of expectancies in achievement behavior
        2. Why do I succeed (or fail)? Forming expectancies (and values) about achievement
    D. Reflections on competence and achievement

Children clearly differ in achievement motivation--that is, their willingness to strive for success and to master new challenges. Infants who are securely attached to responsive companions who provide them with a variety of age-appropriate stimulation are likely to become curious nursery-school children who will later do well at school. Parents may also foster the development of achievement motivation by encouraging their children to do things on their own and to do them well and by reinforcing a child's successes without becoming overly distressed about an occasional failure. Parents who combine all of these practices into one parenting style (authoritative parenting) tend to raise children who seek challenges and who achieve considerable academic success.

Although children differ in achievement motivation, their propensity for achievement in any given context also depends very heavily on the perceived value of success and their expectancies of succeeding. In turn, these two achievement-related cognitions stem from the causal attribution that children have made for previous successes and failures. Mastery-oriented children tend to attribute their successes to stable, internal causes (such as high ability) and their failures to unstable ones (lack of effort); consequently, they feel quite competent and will work hard to overcome failures. By contrast, helpless children often stop trying after a failure because they attribute their failures to stable, internal factors--most notably a lack of ability--that they feel they can do little about. Fortunately, these helpless children can become more mastery oriented if they are taught that their failures can and often should be attributed to unstable causes (such as a lack of effort) that they can overcome.

CHAPTER 12 VOCABULARY FILL-INS
(Definitions below are in order of appearance in text margins)

MATCH VOCABULARY WORD/PHRASE TO ITS DEFINITION.
THEN COVER YOUR ANSWERS TO TEST YOUR MASTERY.

categorical self	self
looking-glass self	self-concept
private self	self-esteem
public self	social comparison

1. _____ The combination of physical and psychological attributes that is unique to each individual.

2. _____ The idea that a child's self-concept is largely determined by the ways other people respond to him or her.

3. _____ One's perceptions of one's unique attributes or traits.

4. _____ A person's classification of the self along socially significant dimensions such as age and sex.

5. _____ Those aspects of self that others can see or infer.

6. _____ Those inner, or subjective, aspects of self that are known only to the individual and are not available for public scrutiny.

7. _____ One's evaluation of one's worth as a person based on an assessment of the qualities that make up the self-concept.

8. _____ The process of defining and evaluating the self by comparing oneself to other people.

foreclosure
identity achievement
identity crisis
identity diffusion

industry versus
inferiority
moratorium

9. _____ The psychosocial crisis of the grade school years, in which children must acquire important social and intellectual skills, or they may view themselves as incompetent.

10. _____ Erikson's term for the uncertainty and discomfort that adolescents experience when they become confused about their present and future roles in life.

11. _____ Identity status characterizing individuals who are not questioning who they are and have not yet committed themselves to an identity.

12. _____ Identity status characterizing individuals who have prematurely committed themselves to occupations or ideologies without really thinking about these commitments.

13. _____ Identity status characterizing individuals who are currently experiencing an identity crisis and are actively exploring occupational and ideological positions in which to invest themselves.

14. _____ Identity status characterizing individuals who have carefully considered identity issues and have made firm commitments to an occupation and ideologies.

ordinal-position effect
role taking

social cognition
sociability

15. _____ Thinking people display about the thoughts, feelings, motives, and behaviors of themselves and other people.

16. _____ The ability to assume another person's perspective and understand his or her thoughts, feelings, and behaviors.

17. _____ Willingness to interact with others and to seek their attention or approval.

18. _____ The finding that first-borns tend to be more socially responsive to their peers than later-borns.

effectance motivation
extrinsic orientation

intrinsic orientation
need for achievement
(n Ach)

19. _____ An inborn motive to explore, understand, and control one's environment (sometimes called mastery motivation).

20. _____ A learned motive to compete and to strive for success in situations where one's performance can be evaluated against some standard of excellence.

21. _____ A desire to achieve in order to satisfy one's personal needs for competence or mastery.

22. _____ A desire to achieve in order to earn external incentives such as grades, prizes, or the approval of others.

authoritarian parenting
authoritative parenting

HOME inventory
permissive parenting

23. _____ A measure of the amount and type of intellectual stimulation provided by a child's home environment.

24. _____ Flexible, democratic style of parenting in which warm, accepting parents provide guidance and control while allowing the child some say in deciding how best to meet challenges and obligations.

25. _____ Inflexible style of parenting in which adults set firm standards and rules for the child to live by while allowing little or no autonomy.

26. _____ Lax or indulgent style of parenting in which adults make few demands of their children and do not closely monitor their conduct.

attribution retraining   locus of control
causal attributions   mastery orientation
learned helplessness

27. _____ Personality dimension distinguishing people who assume that they are personally responsible for their life outcomes (internal locus) from those who believe that their outcomes depend more on circumstances beyond their control (external locus).

28. _____ Inferences made about the underlying causes of one's own or another person's behavior.

29. _____ A tendency to persist at challenging tasks because of a belief that one has high ability and/or that earlier failures can be overcome by trying harder.

30. _____ A tendency to give up or to stop trying after failing because these failures have been attributed to a lack of ability that one can do little about.

31. _____ Therapeutic intervention in which helpless children are persuaded to attribute failure to their lack of effort rather than a lack of ability.

CHAPTER 12 STUDY QUESTIONS

DEVELOPMENT OF THE SELF-CONCEPT

1.   Lewis and Brooks-Gunn found that 18- to 24-month-olds show recognition of themselves in a mirror, an advance that seems to be tied to level of _____ development. Gallup also found that adolescent chimps show self-recognition with the rouge-on-the-cheek test, but only if reared normally. Social isolates do not. The Gallup findings demonstrate that _____ _____ is/are important to development of **knowledge of self.** (p. 449-450)

2. What kind of self-understanding does the notion **"categorical self"** refer to? (p. 450-451)

How early do children show **evidence of distinguishing between their private self and their public self?** (p. 451-452)

How does the 8-year-old's **understanding of the relationship between the private and public self** differ from that of the preschooler's? (p. 452-453)

3. What types of **attributes** have preschoolers, mid-elementary children and adolescents been found to emphasize in their **self-descriptions?** (p. 451-453)

PRESCHOOLERS:

ELEMENTARY:

ADOLESCENT:

What **qualification** does **Eder's** recent research suggest regarding the preschooler's self-understanding? (p. 451)

4.   **Harter** (1982) administered a **self-concept scale** to children 3rd through 9th grades. Children evaluated their competencies in what four areas? (p. 454)

(a)

(b)

(c)

(d)

Did **children rate themselves** uniformly "great" or "awful" on all four competencies? If not, what did they do? (p. 454)

How accurately did their self-ratings reflect how **others** perceive them? (p. 454)

5.   Do Harter's findings confirm or disconfirm **Cooley's notion of the looking-glass self** as an explanation of how we construct self-image? (p. 454)

6.   What factors have been shown to be particularly important **influences on a child's self-esteem**? (p. 454-455)

(a)

(b)

7.   What **two competencies** have been found to **relate to high self-esteem** for elementary-age children? (p. 455)

(a)

(b)

8. Several recent studies have looked at **self-esteem in adolescence** (e.g., Marsh, 1989; Nottelmann, 1987; Petersen, 1988). The results of these studies _____ (agree, disagree) **with Erikson** that adolescents experience an erosion of self-esteem. (p. 455-456)

What **conclusion** does recent research suggest is warranted regarding the **continuity of self-esteem** from childhood through adolescence? (p. 455-456)

What accounts for the erosion of self-esteem in some adolescents? (p. 456)

9. **Erikson** assumed that **identity formation** and a stable notion of who I am and what I am going to be was reached by age _____. Studies by **Meilman** and others found that not until age _____ had most individuals reached **moratorium** or **achieved stable identities**. (p. 457-458 & Fig. 12-1)

10. Erikson assumed that being in moratorium would be stressful for individuals. What did **Marcia** find regarding the **self-esteem** of individuals in **moratorium**? (p. 458)

11. What kind of **parenting** is associated with the following **identity statuses**? (p. 458-459)

FORECLOSURE:

DIFFUSION:

MORATORIUM:

IDENTITY-ACHIEVED:

KNOWING ABOUT OTHERS

12.   **Preschool** children tend to characterize other people using the same level of description they do for themselves, i.e., they tend to **describe others** in terms of their _____ qualities. (p. 459)

Does this mean they have no awareness of other qualities? See research by Miller and Aloise (1989), Eder (1989), and Gnepp and Chilamkurti (1988). Explain. (p. 459)

13.   **Barenboim** found that in describing others, 6- to 8-year-olds focused on behavioral comparisons, 9- to 11-year-olds on psychological constructs, and 12- to 16-year-olds were beginning to generate psychological comparisons. How do these **descriptions of others compare with the description of self?** (p. 451-453, 459-460)

14.   What relationship has been found between the **abstractness of self- and other-descriptions** and Piaget's stages of **cognitive development?** (p. 461)

15.   What aspect of cognition does **Selman** stress as an important **factor underlying** mature social understanding, social behavior, and friendship? (p. 461)

16.   **Selman** argues that his **five stages of social perspective taking** occur in a **fixed developmental sequence.** What findings confirmed this position in the Gurucharri and Selman study? (p. 462-463)

17.   For each of Selman's stages of social perspective taking, **characterize each stage** and give an **example** of how that level of perspective taking is **manifest in** friendships. (p. 461-464 & Table 12-1)

Level 0:

Level 1:

Level 2:

Level 3:

Level 4:

18.   At which level and age range did Selman find children indicating that if they did something nice for a friend, it did **not require immediate reciprocity?** Note: The focus is more on the **sharing of feeling** than things at this level. (p. 463)

19.   What **relationship** has been found between **role-taking skills** and **popularity** (Kurdek & Krile, 1982) and **sociability** (LeMare & Rubin, 1987; McGuire & Weisz, 1982)? (p. 464)

What did **Hudson et al.** find that **mature role takers** are able to do that may account for their popularity and success at social relationships? (p. 464)

20.   Role-taking skills have been found to be related to level of cognitive maturity and to experience interacting with peers. What specific **type of peer-interaction** did **Nelson and Aboud** find to be **important to the development of role-taking skills** and interpersonal understanding? (p. 465)

Why is this kind of interaction believed to be so **effective in promoting social awareness and role taking?** (p. 465)

21. Were the findings of **Nelson and Aboud** consistent or inconsistent with **Piaget's** views on the **kinds of experiences** he believed to contribute to growth in social perspective taking and interpersonal understanding? (p. 464-465)

22. What **two factors** have been found to contribute to the development of children's **self-awareness** and **understanding of other people** (Gnepp, 1989)? (p. 465-466)

   (a)

   (b)

SOCIABILITY: DEVELOPMENT OF THE SOCIAL SELF

23. How does the text **distinguish between sociable interactions** and **emotional attachments?** (p. 466)

24. Infants show signs of **sociability** as early as **3-4 months** by touching each other. However, truly **coordinated play** such as tag or cooperative play does not regularly occur until about _____ months. (p. 467)

25. Shea, Brody et al., and Harper and Huie studied the **effects of preschool on children's sociability.** They found that over time play behavior becomes more _____ and less _____. (p. 468-469)

26.   For a small subgroup of children, the **preschool** experience does **not have positive effects.** Indicate below what subgroup and what kind of outcome is found (Pennebaker et al., 1981). (p. 469)

SUBGROUP:

OUTCOME:

27.   Box 12-2 presents some **techniques for improving** the **social skills** of withdrawn children. Briefly characterize each technique below.
(p. 468-469, Box 12-2)

REINFORCING SOCIALLY APPROPRIATE BEHAVIORS:

MODELING SOCIAL SKILLS:

COGNITIVE APPROACHES TO SOCIAL-SKILLS TRAINING, E.G., COACHING:

28.   **Highly aggressive children** may **require help beyond** that necessary for withdrawn children. Why? (p. 469, Box 12-2)

What **treatment strategies** have been found to be effective? (p. 469, Box 12-2)

29.   Indicate how strong the **evidence** is for each of the following **hypotheses** that have been offered to **account for individual differences in sociability.** (p. 470-472)

GENETIC HYPOTHESIS:

SECURITY-OF-ATTACHMENT HYPOTHESIS:

PARENTAL SOCIALIZATION HYPOTHESIS:

30.   How might the **difference in sociability of first- and later-borns** be explained? (p. 471-472)

31.   The question of whether there is **continuity** between **early sociability** and **adult behavior** is an important one. Using a _____ approach, **Roff** and associates found that children who are unsociable and aggressive or argumentative and are _____ _____ _____ _____ are **more likely to have serious emotional disturbances later in life.** (p. 472)

32.   A survey of 30 cultures indicated that **achievement the world over tends to include valuing** of attributes such as ____-____, _____, and _____ ____ _____ _____ (Fyans et al., 1983). (p. 472-473)

33.   Describe the **difference** between **intrinsically and extrinsically motivated children**. (p. 474)

34.   Home and family variables have been found to influence mastery motivation and achievement. Describe what aspects of each of the following **promote mastery**. (p. 474-476)

SENSORY STIMULATION:

QUALITY OF ATTACHMENT:

HOME ENVIRONMENT:

CHILD REARING:

35.   A child may be shown to generally have a high need to achieve, but what three **factors** are related to whether a child is **motivated to achieve** in some **specific situation?** (p. 476-477)

(a)

(b)

(c)

36.   Individuals differ in whether they attribute responsibility for success or failure on a task to internal or external factors. List the two **internal** and two **external causes to which people attribute outcomes.** (p. 477-478)

INTERNAL CAUSES:

(a)

(b)

EXTERNAL CAUSES:

(a)

(b)

37.   **Weiner** argues that there is more to achievement motivation than the locus of control of one's causal attributions. Whether the attribution is stable or unstable also makes a difference. *Circle those factors listed in your answer to question 36 that are considered **stable causes** of good or bad performance.* Also list them below along with the factors considered to be unstable causes. (p. 478 & Table 12-4)

STABLE CAUSES:

(a)

(b)

UNSTABLE CAUSES:

(a)

(b)

Locus of causality is important to achievement motivation because it determines the _____ to the perceiver; we feel proud if we did well because we worked hard or have high ability. (p. 479)

Stability as well as locus of causality must be considered to understand achievement motivation because the stability dimension determines achievement _____. (p. 478)

38.   What confusion or lack of understanding regarding cause of task successes and failures **protects young children** from the potentially damaging effects of failure? (p. 480)

39.   What **attitudes toward failure experiences** have **Dweck** and associates found in **mastery oriented children** who persist in the face of failure? (p. 480)

In **contrast**, students who show a helpless orientation tend to _____ in the face of failure and **attribute their failures to** _____. (p. 480-481)

40.   Are highly competent children spared from developing learned helplessness? Explain. (p. 481)

41.   Research by **Dweck** and others has shown that how adults respond to children's failures has a marked impact on whether they attribute their failure to lack of ability or to other unstable or external causes that can be changed. What kind of **adult feedback** tends to lead to a helpless feeling and what kind to a mastery pattern in children? (p. 481)

HELPLESS:

MASTERY:

42.   What **kind of task experience and feedback** did Dweck find can **retrain children** who have been using a helpless attribution and giving up? (p. 482)

43.   Box 12-3 presents some further research by **Dweck** and colleagues. They have found that the goal children adopt in achievement situations can affect whether or not they give up after failure. **What type of learning goal was associated with persistence** after failures, even in children who believed they were low ability? (p. 483, Box 12-3)

What are the **implications** of Dweck's research findings for classroom teachers? (Box 12-3)

44.   What **conclusion** did the text author reach regarding the theories offered by McClelland, Crandall, Weiner, and Dweck to explain achievement-related behavior? (p. 482-483)

ACTIVITY 12-1

WHO AM I?

INTRODUCTION: This activity relates to Chapter 12 material on children's conceptions of themselves (p. 451-456). Developing a sense of who we are is one of the great tasks of development. It is a long, gradual process complicated by the fact that abilities and characteristics change with development, sometimes slowly, sometimes rapidly. The self-definition must evolve with development. It is based on the feedback an individual gets from interacting with her physical and social environment. In turn self-definition can influence all areas of our functioning--social, emotional, and cognitive.

One of the ways researchers have attempted to trace the development of children's self-concept has been to ask them to complete sentences beginning, "I am a _____" or "I am a boy/girl who_____." Another strategy has been to ask individuals to give 10-20 responses to the question "Who Am I?" Below you are asked to write down 20 self-descriptors to (a) make you more aware of the many dimensions by which individuals define themselves and (b) to help put you in touch with the personal importance of one's self-concept. Some things we write down will seem mundane, others will make us smile and have a good feeling, others may make us frown and feel sad or anxious. The feelings evoked reflect our self-evaluation or self-esteem, whether we consider that trait to be a "good" one, a "bad" one, or a neutral one. Take stock of yourself in the assignment below. Just who are you and how do you feel about that person? Why do you think you feel the way you do about yourself?

INSTRUCTIONS:

1. Write down 20 answers to the question "Who Am I?"

2. Beside each number, indicate the valence of that descriptor, i.e., how you feel about yourself with respect to that characteristic:
   - **+** = I feel good about this characteristic
   - **-** = I have negative feelings about this characteristic
   - **N** = I feel neutral about this characteristic

3. For those marked by a plus or a minus, briefly indicate any person or incident that you think might have contributed to how you feel about yourself with regard to that trait. (Purpose: To raise awareness of the role of peers, parents, and other significant adults in the formation of how we feel about ourselves.)

WHO AM I?

___ 1.

___ 2.

___ 3.

___ 4.

___ 5.

___ 6.

___ 7.

___ 8.

___ 9.

___10.

___11.

___12.

___13.

___14.

___15.

___16.

___17.

___18.

___19.

___20.

ACTIVITY 12-2

WHO AM I TO BE?

INTRODUCTION: This activity relates to material presented in Chapter 12 (p. 456-459) on the development of a mature identity. Adolescence and young adulthood are often times of search for a vocational, political, and religious identity. According to Erik Erikson and James Marcia, the crisis/search process can sometimes go on for several years before the individual commits to a particular career or to particular beliefs. Not all individuals go through an active search process, but rather, commit to a career or belief system recommended by parents or others. A few never go through an active search nor do they make a commitment, but remain directionless. Sometimes an individual may have settled into a career and set of beliefs, but a change in life circumstances precipitates a renewed search. Some of you may be students now as a result of a search process that led to a decision to change careers. This activity asks that you review your own history with regard to career, political, and religious identity using the identity status descriptions below.

INSTRUCTIONS: Study the descriptions of each of the four identity statuses. Then proceed with Parts A and B of this activity.

IDENTITY STATUSES

Identity Diffusion: The individual identified as diffuse either has not yet experienced an identity search or has abandoned the search prematurely. No commitment has been made to career, values, and beliefs, or to plan for the future. Rather, the individual lives for the moment. These individuals seem directionless and in a state of suspension from life.

Identity Foreclosure: The foreclosed individual has made a commitment without having gone through an identity search process. The foreclosed individual has avoided the uncertainty of the identity search/crisis by accepting whatever role parents or influential friends have prescribed with little questioning of whether it really fits the individual or is what the individual wants.

Moratorium: Diffusion and moratorium often look similar because both statuses are characterized by a lack of commitment to particular career, political, or religious beliefs. The individual in moratorium differs, however, in that the individual is engaged in an active search process, not simply existing from day to day. A moratorium period during which an individual explores alternatives is viewed by Marcia and by Erikson as an essential step to reaching the "identity-achieved" status. The early college years are a period of moratorium for many individuals.

Identity Achieved: The identity-achieved individual has undergone a crisis/search phase (moratorium) and has made a commitment. This individual differs from the foreclosed one in that he has a personal identity that is not borrowed from parents or friends. The individual is self-directed and has strong personal reasons for the choices made for a career, for political orientation, or for religious beliefs. The identity-achieved individual's choice and commitment typically are accompanied by a strong investment in the career or beliefs adopted, making the individual especially effective in carrying through on those self-chosen goals or beliefs.

Part A

Indicate below which status would best describe your career, political, and religious identity status at each of the following times in your life: (NOTE--You may be on the same line at more than one time period.)

five years ago   (use a 5)
one year ago   (use a 1)
now   (write NOW)

	CAREER	POLITICAL IDEOLOGY	RELIGIOUS IDEOLOGY
IDENTITY DIFFUSION	____	____	____
IDENTITY FORECLOSURE	____	____	____
MORATORIUM	____	____	____
IDENTITY ACHIEVEMENT	____	____	____

Part B

Write a personal history about "where you have been" and how you got to "where you are now" in each of the three areas: career choice, political ideology, and religious beliefs. Mention factors that influenced your decisions along the way. Also include how you felt (frustrated, depressed, satisfied, apprehensive, confused, relieved, etc.) at various points along the path to where you are today in your commitment (or lack of commitment) to a career, a political orientation, and to religious beliefs.

ACTIVITY 12-3

SOME PERSONAL AND SOCIAL IMPLICATIONS OF FORMAL THOUGHT

INTRODUCTION: This activity relates to material presented in Chapter 7 (p. 262-263) on the personal and social implications of formal thought and to material in Chapter 12 (p. 461-466) on social perspective taking. A major theme of social and cognitive development is the significance of the child's growing ability to role-take or perspective-take, i.e., an awareness of the perspective of another. Acquisitions in many areas have been linked to growth in formal thought and in perspective taking.

According to Piaget one manifestation of advances in formal thought in adolescence is <u>awareness of logical inconsistencies.</u> Piaget was referring to a growing awareness in adolescence of the discrepancy between what "should be" in a more perfect world and what actually is--in government, our school system, foreign policy, social consciousness, environmental consciousness, our parents, etc. Piaget maintained that this growing awareness of logical inconsistencies that accompanies development of formal thought sometimes feeds rebellion and disrespect for parents and the establishment.

David Elkind has suggested two additional manifestations of formal thought, <u>imaginary audience</u> and <u>personal fable</u>. He viewed these phenomena as forms of adolescent egocentrism that are outgrowths of the development of formal thought. More recently Lapsley has suggested that adolescent self-consciousness and self-focusing reflect advances in perspective taking rather than adolescent egocentrism as Elkind suggested. Lapsley argues that these phenomena reflect a growing awareness in adolescents of how other people might perceive them.

INSTRUCTIONS: The three manifestations of formal thought identified by Elkind are listed and defined on the following page. Give examples from your own experience of times when your own behavior and concerns reflected each of the three manifestations. You can dig back in your memory for examples from your adolescence or use more current examples. We tend to become less concerned about and angry over inconsistencies and injustices, to become less self-conscious and to feel less invulnerable with age, but we still experience these same phenomena from time to time.

A. AWARENESS OF LOGICAL INCONSISTENCIES/FLAWS (in government, in law, in parents, in social policies, etc.; think of people or circumstances or policies that you view as very hypocritical, unjust, or downright stupid and that make you angry)

B. IMAGINARY AUDIENCE (a feeling that everyone knows/cares about how you look, what you just did, what you said, or what you thought)

C. PERSONAL FABLE (a belief that no one else could possibly understand what you're going through; a belief that rules do not apply to you; a belief that nothing bad could happen to you when you engage in risky behavior)

RELATED REFERENCES

Elkind, D. (1967). Egocentrism in adolescence. *Child Development, 38,* 1025-1034.

Lapsley, D.K. (1985). Elkind on egocentrism. *Developmental Review, 5,* 227-236.

Lapsley, D.K., Milstead, M., Quintana, S.M., Flannery, D., & Buss, R.R. (1986). Adolescent egocentrism and formal operations: Tests of a theoretical assumption. *Developmental Psychology, 22,* 800-807.

CHAPTER 12 ANSWERS TO STUDY QUESTIONS

DEVELOPMENT OF THE SELF-CONCEPT

1. (450)   Cognitive, social experiences

2. (450)   Shortly after toddlers can recognize themselves in a mirror or a photograph, they begin to notice some of the ways that people differ and to categorize themselves on these dimensions (e.g., age, gender, etc.).

    (451-452)   3-year-olds show evidence of discriminating private and public self.

    (452-453)   8-year-olds are more aware of the inconsistencies between private and public self.

3. (451-452)   PRESCHOOLERS: 3- to 5-year-olds emphasize physical attributes, interpersonal relations, or actions of which they feel especially proud.
ELEMENTARY: evolve from emphasis on physical, behavioral, and "external" attributes to sketches of their enduring inner qualities--that is, their traits, values, beliefs, and ideologies.
ADOLESCENT: are aware that any number of extenuating circumstances can cause them to act in ways that seem inconsistent with the self-descriptions.

               Eder's work suggests self-description underestimates self-understanding; know more than can verbalize in trait terms

4. (454)   a) cognitive competence
                b) social competence
                c) physical competence
                d) general self-worth

               Harter found that even the 3rd-graders perceived themselves in favorable or unfavorable terms on each of the four subscales--indicating that children's feelings about the self (or self-esteem) are well established in childhood.

               Their self-ratings were accurate reflections of how others perceive them.

5. (454)   Confirm

6. (454)   a) parental acceptance
                b) social comparison with peers

7. (455)   a) success in school
                b) many friends

8. (456)   Disagree

The portrayal of adolescence as a period of personal stress and eroding self-esteem seems to characterize only a <u>small minority</u> of young people.

Erosion of self-esteem occurs primarily in those who experience <u>many life changes</u> all at once.

9. (457-458)   15-18 years, 21 years

10. (458)   Active identity seekers feel much better about themselves and their futures than do agemates in the diffusion and foreclosure statuses.

11. (458)   FORECLOSURE: close relationship with domineering parents
DIFFUSION: distant relationship with aloof or uninvolved parents
MORATORIUM AND IDENTITY-ACHIEVED: solid base of affection at home combined with freedom to be individuals in their own right

KNOWING ABOUT OTHERS

12. (459)   Concrete, observable

Preschoolers are aware of inner qualities; however, traitlike descriptions are often less meaningful for younger than for older children.

13. (460)   Self-concepts and impressions of others develop in a very similar pattern, becoming increasingly integrated and abstract over time.

14. (461)   As children progress through Piaget's stages of cognitive development, they become able to look beyond immediate appearances and to infer underlying invariances about the same time they are actively comparing themselves with peers (7-10 years). These cognitive abilities are necessary in making the psychological comparisons evident in the self-concepts of mature individuals.

15. (461)   Role-taking

16. (462-463)   41 boys were repeatedly tested over a five-year period and 40 showed a steady forward progression from stage to stage with no skipping of stages.

17. (462)   Level 0: Children are unaware of any perspective other than their own. These children do not realize that another person's viewpoint may differ from their own. A friend is anyone with whom there is a pleasant physical interaction.
Level 1: Children now recognize that other people can have perspectives that differ from their own, but believe that this happens only because these individuals have received different information. At this stage, the child believes that if both parties have exactly the same information, they will reach the same conclusion. A friend is someone who fulfills the child's self-interests.
Level 2: Children now know that their own and other's points of view may conflict even if they have received the same information. However, the child cannot consider his own perspective and that of another person at the same time. True friendships are reciprocal relationships.

Level 3: The child can now simultaneously consider her own and other person's points of view and recognize that the other person can do the same. Friendships have expanded to include the exchange of intimate thoughts and feelings and have become less superficial.

Level 4: The young adolescent now attempts to understand another person's perspective by comparing it with that of the social system in which he operates. A close friend must also be a flexible companion who cares enough to adapt to the new demands and new life circumstances that his (or her) partner may introduce into their relationship.

18. (463)   Stage 3: Mutual role taking (10-12 years)

19. (464)   The most popular children among groups of third- to eighth-graders are those who have well-developed role-taking skills. Highly sociable children and those with close friends score higher on tests of role-taking abilities.

Hudson et al. found that more mature role takers were better able to infer the needs of others from subtle cues.

20. (465)   Disagreements between friends

Because friends are more likely to explain their reasons for their point of view thus providing specific information on others' perspectives

21. (465)   Consistent; Piaget assumes equal-status contacts among peers are important contributors to growth in social perspective taking and interpersonal understanding.

22. (465-466) a) social contacts
               b) cognitive competence

SOCIABILITY: DEVELOPMENT OF THE SOCIAL SELF

23. (466)   Attachment is a relatively strong and enduring affectional tie between the child and a particular person (for example, the mother or father). Sociability refers to the friendly gestures that the child makes to a much wider variety of individuals (peers, strange adults, teachers); the resulting social relationships are often temporary and emotionally uninvolving.

24. (467)   24 months

25. (468)   More playful and outgoing; less forceful and aggressive

26. (469)   SUBGROUP: children rated low in sociability
             OUTCOME: children missed more days of nursery school because of illness than children who are rated highly sociable

27. (468-469) REINFORCING SOCIALLY APPROPRIATE BEHAVIORS: to be effective, contingent reinforcement of socially-skilled behaviors must be administered on a regular basis to the entire peer group--a procedure that not only reinforces unsociable peers for their socially skillful acts but also allows them to see others reinforced for this kind of behavior.

MODELING SOCIAL SKILLS: the modeling approach works best when the model is similar to the child, when the model initially acts shy and withdrawn followed by more socially skillful actions accompanied by some form of commentary that directs the observer's attention to the purposes and benefits of behaving appropriately toward others.

COGNITIVE APPROACHES TO SOCIAL-SKILLS TRAINING, e.g., COACHING: cognitive approaches to social-skills training differ from reinforcement or modeling in that children are more actively involved in thinking about, talking about, practicing, and imagining the consequences of varous social overtures. Coaching is a technique in which the therapist displays one or more social skills, explains the rationales for using them, allows children to practice such behavior, and then suggests how the children might improve on their performances.

28. (469) Aggressive children are likely to overattribute hostile intentions to others.

Role playing that gives practice in generating nonaggressive solutions to conflict and family-based interventions have been found to be most effective.

29. (470-471) GENETIC HYPOTHESIS: research has found a significant correlation between the shyness of adopted toddlers and the sociability of their biological mothers; however, a significant correlation has also been found between the shyness of adopted toddlers and the sociability of their adoptive mothers. The text concluded that although sociability appeals to be a heritable trait, environmental factors play a major role in its expression.

SECURITY-OF-ATTACHMENT HYPOTHESIS: most of the available evidence is consistent with Ainsworth's hypothesis that the quality of a child's attachments will affect his or her reactions to other people. Infants who were securely attached to their mother at 12-18 months of age were more likely than those who were insecurely attached to act sociably around other infants and toddlers and to be friendly, outgoing, and popular with their peers some 3-4 years later in nursery school and kindergarten. Apparently two secure attachments are better than one, for toddlers who were secure with both parents were more socially responsive and less conflicted about contacts with strangers than were those who were insecurely attached to one or both parents.

PARENTAL SOCIALIZATION HYPOTHESIS: although the data are somewhat limited, they provide support for this hypothesis. It appears that parents who are warm and supportive and who require their children to follow certain rules of social etiquette (e.g., "Be nice"; "Play quietly"; "Don't hit") are likely to raise well-adjusted sons and daughters who relate well to both adults and peers.

30. (471-472) First-borns tend to be more sociable, perhaps because they receive more individual attention or, perhaps, because later-borns are more wary as a result of being dominated or bullied by older sibs.

31. (472) Longitudinal, rejected by their peers

32. (473)   Self-reliance, responsibility, willingness to work hard

33. (474)   Extrinsic orientation refers to motivation dependent on <u>external incentives</u> such as grades, prizes, or approval, whereas, intrinsic orientation is a strong, <u>internally guided desire</u> to do well based on pride in mastering important challenges.

34. (474-475)   SENSORY STIMULATION: those who score highest in mastery motivation have parents who frequently provide sensory stimulation designed to amuse them and arouse their curiosity--experiences such as tickling, bouncing, games of pat-a-cake, and so on.
    QUALITY OF ATTACHMENT: infants who are securely attached to their mother at age 12-18 months are more likely than those who are insecurely attached to venture away from the mother to explore strange environments and to display a strong sense of curiosity, self-reliance, and eagerness to solve problems some four years later in kindergarten. Securely-attached children are not any more intellectually competent; instead, they seem to be more eager than insecurely-attached children to apply their competencies to the new problems they encounter.
    HOME ENVIRONMENT: it seems that the joy of discovery and problem solving is unlikely to blossom in a barren home environment where the child has few problems to solve and limited opportunities for learning. Variety of stimulation and the age-appropriateness of play materials are strong predictors of children's later scholastic achievement.
    CHILD REARING: parents who stress independence training--doing things on one's own--and who warmly reinforce such self-reliant behavior will contribute in a positive way to the growth of achievement motivation. Direct achievement training--setting high standards and encouraging children to do things well--also fosters achievement motivation. Patterns of praise (or punishment) that accompany the child's acomplishments are also important: children who seek challenges and display high levels of achievement motivation have parents who reward their successes and are not overly critical of occasional failures. Parents of high need-achievers tend to possess three characteristics: 1) warm, accepting, quick to praise the child's acomplishments; 2) provide guidance and control by setting standards; and 3) permit the child some independence or autonomy.

35. (477)   a) value placed on achievement of a particular goal
    b) the individual's expectancies of succeeding (or failing)
    c) attributions made for the successes (or failures)

36. (478)   INTERNAL CAUSES: a) ability
                              b) effort
              EXTERNAL CAUSES: a) task difficulty
                                b) luck

37. (478-479) STABLE CAUSES: a) ability
               b) task difficulty

UNSTABLE CAUSES: a) effort
                  b) luck

Value

Expectancies

38. (480) Young children often believe they can succeed simply by wanting to badly enough. Also, they do not fully understand the notion of ability and how it differs from effort. They are more likely to assume failure indicates lack of effort than older children.

39. (480) Attribute successes to ability and failures to external causes or lack of effort

Give up, low ability

40. (481) No; highly capable children can show learned helplessness if praised for working hard when they succeed, but ability is questioned when they fail.

41. (481) HELPLESS: praised for hard work upon success, but question ability after failure
           MASTERY: praise for abilities upon success, but criticized for lack of effort after failure

42. (482) Attribution retraining, in which helpless children are persuaded to attribute their failures to unstable causes--that they can do something about (e.g., insufficient effort), rather than continuing to view them as stemming from their lack of ability, which is not so easily modifiable.

43. (483) A learning or mastery goal ("Let's try to improve.") was associated with persistence. A performance goal ("Lets's see who can get them all correct.") led to signs of helplessness in children who believed they had low ability.

           These undesirable consequences might be prevented by restructuring classroom goals to emphasize individual mastery of particular learning objectives rather than continuing to place children in direct competition.

44. (482-483) Dweck's learned-helplessness notion, Weiner's notion of causal attribution, and Crandall's work on achievement expectancies and locus of control have all extended and enriched McClelland's notion of achievement motivation.

CHAPTER 13

SEX DIFFERENCES AND
SEX-ROLE DEVELOPMENT

STUDY CHECKLIST

_____ Read Chapter Outline and Summary (Study guide)

_____ Read Chapter (Text)

_____ Completed Vocabulary Fill-Ins (Study guide)

_____ Re-Read Outline and Summary (Study guide)

_____ Reviewed Lecture Notes and Integrated with Text

_____ Reviewed Vocabulary, Study Questions, and Text Chapter

CHAPTER 13 OUTLINE AND SUMMARY

I. **Categorizing males and females: Sex-role standards**
II. **Some facts and fictions about sex differences**
    A.   Actual psychological differences between the sexes
    B.   Cultural myths
    C.   Evaluating the accomplishments of males and females
III. **Developmental trends in sex typing**
    A.   Development of the gender concept
    B.   Acquiring sex-role stereotypes
    C.   Development of sex-typed behavior

Differences between males and females can be detected in the physical, psychological, and social realms. Some sex differences are biological in origin, whereas others arise from socialization pressures. Interests, activities, and attributes that are considered more appropriate for members of one sex than the other are called sex-role standards (or sex-role stereotypes). Sex typing is the process by which children acquire a gender identity and assimilate the motives, values, and behaviors considered appropriate in their culture for members of their biological sex.

Some sex-role stereotypes are more accurate than others. Males tend to be more active and aggressive than females and they tend to outperform them on tests of spatial abilities and arithmetic reasoning; females are more emotionally expressive and compliant than males, and they tend to outperform males on tests of verbal abilities. But on the whole these sex differences are quite small, and males and females are more similar psychologically than they are different. Among the stereotypes that have no basis in fact are the notions that females are more sociable, suggestible, and illogical and less analytical and achievement oriented than males. The persistence of these "cultural myths" is particularly damaging to women. For example, members of both sexes tend to devalue women's accomplishments by attributing them to luck or hard work rather than to competence. This tendency to degrade the achievements of females is well established by middle childhood.

Sex typing begins very early. By age 2 1/2 most children know whether they are boys or girls, they tend to favor sex-typed toys and activities, and they are already aware of several sex-role stereotypes. By the time they enter school (or shortly thereafter), they know that gender is an unchanging aspect of their personalities, and they have learned most of the sex-role standards of their society. Boys face stronger sex-typing pressures than girls do, and consequently males are quicker to develop a preference for sex-appropriate patterns of behavior.

IV. Theories of sex typing and sex-role development
  A.   Money and Ehrhardt's biosocial theory
    1.   An overview of gender differentiation and sex-role development
    2.   Evidence for biological influences on gender differentiation and sex roles
  B.   Freud's psychoanalytic theory
  C.   Social-learning theory
    1.   Direct tuition of sex roles
    2.   Observational learning
  D.   Kohlberg's cognitive-developmental theory
  E.   Gender schema theory
  F.   An attempt at integration

Several theories have been proposed to account for sex differences and sex-role development. Money and Ehrhardt's biosocial theory emphasizes the biological developments that occur before a child is born--developments that parents and other social agents will react to when deciding how to socialize the child. Other theorists have focused more intently on the socialization process itself. Psychoanalytic theorists suggest that sex typing is one result of the child's identification with the same-sex parent. Social-learning theorists offer two mechanisms to explain how children acquire sex-typed attitudes and behaviors: (1) direct tuition (reinforcement for sex-appropriate behaviors and punishment for sex-inappropriate ones) and (2) observational learning. Cognitive-developmental theorists point out that the course of sex-role development will depend, in part, on the child's cognitive development. And proponents of gender schema theory have shown how children's active construction of sex-role stereotypes (gender schemas) colors their interpretations of social events and contributes to the development of sex-types interestes, attitudes, and patterns of behavior.

V. Psychological androgyny: A prescription for the future?
  A.   Do androgynous people really exist?
  B.   Are there advantages to being androgynous?

The psychological attributes of "masculinity" and "femininity" are generally considered to be at opposite ends of a single dimension. However, one "new look" at sex roles proposes that masculinity and femininity are two separate dimensions and that the androgynous person is someone who possesses a fair number of masculine and feminine characteristics. Recent research shows that androgynous people do exist, are relatively popular and well adjusted, and may be adaptable to a wider variety of environmental demands than people who are traditionally sex typed.

VI. Development of sexuality and sexual behavior
    A.   Origins of "sexual" activities
    B.   Sexual behavior during childhood
    C.   Adolescent sexuality

As Freud thought, infants are sexual beings from the start, reacting physiologically to genital stimulation even though they have no awareness that their responses are "sexual" ones. Moreover, Freud's portrayal of preschool children as sexually curious beings was also correct, although he was very wrong in assuming that school-age children have repressed their sexual urges; in fact, sexual activity actually increases rather than declines during Freud's so-called latency period. Sexual matters become very important to adolescents, who, having reached sexual maturity, must incorporate their sexuality into their changing self-concepts. During this century, sexual attitudes have become much more permissive. The belief that premarital sex is immoral has given way to the view that sex with affection is acceptable; the double standard has weakened; and conflicting norms have increased confusion about what constitutes acceptable sexual conduct. Sexual behavior has increased as well, as more adolescents are engaging in various forms of sexual activity at earlier ages than in the past.

CHAPTER 13 VOCABULARY FILL-INS
(Definitions below are in order of appearance in text margins)

MATCH VOCABULARY WORD/PHRASE TO ITS DEFINITION.
THEN COVER YOUR ANSWERS TO TEST YOUR MASTERY.

expressive role	sex-role standard
gender identity	sex typing
instrumental role	

1. _____   The process by which a child becomes aware of his or her gender and acquires motives, values, and behaviors considered appropriate for members of that sex.

2. _____   A behavior, value, or motive that members of a society consider more typical or appropriate for members of one sex than the other.

3. _____   A social prescription, usually directed toward females, that one should be cooperative, kind, nurturant, and sensitive to the needs of others.

4. _____   A social prescription, usually directed toward males, that one should be dominant, independent, assertive, competitive, and goal oriented.

5. _____   One's awareness of one's gender and its implications.

---

androgenized females
testicular feminization syndrome
"timing of puberty" effect

6. _____   A genetic anomaly in which a male fetus is insensitive to the effects of male sex hormones and will develop female-like external genitalia.

7. _____   The finding that people who reach puberty late perform better on visual/spatial tasks than those who mature early.

8. _____   Females who develop male-like external genitalia because of exposure to male sex hormones during the prenatal period.

---

castration anxiety   **latency period**
Electra complex   **Oedipus complex**
identification   **phallic stage**

9. _____   Freud's term for the child's tendency to emulate another person, usually the same-sex parent.

10. _____   Freud's third stage of psychosexual development (from 3 to 6 years of age) in which children gratify the sex instinct by fondling their genitals and developing an incestuous desire for the parent of the other sex.

11. _____   In Freud's theory, a young boy's fear that his father will castrate him as punishment for his rivalous conduct.

12. _____   Freud's term for the conflict that 3- to 6-year-old boys were said to experience when they develop an incestuous desire for their mothers and a jealous and hostile rivalry with their fathers.

13. _____ Female version of the Oedipus complex, in which a 3- to 6-year-old girl was thought to envy her father for possessing a penis and would choose him as a sex object in the hope that he would share with her this valuable organ that she lacked.

14. _____ Freud's fourth stage of psychosexual development (age 6 to puberty) in which sexual desires are said to be repressed and the child's energy is channeled into socially acceptable outlets such as school work or vigorous play.

==========

androgyny
basic gender identity
gender consistency

gender stability
in-group/out group
schema
own-sex schema

15. _____ The stage of gender identity in which the child first labels the self as a boy or a girl.

16. _____ The stage of gender identity in which the child recognizes that gender is stable over time.

17. _____ The stage of gender identity in which the child recognizes that a person's gender is invariant despite changes in the person's activities or appearance (also known as gender constancy).

18. _____ One's general knowledge of the mannerisms, roles, activities, and behaviors that characterize males and females.

19. _____ Detailed knowledge or plans of action that enable a person to perform gender-consistent activities and to enact his or her sex role.

20. _____ A sex-role orientation in which the individual has incorporated a large number of both masculine and feminine attributes into his or her personality.

==========

CHAPTER 13 STUDY QUESTIONS

CATEGORIZING MALES AND FEMALES: SEX-ROLE STANDARDS

1.   To what extent has research found that **societies value** and encourage **different attributes in males in females**--attributes such as nurturance, achievement, self reliance, etc.? (p. 489-490 & Table 13-1)

2.   The text lists nine **attributes on which males and females have been found to differ.** List the nine attributes and indicate the direction of the effects. (p. 491-492)

     (a)

     (b)

     (c)

     (d)

     (e)

     (f)

     (g)

     (h)

     (i)

SOME FACTS AND FICTIONS ABOUT SEX DIFFERENCES

3. What conclusion does the text author suggest is warranted regarding the **magnitude** of **sex differences?** (p. 493)

4. There are many sex stereotypes that seemed to be unfounded. List the six from Table 13-3. **Reword so they are "truths"** rather than myths, e.g., "girls are not more sociable than boys." (p. 493-494 & Table 13-3)

(a)

(b)

(c)

(d)

(e)

(f)

What two reasons for the persistence of inaccurate sex stereotypes have received research support (Martin & Halverson, Cann & Newbern)? (p. 493-495, Box 13-1)

(a)

(b)

5. The text author suggests that sex stereotypes influence how we evaluate males and females and what expectations we have. At what **ages** did Haugh and associates and Pollis and Doyle find that **girls** were already **judged as less competent** than males? (p. 494-495)

6.   How has research shown that home and school may **promote** these **false stereotypes?** (p. 495-496)

HOME:

SCHOOL:

DEVELOPMENTAL TRENDS IN SEX TYPING

7.   Even though children know that they are a boy or girl quite early, they do not fully realize that **gender is constant** until about age _____ years. (p. 497)

8.   Research (e.g., Damon, 1977) has shown **sex-stereotypes** to be particularly **strong** and **rigid during two age periods,** ages _____ and _____ years. (p. 497-498)

9.   How early and how universal have **preference for same-sex playmates** and **sex differences in toy preferences** and **play patterns** been found to be? (p. 499-500 & Fig. 13-1)

EARLINESS:

UNIVERSALITY:

Does the preference for **same-sex friends** increase or decline when children start school (i.e., from 4 1/2 to 6 years is there an increase or decline)? (p. 499)

How does **Maccoby explain** the strong **same-sex affiliative preferences** found already in 2- to 3-year-old toddlers? (p. 499-450 & Fig. 13-1)

10. Explain Emmerich's statement that "the major task for young girls is to learn how not to be babies, whereas **young boys must learn how not to be girls.**" (p. 500-501)

11. How **stable** has research found **sex typing** to be? (p. 501)

THEORIES OF SEX TYPING AND SEX-ROLE DEVELOPMENT

12. Provide a brief statement of **Money** and **Ehrhardt's biosocial theory** of sex differences and then summarize the evidence for the biological and for the social components. (p. 502-506 & Box 13-2)

BIOSOCIAL THEORY:

EVIDENCE FOR BIOLOGICAL COMPONENT:

EVIDENCE FOR SOCIAL COMPONENT:

13. Box 13-2 presents data that question the viewpoint that sex-typing is entirely a function of child-rearing practices and seem to support the view that **biology is "destiny." What conclusion** does the text author argue is **warranted** at this time? (p. 507 & Box 13-2)

14.	Freud's **psychoanlytic theory** explains **sex typing** by suggesting that it occurs through a process of _____, a product of the resolution of the Oedipus/Electra complex. Give an example of evidence consistent with this view and one that is inconsistent. (p. 507-508)

CONSISTENT EVIDENCE:

INCONSISTENT EVIDENCE:

What conclusion does the text author draw?

15.	**Social-learning theory** maintains that children learn sex roles primarily through two means, differential reinforcement and observational learning. Cite evidence for each. (p. 509-510)

DIFFERENTIAL REINFORCEMENT:

OBSERVATIONAL LEARNING:

16.	What reactions have **Langlois and Downs** and **Fagot** found that adults and peers have to **cross-sex play**? (p. 509)

Who was the most permissive of cross-sex play in these studies (fathers, mothers, or peers)? (p. 509)

17.	What **findings** does the text indicate are <u>inconsistent</u> with **Bandura's emphasis on observational learning as a mechanism for acquiring early sex-typed behaviors?** (p. 510)

18. Research that has looked at sex-role development in the context of the family system has found that **sex-role socialization depends** _____ (more, less) **on the total family environment than on the influence of the same-sex parent**. Explain. (p. 510-511)

What **combination of siblings** did **Tauber** and **Grotevant** find to be more stereotyped (same sex or opposite sex)? How can this finding be explained? (p. 510-511)

19. What impact have **Frueh and McGhee** found high levels of **television** viewing to have on how stereotyped young children's **sex-role views** are? (p. 511)

20. **Kohlberg's cognitive-developmental theory** emphasizes what two **major themes**? (p. 511)

(a)

(b)

21. **Kohlberg** maintains that children pass through **three stages** as they acquire a **mature gender identity**. Characterize each stage. (p. 512)

BASIC GENDER IDENTITY:

GENDER STABILITY:

GENDER CONSISTENCY:

Although there is some support for the three stages that **Kohlberg** has hypothesized children go through, there is a **major problem** with this theory. Describe the problem. (p. 512)

22. **Martin and Halverson's gender schema theory** agrees with Kohlberg's view that children socialize themselves into sex roles; however, they disagree with Kohlberg, saying that self-socialization begins at age _____ years, once children acquire _____. (p. 513)

According to **gender schema theory**, establishment of a basic gender identity (e.g., "I'm a girl") motivates children to learn about the sexes. This information they learn is incorporated into one of two schemas. Characterize each. (p. 513)

IN-GROUP/OUT-GROUP SCHEMA:

OWN-SEX SCHEMA:

Once these schemas are formed, children are more likely to **remember information consistent with those schemas** (e.g., see Box 13-1) and are **likely to show more interest and learn more about objects that fit their own sex schemas.** For example, **Bradbard** et al. (1986) found: (p. 513-514)

23. Table 13-5 provides an **overview of sex typing** that incorporates the "truths" from each of the different viewpoints presented in the text. For each developmental period indicate the **predominant theme(s)**: biological development, learning limitation and/or cognitive development/schema development. (p. 514-515 & Table 13-5)

PRENATAL:

BIRTH TO 3 YEARS:

3-6 YEARS:

6-7 YEARS:

PSYCHOLOGICAL ANDROGYNY: A PRESCRIPTION FOR THE FUTURE?

24.   An **androgynous** person is one who has _____ number of both masculine and feminine attributes, whereas people characterized as **undifferentiated** display _____ masculine or feminine characteristics. (p. 516)

25.   Surveys of college students and of children have indicated that about **what proportion** of individuals could be classified as **androgynous?** (p. 516)

26.   What effect has an androgynous role or orientation been shown to have on **self-esteem** and **achievement attribution?** (p. 517)

Are these effects attributable to androgyny per se, the possession of "feminine" traits, or possession of "masculine" traits? (p. 517)

DEVELOPMENT OF SEXUALITY AND SEXUAL BEHAVIOR

27.   What **evidence contradicts Freud's** claim that interest in sexual matters and genital stimulation declines during the grade-school years? (p. 519)

28.	What three **changes** from earlier eras in **teenage sexual attitudes** does **Dreyer** describe ? (p. 520-521)

(a)

(b)

(c)

29.	Sexual involvement has become the norm for adolescents today. **What kind of "report card" does research suggest we can give a sexually active adolescent** regarding practice of birth control, knowledge of reproduction, and use of safe-sex practices to guard against AIDS? (p. 522)

ACTIVITY 13-1

MEDIA (ADS, TELEVISION, FILMS) AS A POTENTIAL INFLUENCE ON SEX TYPING AND SELF-CONCEPT

INTRODUCTION: This activity relates to material in several chapters: Chapter 5 on the psychological importance of physical maturation, Chapter 12 on self-concept, Chapter 13 on sex typing, and Chapter 16 on extrafamilial influences on development. An important task in childhood is learning what are gender-appropriate behaviors and how to interact appropriately with the opposite sex (i.e., in accordance with cultural norms). In addition, each child develops some feeling about how adequately he or she meets the cultural ideal of maleness or femaleness and the cultural ideal of attractiveness. At adolescence individuals become particularly concerned with how well they meet those cultural ideals.

Children are dependent on external feedback throughout childhood for developing self-concept and self-esteem. Parents, peers, teachers, and other important people in a child's life are all potential sources of input. Children also actively compare themselves to others. How well they perceive that they measure up to what is culturally valued in that comparison will affect how children feel about themselves. A potential source of input about what that cultural ideal is comes from the media--television, films, and advertisements.

Many individuals today are concerned about what kind of messages the media may be giving our children about appearance and about sex roles. For example, are ads contributing to a cultural definition of beauty so narrow that no one can possible meet that ideal? The message seems to be that whatever we look like, it is not good enough--that what we really need is the right make-up, the right diet program, the right exercise machine, the right deodorant, etc. before we can possibly be attractive to the opposite sex. Are ads telling our young people that they will magically be attractive and popular if they drink the right beer or smoke the right cigarette? Do character portrayals in television programs and in films perpetuate stereotypes about roles by defining them very narrowly? Do they convey the message that sex is the route to intimacy and acceptance, etc.?

The purpose of this activity is to explore the kinds of messages that one source of input, the media, may be giving to our children and to think about (a) how those messages might influence how a teen feels about his physical attractivess and (b) how they might affect his behavior and attitudes about himself and about others.

INSTRUCTIONS:

1. Using films, television, and/or magazines, "collect" five examples of ad and character portrayals of males and five of females. Describe each example (identify source; attach magazine ads).

2. Then comment on what "message" you think a child seeing that particular advertisement or seeing that character portrayal in a film or on TV may be receiving and what impact that message might have on the child's notion of what is sex appropriate and on the child's notion of the basis for close relationships. Also, comment on how each example could influence how an individual feels about himself.

CHAPTER 13 ANSWERS TO STUDY QUESTIONS

CATEGORIZING MALES AND FEMALES: SEX-ROLE STANDARDS

1. (490) All cultures, even ours today, encourage different attributes in males and females.

2. (491-492)
   a) verbal abilities--females outperform males
   b) visual/spatial abilities--males outperform females
   c) arithmetic reasoning--boys show a small but consistent advantage over girls
   d) aggressiveness--males are more physically and verbally aggressive than females
   e) activity level--starting in infancy, boys are more physically active than girls
   f) fear, timidity, and risk taking--girls report being more fearful or timid and taking fewer risks
   g) developmental vulnerability--boys are more vulnerable than girls
   h) emotional sensitivity/expressivity--from age 4-5 on, girls and women tend to be more sensitive and expressive
   i) compliance--girls tend to be more compliant than boys

SOME FACTS AND FICTIONS ABOUT SEX DIFFERENCES

3. (493) Very small; males and females are far more psychologically similar than they are different. It is impossible to accurately predict the aggressiveness, the mathematical skills, the activity level, or the emotional expressivity of any individual simply by knowing his or her gender. Only when group averages are computed do the sex differences emerge.

4. (494)
   a) Girls are not more social than boys.
   b) Girls are not more suggestible than boys.
   c) Girls do not have lower self-esteem than boys
   d) Boys do not excel at tasks that require higher-level cognitive processing (although boys are better than girls at simple repetitive tasks).
   e) Boys are not more analytic than girls.
   f) Girls do not show lower achievement motivation.

   (493, 495)   a) Input that is gender-inconsistent is poorly recalled.
   (Box 3-1)   b) Input that is gender-inconsistent is often incorrectly recalled (i.e., distorted)

5. (495) 3-5 years

6. (495-496) HOME: Parents have different expectancies for boys and girls and differentially respond to boys and girls.
   SCHOOL: Teachers often respond differently to the accomplishments of male and female students (with mastery responses to boys and helplessness messages to girls).

DEVELOPMENTAL TRENDS IN SEX TYPING

7. (497) 5-7 years

8. (498) ages 6-7, 12-15 years

9. (499)   EARLINESS: 14 to 22 months (toddlerhood)
   (Fig. 13-1)   UNIVERSALITY: gender segregation has been observed in 12 different cultures from widely-scattered parts of the world.

   Increase; at age 4 1/2 children spend three times as much time playing with same-sex partners as they do with cross-sex partners. By age 6 1/2 the ratio of same-sex to opposite-sex playtime has increased to 11 to 1.

   (499-500)   Maccoby suggests same-sex preferences reflect a basic incompatibility in boys' and girls' play styles.

10. (500)   The male role is more clearly (and narrowly) defined than the female role. Boys are more likely to be criticized for deviating from approved sex-role standards than are girls.

11. (501)   At least one longitudinal study of middle-class children suggests that sex typing is reasonably stable over time.

THEORIES OF SEX TYPING AND SEX-ROLE DEVELOPMENT

12. (502)   BIOSOCIAL THEORY: Emphasizes biological forces while acknowledging that early biological developments will affect other people's reactions to the child. These social forces are also believed to play a major part in steering the child toward a particular sex role.
   (504-505)   EVIDENCE FOR BIOLOGICAL COMPONENT: (a) Adolescent twin
   (Box 13-2)   studies suggest that genotype accounts for about 50% of the variability in people's masculine self-concepts (but only 0-20% of the variability in their feminine self-concepts). (b) Exposure to masculine hormones prenatally can lead to masculinization of a female's external genitalia and her behavior.
   (505-506)   EVIDENCE FOR SOCIAL COMPONENT: (a) Adults respond differently
   (Box 13-2)   to children, even young infants, depending on gender. (b) Money's research findings indicate that early social labeling and sex-role socialization can play a very prominent role in determining a child's gender identity and sex-role preference.

13. (507)   The first three years is a sensitive period rather than a critical period for sex-role
   (Box 13-2)   development, and both biology and society influence a child's gender identity and sex-role preferences. Neither biology nor social labeling is "destiny."

14. (507)   Identification

   CONSISTENT EVIDENCE: Boys whose fathers are absent from the home (because of divorce, military service, or death) during the Oedipal period frequently have no male role model to emulate and are often found to be less masculine in their sex-role behaviors than boys from father present homes.
   INCONSISTENT EVIDENCE: Many preschool children are so ignorant about differences between male and female genitalia that it is hard to see how most boys could fear castration or how most girls could feel castrated and envy males for having a penis.
   CONCLUSION: Freud's explanation of sex typing has not received much empirical support even though children do begin to develop sex-role preferences at about the time that he specified.

15. (509-510) DIFFERENTIAL REINFORCEMENT: Fagot and Leinbach (1989) found that parents are already encouraging sex-appropriate play and are responding negatively to cross-sex behaviors during the second year, before the children acquire a basic gender identity or display a clear preference for male or female activities.

(510) OBSERVATIONAL LEARNING: Once children recognize that gender is an unchanging aspect of their personalities (at age 6 to 7), they begin to attend selectively to same-sex models and are likely to avoid toys and activities that other-sex models seem to enjoy (Ruble et al., 1981).

16. (509) Fathers showed the clearest pattern by rewarding their children for playing with the same-sex items while actively suppressing cross-sex play. Mothers showed a similar pattern with their daughters but permitted their sons to play with either masculine or feminine toys. Finally, peers were quite critical of children who played with cross-sex toys, often ridiculing the offender or disrupting this "inappropriate" play.

Mothers were the most permissive of cross-sex play in these studies.

17. (510) Children do not pay more attention to same-sex models until relativley late--about 6 to 7 years of age (Ruble et al., 1981). Masters and his associates (1979) found that preschool children were more concerned about the sex appropriateness of the behavior they observed than the sex of the model who displayed it.

18. (510-511) More

The number of children in a family and their ages and sexes affect the sex-role behaviors of all family members. Fathers who have two daughters tend to portray a more "masculine" image than fathers who have a son and a daughter.

Children in families with opposite-sex siblings are more stereotyped than those with same-sex siblings because same-sex siblings may avoid sex-stereotyped activities as a way of differentiating themselves from the other boys or girls in their families.

19. (511) Children who watch more than 25 hours of TV per week are more likely to prefer gender-appropriate toys and to hold highly stereotyped views of men and women.

20. (511) a) the role of cognitive development in sex-role development
b) the role children play in their sex-role socialization by actively seeking information about how to act like a boy or girl

21. (512) BASIC GENDER IDENTITY: children correctly identify themselves as a boy or girl by age 3
GENDER STABILITY: understand that boys become men and girls become women
GENDER CONSISTENCY: understand that one's sex cannot be changed by dressing in opposite-sex clothes or engaging in opposite-sex activites

Problem: Sex typing is already well underway before the child acquires a mature gender identity.

22. (513)   2 1/2 - 3 years, basic gender identity

IN-GROUP/OUT-GROUP SCHEMA: a basic categorization of objects, behaviors, and roles as "for females" or "for males"
OWN-SEX SCHEMA: detailed information about how to behave consistent with one's sex

(514)   Boys recalled much more in-depth information about "boy" items than did girls, whereas girls recalled more than boys about these very same objects if they had been labeled "girl" items. Children's information-gathering efforts seemed consistently guided by their own-sex schemas.

23. (515)   PRENATAL: biological
BIRTH TO 3 YEARS: learning, cognitive development
3-6 YEARS: schema development, imitation of models
6-7 YEARS: cognitive development, imitation of same-sex models

PSYCHOLOGICAL ANDROGYNY: A PRESCRIPTION FOR THE FUTURE?

24. (516)   A large (number), few

25. (516)   27-32%

26. (517)   Androgynous children and adolescents enjoy higher self-esteem (than feminine sex-typed or undifferentiated persons) and are perceived by peers as more likable and better adjusted than classmates. Androgynous females are more likely than sex-typed females to attribute their achievements to ability (rather than effort or luck).

Possession of "masculine" traits

DEVELOPMENT OF SEXUALITY AND SEXUAL BEHAVIOR

27. (519)   Masturbation and erotic play are quite common among grade-school children and may actually increase rather than decrease during this period.

28. (520-521)   a) sex with affection is acceptable
b) decline of the double standard (i.e., it is not more acceptable for males to be sexually active than for females to be sexually active)
c) increased confusion about sexual norms

29. (522)   A low grade; many fail to consistently practice birth control; 1 in 10 girls give birth; there has been little shift toward the direction of safer sexual practices (to guard against AIDS)

CHAPTER 14

AGGRESSION, ALTRUISM, AND MORAL DEVELOPMENT

STUDY CHECKLIST

_____ Read Chapter Outline and Summary (Study guide)

_____ Read Chapter (Text)

_____ Completed Vocabulary Fill-Ins (Study guide)

_____ Re-Read Outline and Summary (Study guide)

_____ Reviewed Lecture Notes and Integrated with Text

_____ Reviewed Vocabulary, Study Questions, and Text Chapter

CHAPTER 14 OUTLINE AND SUMMARY

I. **The development of aggression**
  A. What is aggression?
  B. Origins of aggression
  C. Age-related changes in the nature of aggression
    1. Individual differences in aggression
    2. Is aggression a stable attribute?
    3. Sex differences in aggression
  D. Cultural influences on aggression
  E. Familial influences on aggression
    1. Parental child-rearing practices and children's aggressive behavior
    2. The home as a breeding ground for aggression
  F. Methods of controlling aggression
    1. Catharsis: A dubious strategy
    2. Eliminating the payoffs for aggression
    3. Modeling and coaching strategies
    4. Creating "nonaggressive" environments
    5. Training children to empathize with victims

This chapter focuses on three interrelated aspects of moral development that are often considered when making judgments about a child's moral character: the emergence and control of aggressive behavior, the development of altruism and prosocial behavior, and the broader (or more inclusive) topic of moral socialization and moral development.

Aggression is defined as any act designed to harm or injure another living being who is motivated to avoid such treatment. Aggression emerges during the second year as older infants and toddlers begin to quarrel with siblings and peers over toys and other possessions. During early childhood, aggression becomes less physical and increasingly verbal, as well as somewhat less instrumental and increasingly hostile. Compared to nonaggressive peers, highly aggressive children (1) expect aggression to be personally rewarding, (2) value these outcomes highly, and (3) display a hostile attributional bias that predisposes them to favor aggressive solutions to conflict. One's characteristic level of aggression (aggressiveness) is a reasonably stable attribute for both boys and girls; however, boys are more physically and verbally aggressive than girls and are more likely than girls to become targets of aggression.

A person's aggressive inclinations will depend, in part, on the cultural, subcultural, and family settings in which he or she is raised. Cold and rejecting parents who rely on physical punishment and often permit aggression are likely to raise highly aggressive children. Yet the socialization of aggression is a two-way street, for characteristics of the child (such as an active, impetuous temperament) can affect the child-rearing practices that parents use. Highly aggressive youngsters who are "out of control" often live in coercive home environments where family members are constantly struggling with one another. In order to help these highly combative children, it may be necessary to treat the entire family.

Proceeding in accordance with the catharsis hypothesis--the belief that children become less aggressive after letting off steam against an inanimate object--is an ineffective control tactic that may instigate aggressive behavior. Some proven methods of controlling children's aggression are (1) using the incompatible-response technique, (2) using the time-out procedure to punish aggression, (3) coaching and modeling nonaggressive solutions to conflict, (4) creating play environments that minimize the likelihood of conflict, and (5) encouraging children to recognize the harmful effects of their aggressive acts and to empathize with the victims of aggression.

II. **Altruism: Development of the prosocial self**
   A. Origins of altruism and altruistic concern
   B. Developmental trends in altruism
   C. Cognitive and affective contributors to altruism
      1. Prosocial moral reasoning
      2. Empathy
      3. Viewing oneself as altruistic: A social-cognitive contributor
   D. Promoting altruism: Cultural and social influences
      1. Cultural influences
      2. Reinforcing altruism
      3. Practicing and preaching altruism
      4. Who raises altruistic children?

Although infants and toddlers will occasionally offer toys to playmates, help their parents with household chores, and try to soothe distressed companions, examples of altruism become increasingly common over the course of childhood. The growth of altruistic concern is closely linked to the development of role-taking skills, empathy, and prosocial moral reasoning; and children who have incorporated altruism into their self-concepts are inclined to perform many acts of kindness in order to live up to their positive self-images.

Like aggression, a person's altruistic tendencies are influenced by the cultural and family settings in which he or she is raised. Parents can promote altruistic behavior by encouraging their child to perform acts of kindness, by showing approval for such kindly deeds, and by practicing themselves the prosocial lessons they have preached. Moreover, parents who discipline harmdoing with nonpunitive, affective explanations that point out the negative effects of misconduct for the child's victims are likely to raise children who become sympathetic, self-sacrificing, and concerned about the welfare of others.

Morality has been defined in many ways, although almost everyone agrees that it implies a set of principles or ideals that help the individual to distinguish right from wrong and to act on this distinction. Morality has three basic components: moral affect, moral reasoning, and moral behavior.

Psychoanalytic theorists emphasize the affective, or "emotional," aspects of morality. According to Freud, the character of the parent/child relationship largely determines the child's willingness to internalize the moral standards of his or her parents. This internalization is said to occur during the phallic stage and to result in the development of the superego. Once formed, the superego functions as an internal censor that will reward the child for virtuous conduct and punish moral transgressions by making the child feel anxious, guilty, or shameful. Although Freud's broader themes about the importance of moral emotions have some merit, the particulars of his theory have not received much empirical support.

Cognitive-developmental theorists have emphasized the cognitive component of morality by studying the development of moral reasoning. Jean Piaget was the pioneer. He formulated a two-stage model of moral development based on changes that occur in children's conceptions of rules and their sense of social justice. Although Piaget did identify some important processes and basic trends in the development of moral reasoning, recent research suggests that his two-stage theory badly underestimated the moral sophistication of preschool and young grade-school children while overestimating the moral maturity of adolescents.

Lawrence Kohlberg's revised and extended version of Piaget's theory views moral reasoning as progressing through an invariant sequence of three levels, each composed of two distinct stages. According to Kohlberg, the order of progression through the levels and stages is invariant because each of these modes of thinking depends, in part, on the development of cognitive abilities that evolve in a fixed sequence. Yet Kohlberg also claimed that no moral growth occurs in the absence of social experiences that would cause a person to reevaluate her existing moral concepts.

Research indicates that Kohlberg's stages do form an invariant sequence and that both cognitive development and such relevant social experiences as higher education and peer interaction contribute to the growth of moral reasoning. Moreover, each of Kohlberg's stages is a reasonably consistent mode of thinking that is likely to guide an individual's reasoning about both hypothetical and real-world dilemmas. And research has consistently failed to support the claims that Kohlberg's theory is biased against women.

VI. **Morality as a product of social learning**
    A.   How consistent are moral conduct and moral character?
    B.   Learning to resist temptation
        1.   Reinforcement as a determinant of moral conduct
        2.   The role of punishment in establishing moral prohibitions
        3.   Effects of social models on children's moral behavior

Social-learning theorists emphasize the behavioral component of morality, and their research has helped us to understand how children are able to resist temptation and to inhibit acts that violate moral norms. Among the processes that are important in establishing inhibitory controls are (1) reinforcing the child for following rules and (2) punishing transgressions. The most effective punitive tactics are those that include cognitive rationales explaining why the punished act is wrong and why the child should want to inhibit such conduct. Nonpunitive techniques such as teaching the child how to instruct herself to avoid temptations or convincing the child that she is a "good" or "honest" person are also quite effective at promoting moral self-restraint. Indeed, any technique that induces children to make internal attributions for their uneasiness in the face of temptation or for their compliance with rules is likely to contribute to their moral maturity. Children may also acquire inhibitory controls by observing models who show moral restraint or by serving as rule-following models for other children.

VII. **Who raises children who are morally mature?**

Martin Hoffman has looked at the relationship between parental disciplinary practices and children's moral development. His findings indicate that warm and loving parents who rely mainly on inductive discipline tend to raise children who are morally mature. Induction is an effective method of moral socialization because it often illustrates and may help the child to integrate the affective, cognitive, and behavioral aspects of morality. And because children generally prefer induction to other disciplinary techniques, viewing it as the wise choice for handling most transgressions, they may be highly motivated to accept influence from an inductive adult whose methods they can respect.

CHAPTER 14 VOCABULARY FILL-INS
(Definitions below are in order of appearance in text margins)

MATCH VOCABULARY WORD/PHRASE TO ITS DEFINITION.
THEN COVER YOUR ANSWERS TO TEST YOUR MASTERY.

| aggression | hostile attributional bias |
| hostile aggression | instrumental aggression |

1. _____ Behavior performed with the intention of harming a living being who is motivated to avoid this treatment.

2. _____ Aggressive acts for which the actor's major goal is to harm or injure a victim.

3. _____ Aggressive acts for which the actor's major goal is to gain access to objects, space, or privileges.

4. _____ Tendency to view harm done under ambiguous circumstances as having stemmed from a hostile intent on the part of the harmdoer; characterizes highly aggressive children and adolescents.

catharsis hypothesis	incompatible-response
cathartic technique	technique
coercive home environment	negative reinforcer
	time-out technique

5. _____ A home in which family members often annoy one another and use aggressive tactics as a methods of coping with these aversive experiences.

6. _____ Any stimulus whose removal or termination as the consequence of an act will increase the probability that the act will recur.

7. _____ The notion that aggressive urges are reduced when people commit real or symbolic acts of aggression.

8. _____ A strategy for reducing aggression by encouraging children to vent their anger or frustrations on inanimate objects.

9. _____ A nonpunitive method of behavior modification in which adults ignore undesirable conduct while reinforcing acts that are incompatible with these responses.

10. _____ A strategy in which the disciplinary agent "punishes" a child by disrupting or preventing the prohibited activity that the child seems to enjoy.

---

altruism
altruistic exhortations
empathy

norm of social
    responsibility
prosocial moral
    reasoning

11. _____ The ability to experience the same emotions that someone else is experiencing.

12. _____ A concern for the welfare of others that is expressed through prosocial acts such as sharing, cooperating, and helping.

13. _____ The thinking that people display when deciding whether to help, share with, or comfort others when these actions could prove costly to themselves.

14. _____ The principle that we should help others who are in some way dependent on us for assistance.

15. _____ Verbal encouragements to help, comfort, share, or cooperate with others.

---

internalization
moral affect
moral behavior
moral development

moral reasoning
morality
Oedipal morality

16. _____ The process by which children acquire society's standards of right and wrong.

17. _____ A set of principles or ideals that help the individual to distinguish right from wrong and to act on this distinction.

18. _____ The process of adopting the attributes or standards of other people--taking these standards as one's own.

19. _____ The emotional component of morality including feelings such as guilt, shame, and pride in ethical conduct.

20. _____ The cognitive component of morality; the thinking that people display when deciding whether various acts are right or wrong.

21. _____ The behavioral component of morality; actions that are consistent with one's moral standards in situations in which one is tempted to violate a prohibition.

22. _____ Freud's theory that moral development occurs during the phallic period (ages 3 to 6) when children internalize the moral standards of the same-sex parent as they resolve their Oedipus or Electra conflicts.

---

autonomous morality   invariant sequence
expiatory punishment   premoral period
heteronomous morality   reciprocal punishment
immanent justice

23. _____ A series of developments that occur in one particular order because each development in the sequence is a prerequisite for those appearing later.

24. _____ In Piaget's theory, the first 5 to 6 years of life, when children have little respect for or awareness of socially defined rules.

25. _____ Piaget's first stage of moral development, in which children view the rules of authority figures as sacred and unalterable.

26. _____ The notion that unacceptable conduct will invariably be punished and that justice is ever present in the world.

27. _____ Piaget's second stage of moral development, in which children realize that rules are arbitrary agreements that can be challenged and even changed with the consent of the people they govern.

28. _____ Punitive consequences that bear no relation to the nature of the forbidden act.

29. _____ Punitive consequences that are tailored to the forbidden act so that a rulebreaker will understand the implications of a transgression.

---

conventional morality
morality of care
postconventional morality

preconventional morality
transactive interactions

30. _____ Kohlberg's term for the first two stages of moral reasoning, in which moral judgments are based on the tangible punitive consequences (Stage 1) or rewarding consequences (Stage 2) of an act for the actor rather than on the relationship of that act to society's rules and customs.

31. _____ Kohlberg's term for the third and fourth stages of moral reasoning, in which moral judgments are based on a desire to gain approval (Stage 3) or to uphold laws that maintain social order (Stage 4).

32. _____ Kohlberg's term for the fifth and sixth stages of moral reasoning, in which moral judgments are based on social contracts and democratic law (Stage 5) or on universal principles of ethics and justice (Stage 6).

33. _____ Gilligan's term for what she presumes to be the dominant moral orientation of females--an orientation focusing more on compassionate concerns for human welfare than on socially defined justice as administered through law.

34. _____ Verbal exchanges in which individuals perform mental operations on the reasoning of their discussion partners.

---

doctrine of specificity
"forbidden toy" paradigm

inhibitory control
unitary morality

35. _____ A viewpoint shared by many social-learning theorists that holds that moral affect, moral reasoning, and moral behavior depend more on the situation one faces than on an internalized set of moral principles.

36. _____ The notion that moral affect, moral reasoning, and moral behavior are interrelated components of a "moral character" that is consistent across situations.

37. _____ An ability to display acceptable conduct by resisting the temptation to commit a forbidden act.

38. _____ A method of studying children's resistance to temptation by noting whether youngsters will play with forbidden toys when they believe that this transgression is unlikely to be detected.

---

induction   **power assertion**
love withdrawal

39. _____ A form of discipline in which an adult withholds attention, affection, or approval in order to modify or control a child's behavior.

40. _____ A form of discipline in which an adult relies on his or her superior power (for example, by administering spankings or withholding privileges) to modify or control a child's behavior.

41. _____ A nonpunitive form of discipline in which an adult explains why a child's behavior is wrong and should be changed by emphasizing its effects on others.

CHAPTER 14 STUDY QUESTIONS

THE DEVELOPMENT OF AGGRESSION

1. What "defines" an act as aggressive? (p. 527)

Distinguish between hostile aggression and instrumental aggression. (p. 527)

HOSTILE:

INSTRUMENTAL:

At about what age do acts of force begin to show the "seeds" of instrumental aggression? (p. 527)

2. _____ aggression has been found to decline with age but _____ aggression **increases** with age. (p. 528) This increase occurs despite the findings of Dodge et al. that older children are better able to discriminate intentional harmdoing from nonintentional. One **possible reason for the increase in hostile aggression** is suggested by the findings of **Sancilio** et al. and **Ferguson and Rule.** Peers _____ retaliation irrespective of intent. (p. 529)

3. Indicate the ways **highly aggressive children** have been shown to differ from less aggressive children. (p. 529)

MORE POSITIVE EXPECTANCIES SUCH AS . . .

VALUE OUTCOMES OF AGGRESSION MORE, i.e., . . .

SHOW HOSTILE ATTRIBUTIONAL BIAS THAT . . .

4. **Dodge** and others have found that aggressive children are more likely than nonaggressive children to **interpret ambiguous events as having hostile intent** and see retaliation as appropriate. **Is their expectation that the intentions of others are hostile warranted?** Research by **Dodge** and associates and by **Sancilio** et al. indicates that the answer to that question is _____ because _____. (p. 530-531)

5.   Have aggressive children been found to attack a variety of other children or do they tend to single out a few children to bully? (p. 530-531, Box 14-1)

What are the **characteristics of children who repeatedly get attacked** according to **Olweus?** (p. 530-531, Box 14-1)

(a)

(b)

(c)

(d)

(e)

What two types of victims have been identified by **Olweus** and by **Perry** et al.? Which type is more common? (p. 530, Box 14-1)

What have **Perry** et al. (1990) found to be the **perceived rewards for the aggressor of aggression** toward regularly victimized peers? (p. 531, Box 14-1)

6.   What conclusion can be drawn regarding the **continuity** or predictability of aggression from childhood to adulthood for males? for females? (p. 532)

7.   Data from over 100 studies have indicated that men and **boys** are **more aggressive** than females in which type(s) of aggression? (p. 532)

8.   What **causal factors** does the text suggest lie behind the **sex differences** found in aggression? (p. 532-533)

9.   Does aggression occur at a fairly constant level across diverse cultures, or does the level vary considerably from culture to culture? (p. 533)

How does the **U.S.** rank on aggressiveness among stable democracies?

10.   What **parenting practices** have been repeatedly found to be related to aggressiveness in children? (p. 533-534)

11.   **Olweus** found that the **best predictor** of aggression among adolescent males was _____ and the next best predictor was _____. (p. 534)

12.   What relationship has parental **monitoring** been found to have with aggression and antisocial acts outside the home? (p. 534)

13. **Patterson's** work indicates that aggression is often a family problem, not just a child's problem. What strategy has he found to be effective in **treating aggression** in children? (p. 535-536 & Box 14-2)

(a)

(b)

(c)

(d)

(e)

14. The catharsis view maintains that children should be encouraged to vent their aggression on inanimate objects so they will be less inclined to hurt other people. **What is the status of the catharsis view?** (p. 537)

15. Briefly characterize each of the following **strategies for controlling aggression.** (p. 537-539)

INCOMPATIBLE-RESPONSE TECHNIQUE:

TIME-OUT TECHNIQUE:

MODELING/COACHING:

NONAGGRESSIVE ENVIRONMENTS:

EMPATHY TRAINING:

16.   What did **Zahn-Waxler** and associates find that **mothers of compassionate children do when disciplining** their child that was different from what mothers of less compassionate children do? (p. 539)

17.   Children show altruistic responses at a very early age (2-3 years) but not in all areas. List two types of altruistic responses that appear early and two that are relatively infrequent among preschoolers but increase over the elementary years. (p. 540)

> EARLY ALTRUISTIC BEHAVIOR
>
>> (a)
>>
>> (b)
>
> LATER ALTRUISTIC BEHAVIOR
>
>> (a)
>>
>> (b)

18.   What finding in the **Green and Schneider** study indicates that **under some circumstances** children of quite **diverse ages all respond in an altruistic way, e.g.,** sacrificing playtime? (p. 540-541 & Table 14-1)

Note--This finding suggests that altruism is probably circumstantial and that the low levels in some studies could be due to the artificiality of the context, thereby underestimating altruism, especially among younger children.

19. Has the literature shown one **gender** to be more altruistic than the other? (p. 540-541)

20. The text presents evidence for four factors as **contributors to altruism**. Briefly describe the evidence for each and the nature of the link to altruism. Identify a key reference for each factor. (p. 541-544)

ROLE-TAKING SKILLS

Evidence and Reference:

PROSOCIAL MORAL REASONING

Evidence and Reference:

EMPATHY

Evidence and Reference:

VIEWING ONESELF AS ALTRUISTIC

Evidence and Reference:

21. **Cultures** vary markedly in the degree to which they encourage altruism. Where did the **U.S.** place in percentage of children scoring high on altruism in the **Whitings'** six-culture study? (p. 545 & Table 14-3)

What two explanations were offered?

22. Giving tangible reinforcers has not been found to promote altruism. What other types of adult responses, child-rearing strategies, or ways of structuring activities have been found to **promote altruism**? (p. 546-548)

(a)

(b)

(c)

(d)

(e)

What are some reasons why discipline that involves rationales might inspire children to become more altruistic? (p. 547-548)

WHAT IS MORALITY (AND MORAL DEVELOPMENT)?

23. Why is the **transmission** of moral standards to each generation so important? (p. 548)

(a)

(b)

24. Morality involves more than just avoiding punishment or being compliant to receive rewards. **Morally mature individuals are believed to be so because they have** _____ **a set of moral standards.** (p. 548)

25. After each of the following **components of morality,** indicate which theoretical orientation(s) has(have) contributed most to the understanding of that component. (p. 548-549)

AFFECTIVE:

COGNITIVE:

BEHAVIORAL:

PSYCHOANALYTIC EXPLANATIONS OF MORAL DEVELOPMENT

26. What is the **status of Freud's view of the development of morality,** a view that focuses on the resolution of the Oedipus complex? Why? (p. 550)

27. **Erikson's view** differs from Freud's in that Erikson **emphasizes the role of** _____ **parents,** not just the father, in moral development and emphasizes the interplay of the restraining forces of the _____ and the internalized rules of the superego in moral behavior.
(p. 550)

COGNITIVE-DEVELOPMENTAL THEORY--PIAGET

28. Characterize each of **Piaget's three stages of moral reasoning.** (p. 551-553)

PREMORAL:

MORAL REALISM/HETERONOMOUS MORALITY:

MORAL RELATIVISM/AUTONOMOUS MORALITY:

29. What type of **peer experience** did Piaget believe would **promote** moral development? (p. 552-553)

What type of **parent behavior** did he believe would **inhibit** development of mature moral reasoning? (p. 553)

30. In general, has **subsequent research** supported Piaget's hypothesized levels of moral reasoning and his emphasis on role-taking skills and peer participation as mediators of advances in moral reasoning? (p. 553-554)

Have subsequent studies confirmed the **ages** that Piaget associated with reaching each level of moral reasoning? (p. 554-555)

31. The results of studies by **Nelson** suggest that Piaget underestimated the moral maturity of preschool children. What finding demonstrated more **sophisticated moral reasoning** than Piaget attributed to **preschoolers**? (p. 554)

Were any aspects of Piaget's views confirmed? (p. 554)

32. By what **age** do children show evidence of viewing **violation of moral rules as more serious** than violation of social-conventional rules? (p. 554-555)

Why is this a problem for Piaget's theory of moral development? (p. 555)

COGNITIVE-DEVELOPMENTAL THEORY--KOHLBERG

33. **Kohlberg's** research indicates that development of moral reasoning is a long process continuing into adulthood. **What type of theory** did he propose to characterize moral development? (p. 555-556)

What does Kohlberg maintain develops with age that **lies behind** children's changing responses to moral dilemmas? (p. 556)

34.   Briefly characterize each of **Kohlberg's three levels** of moral reasoning. (p. 556-558)

LEVEL 1 PRECONVENTIONAL MORALITY:

LEVEL 2 CONVENTIONAL MORALITY:

LEVEL 3 POSTCONVENTIONAL MORALITY:

35.   What answers does research evidence provide to the questions of how universal **Kohlberg's stages** are and how invariant the sequence of stages is? Indicate direction the weight of evidence points and the type of evidence. (p. 559-560)

UNIVERSALITY:

INVARIANCE OF SEQUENCE:

36.   What level of moral reasoning did **Colby** et al. find to predominate among 14- to 20-year-olds? among young adults 22 to 36 (preconventional, conventional or postconventional)? (p. 560-561 & Fig. 14-5)

14- to 20-year-olds:

22- to 36-year-olds:

37.   Box 14-3 offers support for what **mode of fostering change** in maturity of **moral reasoning**? (p. 560, Box 14-3)

What specific characteristic does research by **Berkowitz and Gibbs** indicate this mode of change must have?

38.   What **minimal cognitive level** has been found to be prerequisite for conventional morality? for postconventional morality? (p. 561)

CONVENTIONAL:

POSTCONVENTIONAL:

Does achieving these prerequisite cognitive levels **guarantee** conventional or postconventional moral reasoning? (p. 561)

39. What kinds of social **experiences/contextual factors** have been shown to be related to **moral growth**? (p. 562 & Box 14-3)

(a)

(b)

(c)

(d)

40. How strong is the **relationship** between **moral reasoning** and **moral behavior**? (p. 562-563)

41. What conclusion can be drawn about the **consistency of moral reasoning** from the results of the **Walker** et al. study comparing responses to hypothetical and real-life moral dilemmas? (p. 563)

42. Although **Gilligan's** view that there are sex differences in moral reasoning has not been supported, her work has **broadened the definition of morality** from just concern with laws, rules, rights, and justice to also include concern with _____ by both males and females. (p. 564-565)

43. Kohlberg's work emphasized moral reasoning as an important factor in understanding the choices people make. **Haan** believes, however, there is another factor that is also important, namely, _____. (p. 564-565)

44.   What conclusion does the text author suggest is warranted regarding the **consistency of moral behavior**; i.e., if a child cheats in one context, is she likely to also cheat in other contexts? (p. 565-566)

45.   What **discipline strategies** and **characteristics of the discipliner** have been found to **promote** resistance to temptation/**self-control**? (p. 566-569 & Box 14-4)

(a)   (p. 566) **Perry & Parke; Sears et al.:**

(b)   (p. 567) **Parke; Hoffman:**

(c)   (p. 568) **Toner, Parke, & Yussen; Grusec et al.:**

(d)   (p. 569) **Toner, Moore, & Ashley:**

(e)   (Box 14-4) **Mischel & Patterson; Toner & Smith:**

(f)   (Box 14-4) **Casey & Burton:**

46.   **Explain why giving rationales** increases the effectiveness of punishment and **promotes true self-control.** (p. 567)

47.   Box 14-4 describes two **nonpunitive strategies** for helping children gain self-control. What three **advantages** do these strategies have over punishment-based strategies? (p. 569, Box 14-4)

(a)

(b)

(c)

WHO RAISES CHILDREN WHO ARE MORALLY MATURE?

48.   What type of **parent disciplinary strategy** has been found by **Hoffman** and others to be most effective in promoting mature moral reasoning and behavior? Why is it believed to be effective? (p. 569-571)

Note the similarity between the description of effective parenting for moral reasoning and behavior and the strategies found in the laboratory that lead to resistance to temptation (Study Question 45).

49.   How has a **child's response to discipline** been found to affect subsequent discipline? (p. 571)

50.   What strategy for dealing with inappropriate behavior did **Siegal and Cowen** find to be **viewed by children** as **most appropriate**? (p. 571-572)

How does their perception of the "best" approach match with what has been found about what strategies are actually most effective?

———————————————————————————————

ACTIVITY 14-1a

FAMILY VARIABLES ASSOCIATED WITH AGGRESSION: ONE CASE

INTRODUCTION: This activity is related to the material on factors contributing to aggression discussed in Chapter 14 (p. 533-539). Several family variables have been found to be related to aggression, such as lack of parental monitoring, permissiveness of aggression, and coercive discipline that models aggression.

INSTRUCTIONS: For this activity think of an example of someone you have known who was/is highly aggressive; someone whose family you know something about.

1. Describe the individual's behavior and attitudes that led you to classify this person as highly aggressive.

2. Describe the family, characterizing parental practices in each of the following areas:

   a. Monitoring of child's activities and friends

   b. Mother's willingness to tolerate aggression

   c. Punishment strategies used by parents

   d. Child's relationship with the parents

   e. Parents' attitude toward the child

   f. Extent aggression was modeled in the home as a way to solve problems or get what was wanted

   g. Other (specify)_____

3. Were all the children in the family aggressive? If not, how might you explain why the person you have described was so highly aggressive and siblings were not?

4. What is your personal theory of what factors are associated with aggressive behaviors in children?

5. How does your theory compare to the Olweus model presented in your text, p. 534?

ACTIVITY 14-1b

FAMILY VARIABLES ASSOCIATED WITH NONAGGRESSION: ONE CASE

INTRODUCTION: This activity is an extension of Activity 14-1a on family variables associated with aggression. (Activity 14-1b is not intended to be used alone, but to accompany Activity 14-1a.)

INSTRUCTIONS: For this activity think of an example of someone you have known who was/is <u>not</u> an aggressive individual, someone whose family you know something about. The first three parts below are the same as for Activity 14-1a, except that this time you are describing a nonaggressive child and the parents' behavior. The fourth and fifth parts differ from those in Activity 14-1a, focusing on the parenting patterns of aggressive and nonaggressive children.

1. Describe the individual's behavior and attitudes that led you to classify this person as nonaggressive (e.g., how does this person handle conflict, get what he wants, respond to verbal or physical attack, etc.?).

2. Describe the family, characterizing parental practices in each of the following areas:

    a. <u>Monitoring of child's activities and friends</u>

    b. <u>Mother's willingness to tolerate aggression</u>

    c. <u>Punishment strategies used by parents</u>

    d. <u>Child's relationship with the parent</u>

    e. <u>Parents' attitude toward child</u>

    f. <u>Extent aggression was modeled in the home as a way to solve problems or get what was wanted</u>

    g. <u>Other</u> (specify) _____

3. Were all the children in the family nonaggressive? If not, how might you explain why the person you have described was less aggressive than one or more siblings?

4. How did the parenting of the aggressive child and the nonaggressive child differ?

5. How closely do the parenting patterns of the two children match the "profile" of the parents of aggressive children and (by inference) the parents of nonaggressive children described in the text (p. 533-539)? If they do not match well, describe what other factors you think might have contributed to the development of the child's behavior patterns.

ACTIVITY 14-2

KOHLBERG'S STAGES OF MORAL DEVELOPMENT

INTRODUCTION: This activity relates to the material in Chapter 14 (p. 555-565) on Kohlberg's stages of moral reasoning. Kohlberg's stages characterize a developmental sequence in the types of reasons that individuals give for their moral decisions. This activity is intended to give you some exposure to the kinds of reasons that different individuals give to back up their positions on moral issues and to give you practice in applying Kohlberg's stage definitions.

INSTRUCTIONS: Select two individuals to interview. These individuals can be adults or children, same age or different age, same sex or different sex. If they are the same sex and age category, try to select one individual whose principles and behavior you admire and one who is less admirable.

Part A: The Interview

Two possible dilemmas and probes are presented below. Select one to present to both individuals or make up one to present to the two individuals you interview. Be sure to write down each probe you present and each response given.

Part B: Classification of Responses

Classify each response given according to Kohlberg's levels of moral reasoning: preconventional (pre), conventional (conv), or postconventional (post). See p. 556-558 of the text for descriptions of each level. Then answer the following questions.

Part C: Questions to Answer

1. Was it easy or difficult to classify individuals' responses? Describe any problems you encountered.

2. How many different levels did each individual use? What was the highest level used by each individual?

3. Were the responses that were given by the two individuals consistent or inconsistent with your expectations of how they would respond? Explain.

DILEMMA 1 INTERVIEW

1. "The **abortion** issue is a pretty hot one this year. What is your position?"

2. "Why do you feel that way?"

3. "Any other reasons you can think of?" (Keep probing with this to encourage multiple reasons.)

4. (if pro-choice) "Anti-abortionists argue that it is not our right to take the life of a child, even one that is in the early stages of development. What would you say to an anti-abortionist to justify your position that it is sometimes appropriate to terminate the life of an unborn child?"

5. (if pro-choice) "Are there any circumstances when you think the mother has the moral obligation to carry the child to term?"

6. (if anti-abortion) "Pro-choicers argue that the mother should have the right to decide what happens to her body and whether she wants to mother a child. What arguments could you give to justify ignoring the mother's viewpoint?"

7. (if anti-abortion) "Are there any circumstances when you think it would be morally right for a mother to abort her developing child?"

8. (Question of your choice; specify)

DILEMMA 2 INTERVIEW

1. "The **temptation to cheat** is something that plagues all students and income tax payers. Do you think there are any circumstances when an individual would be justified in cheating to get a higher grade or a more favorable tax return?" (Adapt to age of interviewee.)

2. (if against cheating) "What justifications can you give for your position, i.e., why do you feel a person should not cheat for personal gain?"

3. (if against cheating) "Are there any circumstances when you think it would be justifiable to cheat?"

4.. (if cheating is OK) "What justifications can you give for your view, i.e., why do you feel that it is OK for a person to cheat?"

5. (if cheating is OK) "Are there any circumstances when you think it would not be morally appropriate to cheat?"

6. (Question of your choice; specify)

DILEMMA 3 INTERVIEW
(Dilemma of your choice; specify topic and probes)

THE DEVELOPMENT OF AGGRESSION

1. (527)   The <u>actor's intentions</u> define an act as "aggressive," not the act's consequences.

HOSTILE: the major goal of hostile aggression is to <u>injure</u> a victim.
INSTRUMENTAL: instrumental aggression describes those situations in which one person harms another as a <u>means to a nonaggressive end</u>.

About 20-23 months

2. (528-529)   Instrumental, hostile, sanction

3. (529)   MORE POSITIVE EXPECTANCIES SUCH AS
1) more confident that aggression will yield tangible rewards (such as control of a disputed toy)
2) more certain that aggression would be successful in terminating others' noxious behavior
3) more inclined to believe that aggression will enhance their self-esteem and will not cause their victims any permanent harm

VALUE OUTCOMES OF AGGRESSION MORE, i.e., they attach much significance to their ability to dominate and control their victims, and they are not particularly concerned about the suffering they may cause or the possibility of being rejected by their peers.
SHOW HOSTILE ATTRIBUTIONAL BIAS THAT causes them to overattribute harmful intentions to their peers, thus viewing them as belligerent adversaries who deserve to be dealt with in a forceful manner.

4. (530-531)   Yes, because not only do aggressive children provoke a large number of conflicts, but they are also more likely than nonaggressive children to be disliked and to become targets of aggression.

5. (530)   <u>A few</u> children are singled out who tend to be:
a) highly anxious
b) low in self-esteem
c) socially isolated
d) physically weak
e) afraid to be assertive or to defend themselves

<u>Passive</u> victims outnumber <u>provocative</u> victims 5:1.

Perceive a high likelihood of acquiring some tangible reward, rewards that are highly valued because of their source--a victimized peer.

6. (532)   Aggression measured as early as age 8 has been shown to be <u>quite a good predictor</u> of adult aggression at age 30 <u>for both males and females</u> (as indexed by criminal behavior, spouse abuse, and self-reported physical aggression).

7. (532)   Physical <u>and</u> verbal aggression

8. (532-533)   Differential reinforcement, hormones

9. (533)   Cross-cultural studies consistently indicate that some societies and subcultures are more violent and aggressive than others.

   The United States is an aggressive society. On a percentage basis, the incidence of rape, assault, robbery, and homicide is higher in the United States than in any other stable democracy (Seabrook, 1990b).

10. (533)   Cold and rejecting parents who apply physical punishment in an erratic fashion and often permit their child to express aggressive impulses are likely to raise hostile, aggressive children.

11. (534)   Mothers' permissiveness toward, or willingness to tolerate, the boys' aggressive behavior early in childhood; the boys' own temperamental impulsivity (highly active, impulsive boys tend to be the most aggressive).

12. (534)   Positive relationship; lack of parental monitoring is associated with aggressive or delinquent adolescent behaviors such as fighting with peers, sassing teachers, destroying property, and generally breaking rules outside the home.

13. (536)   Patterson recommends training parents to:
    a) not give in to their child's coercive behavior
    b) control their own coercive tendencies
    c) control the child's coercion through time-out, etc.
    d) identify irritating behaviors in the child and establish a point system (or contract for older children) to reward or punish the child's behavior
    e) be on the lookout for occasions when they can respond to the child's prosocial conduct

14. (537)   Cathartic techniques do not reduce children's aggressive urges. In fact, they may teach youngsters that hitting and kicking are acceptable methods of expressing their anger or frustrations.

15. (537-539)   INCOMPATIBLE-RESPONSE TECHNIQUE: involves ignoring all but the most serious aggressive antics (thereby denying an "attentional" reward) while reinforcing such acts as cooperation and sharing, which are incompatible with aggression.
    TIME-OUT TECHNIQUE: the aggressive act that the child finds reinforcing is disrupted (e.g., by sending the aggressor to his room until he is ready to behavior appropriately).
    MODELING/COACHING: when children see a model choose a nonaggressive solution to a conflict or are explicitly coached in the use of nonaggressive methods of problem solving, they become much more inclined and able to enact similar solutions to their own problems.
    NONAGGRESSIVE ENVIRONMENTS: involves adults creating play areas that minimize the likelihood of conflict, e.g., removing (or refusing to buy) such "aggressive" toys as cap guns, tanks, and rubber knives, which are known to provoke hostilities.
    EMPATHY TRAINING: empathy can be developed by 1) modeling empathic concern and using disciplinary techniques that point out the harmful consequences of the child's aggressive actions and 2) encouraging the child to put himself in the victim's place and imagine how the victim feels.

16. (540)   Used <u>affective explanations</u> that helped the child to see the relation between his or her own acts and the distress they had caused (e.g., "You made Doug cry; it's not nice to bite"; "You must never poke anyone's eyes!")

17. (540)   EARLY ALTRUISTIC BEHAVIOR
              a) sympathy
              b) compassion

              LATER ALTRUISTIC BEHAVIOR
              a) helping
              b) sharing

18. (540)   To help needy children.

19. (540-541) Most studies find no sex difference in altruism.

20. (541)   ROLE-TAKING SKILLS
                  <u>Evidence & Reference</u>: Chalmers & Townsend and others have found that children who received training in role taking became more charitable, more cooperative, and more concerned about the needs of others.

    (541-543) PROSOCIAL MORAL REASONING
    (Tbl. 14-2)   <u>Evidence & Reference</u>: Eisenberg and her associates have identified five levels of prosocial moral reasoning and have noted that the child's level of prosocial moral reasoning predicts altruistic behavior, e.g., mature high school social reasoners were more likely than immature moral reasoners to help someone they disliked.

    (543-544) EMPATHY
                  <u>Evidence & Reference</u>: Hoffman and others believe empathic arousal (feeling someone else's distress) becomes an important mediator of altruism. Further study suggests that empathic arousal alone does not automatically result in altruism; mature role-taking skills and a feeling/norm of responsibility for others are also needed. Empathic arousal is present in infants and toddlers but role-taking skills and the norm of social responsibility are developing throughout childhood; hence, we see an increase in altruism with age.

    (544)   VIEWING ONESELF AS ALTRUISTIC
                  <u>Evidence & Reference</u>: Grasec and Redler found that labeling children as "nice" or "helpful" after an altruistic act led to in increased altruism. The training was more effective with 8-year-olds than 5-year-olds, perhaps because 8-year-olds are just begining to spontaneously describe themselves in psychological terms and view traits as stable aspects of character. In general, the evidence suggests that if individuals think of themselves as altruistic, they are more likely to behave charitably or helpfully toward others.

21. (545)   Lowest of the six cultures <u>because</u> children in less industrialized societies practice cooperation as a way of life and <u>because</u> of the strong emphasis on competition and individual goals in Western societies.

22. (546-547)
a) verbal reinforcement by a liked and respected person
b) structured play activities where the benefits of helping and cooperating are likely to be discovered
c) regular exposure to adult modeling and altruistic exhortations provide opportunities to internalize altruistic principles
d) warm and affectionate relationship with parents who themselves are highly concerned about the welfare of others
e) rational discipline that is heavy on reasoning

(547-548)
Helps see perspective of another (role-taking), helps in understanding the distress of another (empathy training), teaches the child comforting acts, and might convey the message that the child is "nice" or "helpful."

WHAT IS MORALITY (AND MORAL DEVELOPMENT)?

23. (548)
a) to maintain the social order
b) while making it possible for the individual to function appropriately within his or her culture (or subculture)

24. (548)
Internalized

25. (548-549)
AFFECTIVE: Psychoanalytic
COGNITIVE: Cognitive-developmental
BEHAVIORAL: Social-learning and social information-processing

PSYCHOANALYTIC EXPLANATIONS OF MORAL DEVELOPMENT

26. (550)
Even though Freud's broader themes about the significance of moral emotions have some merit, the "specifics" of his theory are largely unsupported, because children who fear their parents are not more likely to behave ethically or show remorse, and 6- to 7-year-olds who supposedly have resolved the Oedipal crisis are not all that morally mature.

27. (550)
Both, ego

COGNITIVE-DEVELOPMENTAL THEORY--PIAGET

28. (551-553)
PREMORAL: preschool children show little concern for or awareness of rules
MORAL REALISM/HETERONOMOUS MORALITY: between the ages of 5 and 10 the child develops a strong respect for rules and a belief that they must be obeyed at all times
MORAL RELATIVISM/AUTONOMOUS MORALITY: by age 10 or 11 most children realize that social rules are arbitrary agreements that can be challenged and even changed with the consent of the people they govern

29. (553)
Equal-status contact

Dictatorial; parents may actually slow the progress of moral development by reinforcing the child's unilateral respect for authority figures.

30. (554)   Yes; there is support for Piaget's hypothesized levels of moral reasoning and his emphasis on role-taking skills and peer participation.

No; he underestimated the moral sophistication of preschool and young grade-school children and perhaps overestimated the full development of moral reasoning by age 10 to 11.

31. (554)   Took into consideration consequences; the well-intentioned child who had wanted to play was evaluated much more favorably than the child who intended to hurt his friend, regardless of the consequences of his actions.

Piaget was right in one respect: younger children do assign more weight to consequences and less weight to intentions than older children do, even though both younger and older children consider both sources of information when evaluating others' conduct.

32. (555)   Age 2 1/2 - 3

It is a much earlier age than Piaget assumed children could make this distinction.

COGNITIVE-DEVELOPMENTAL THEORY--KOHLBERG

33. (556)   Stage theory

Development of certain cognitive abilities, including perspective taking

34. (556-557)   LEVEL 1 PRECONVENTIONAL MORALITY: Concern is with conforming to rules to avoid punishment or obtain personal rewards; morality is self-serving. Goodness or badness of an act is judged by its consequences rather than the intentions of the person

LEVEL 2 CONVENTIONAL MORALITY: Moral behavior is now defined by what pleases, helps, or is approved of by an important reference person or group. There is increasing concern with maintaining social order. Social praise and avoidance of blame have replaced tangible rewards and punishments as motivators of ethical conduct. The perspectives of others are clearly recognized and considered.

LEVEL 3 POSTCONVENTIONAL MORALITY: Moral behavior is now defined in terms of broad principles of justice rather than by an authority person or group. Morally right and legally proper are not always the same.

35. (559)   UNIVERSALITY: Studies in Mexico, the Bahamas, Taiwan, Turkey, Honduras, India, Nigeria, and Kenya confirm that adolescents and young adults typically reason about moral issues at higher levels than preadolescents and younger children do. This evidence points to Kohlberg's levels and stages of moral reasoning being "universal" structures that are age related.

(560)   INVARIANCE OF SEQUENCE: In a 20-year longitudinal study of 58 American males who were 10, 13, or 16 years old at the beginning of the project, Colby et al. found that subjects proceeded through the stages in precisely the order Kohlberg predicted and that no subject ever skipped a stage. Similar results have been reported in a nine-year longitudinal study of adolescents in Israel and a 12-year longitudinal project conducted in Turkey. Kohlberg's moral stages seem to represent an invariant sequence.

36. (561)   14- to 20-year-olds: Conventional, Stage 3, "Good boy" or "Good girl" orientation

             22- to 36-year-olds: Conventional, Stage 4, Social-order-maintaining morality

37. (560)   Peer discussion

             Peer discussion is effective when characterized by <u>transactive interactions</u>--that is, exchanges in which each discussant performs mental operations on the reasoning of his or her partner (e.g., "Your reasoning misses an important distinction" or "Here's an elaboration of your position").

38. (561)   CONVENTIONAL: clearly requires some role-taking abilities; e.g., a person at stage 3, must recognize others' points of view before she will evaluate intentions that would win their approval as "good" or morally acceptable.
PeOSTCONVENTIONAL: formal operations; the person who bases moral judgments on abstract principles must be able to reason abstractly and take all possible perspectives on a moral issue rather than simply adhering to the rule of law or to concrete moral norms.

             No; having achieved the prerequisite levels of cognitive reasoning for conventional or postconventional moral reasoning is necessary but not sufficient.

39. (562)   a) social experience
(Box 14-3) b) advanced education
             c) being a leader among one's peers
             d) living in a complex, diverse, democratic society

40. (562-563)   Only a moderately strong relationship, indicating that there must be personal qualities other than one's level of moral reasoning, and many situational factors as well, that influence a person's moral conduct in daily life. The relationship does increase with age.

41. (563)   Results showed an underlying consistency of moral reasoning (although not perfect) on hypothetical and real-life moral dilemmas.

42. (564)   Compassion and interpersonal responsibility

43. (564)   Emotion

MORALITY AS A PRODUCT OF SOCIAL LEARNING

44. (565-566)   Not strong evidence for the doctrine of specificity; evidence indicates that morality is not a wholly stable and uniform attribute, and that moral behavior is not as context specific as Hatshorne and May thought.

45. (566)   a) <u>Perry & Parke; Sears et al.</u>: rewarding alternative behaviors that are incompatible with prohibited acts can be an effective method of instilling moral controls. In addition, punishment administered by a warm, loving (socially reinforcing) parent is more successful at producing resistance to temptation than the same punishment given by a cold, rejecting parent.

(567)   b) <u>Parke; Hoffman</u>: punishment when accompanied by a cognitive rationale

(568)   c) <u>Toner, Parke, & Yussen; Grusec et al.</u>: a temptation-resisting model, particularly if he clearly verbalizes that he is following a rule and states a rationale for not committing the deviant act

(569)   d) <u>Toner, Moore & Ashley</u>: the child serving as a model of moral restraint for other children

(Box 14-4)   e) <u>Mischel & Patterson; Toner & Smith</u>: self-instruction using very simple plans or "blueprints for action"

(Box 14-4)   f) <u>Casey & Burton</u>: labeling children as "good" or "honest"

46. (567) Children are able to tell themselves <u>why</u> the deed is wrong, not just that it is wrong, which places their behavior under cognitive control. Come to inhibit misdeed to avoid <u>internal</u> feelings of uneasiness rather than to avoid <u>external</u> consequences.

47. (569)   a) parent is perceived as caring and loving, which should increase the child's
(Box 14-4)   willingness to comply with the parent.
     b) inhibition will be based on development of internal controls rather than fear of external punishment
     c) (therefore) there will be few, if any, undesirable side effects.

WHO RAISES CHILDREN WHO ARE MORALLY MATURE?

48. (570) Inductive discipline, <u>because</u> it (1) fosters the development of empathy and mutual role taking, (2) provides the child with potentially useful self-talk, (3) communicates what he or she should have done when tempted to violate a prohibition and (4) communicates what he or she can now do to make up for a transgression.

49. (571) Parke (1977) found that children who had ignored a disciplinarian or who had pleaded for mercy were dealt with much more forcefully during the next disciplinary encounter than those who had reacted to the earlier discipline by offering to undo the harm they had done. Children with a history of good conduct who respond more favorably to disciplinary encounters are the ones who are likely to be treated in a rational, nonpunitive manner by their parents.

50. (572) Induction was the most preferred disciplinary strategy for subjects of all ages (even preschoolers), and physical punishment was the next most favorably evaluated technique.

A good match; the disciplinary style that children favor (induction backed by occasional use of power assertion) is the one most closely associated with measures of moral maturity in the child-rearing studies and with resistance to temptation in the laboratory.

CHAPTER 15

THE FAMILY

STUDY CHECKLIST

_____ Read Chapter Outline and Summary (Study guide)

_____ Read Chapter (Text)

_____ Completed Vocabulary Fill-Ins (Study guide)

_____ Re-Read Outline and Summary (Study guide)

_____ Reviewed Lecture Notes and Integrated with Text

_____ Reviewed Vocabulary, Study Questions, and Text Chapter

CHAPTER 15 OUTLINE AND SUMMARY

    I.   **Functions of the family**
    II.   **Understanding the family and its contributions to human development**
        A.   The family as a system
        B.   A changing family system in a changing world
    III.   **Interchanges between parents and their infants**
        A.   The transition to parenthood
        B.   Effects of parents on their infants

The family is the primary agent of socialization--the setting in which children begin to acquire the beliefs, attitudes, values, and behaviors considered appropriate in their society. Basic goals of parenting in all societies include (1) ensuring the child's survival, (2) preparing the child for economic self-sufficiency, and (3) encouraging the child to maximize other cultural values such as morality, religion, and achievement.

Whether nuclear or extended in form, families are best viewed as changing social systems embedded in larger social systems that are also changing. Social trends affecting family life today include greater numbers of single adults, later marriages, a decline in childbearing, more female participation in the work force, and more divorces, single parent families, and remarriages.

The birth of a child is a highly significant event that alters the behavior of both parents and may change the character of their marital relationship. The transition to parenthood tends to be less severe or disruptive when parents are older and have been married for some time before the child is conceived. Warm, responsive parenting during infancy contributes to the establishment of secure parent/child attachments and promotes the child's exploratory competence and intellectual growth. Although fathers interact less with their very young infants than mothers do, they soon become more involved with their children and begin to play an important role in the child's life. The quality of the marital relationship is very important. Unhappily married couples often establish shaky emotional relations with their children, whereas parents who are happily married provide the mutual support and encouragement that usually enable them to establish good relations with their infants, even those who require special care or are temperamentally difficult.

IV. Parental socialization during childhood and adolescence
    A.   Two major dimensions of child rearing
        1.   Parental warmth/hostility
        2.   Patterns of parenting
    B.   Social-class differences in parenting
        1.   Patterns of child rearing in high-SES and low-SES families
        2.   Explaining social-class differences in child rearing
    C.   The quest for autonomy: Renegotiating the parent/child relationship during adolescence

Parents differ along two broad dimensions--warmth/hostility and permissiveness/restrictiveness (or control)--that, when considered together, yield four styles of parenting. Generally speaking, warm and restrictive (that is, authoritative) parents who appeal to reason in order to enforce their demands are likely to raise highly competent, well-adjusted children. Outcomes of other parenting styles are not as favorable; indeed, children of hostile and permissive (that is, uninvolved) parents are often deficient in all aspects of psychological functioning.

Parents from different cultures and social classes have different values, concerns, and outlooks on life that influence their child-rearing strategies. Lower- and working-class parents, who tend to be more punitive and authoritarian than their middle-class counterparts, stress obedience, respect, neatness, cleanliness, and avoidance of trouble--precisely the attributes their children will need to succeed in a blue-collar economy. By contrast, middle-class parents are more likely to stress independence, creativity, ambition, and self-control--the attributes that their children will need to succeed in business or a profession. Thus parents from all socioeconomic strata (and from different cultures) emphasize the characteristics that contribute to success as they know it, and it is inappropriate to conclude that one particular style of parenting is somehow "better" or more competent than all others.

Parent/child relationships are renegotiated as adolescents seek to become more autonomous. Although family conflict escalates during this period, adolescents are likely to become appropriately autonomous if their parents willingly grant them more freedom, explain the rules and restrictions that they do impose, and continue to be loving and supportive guides.

V. The influence of siblings and sibling relationships
    A.   And baby makes four: Changes in the family system with the birth of a second child
    B.   Sibling relationships over the course of childhood
    C.   Positive aspects of sibling interactions
    D.   Characteristics of only children

Although sibling rivalries are a normal aspect of family life and may begin as soon as a younger sibling arrives, there is a positive side to having siblings. Siblings are typically viewed as intimate associates who can be counted on for support. Older sibs frequently serve as attachment objects, models, and teachers for their younger siblings, and they often profit themselves from the instruction and guidance they provide. Yet sibling relationships are not essential for normal development, for only children are just as socially, emotionally, and intellectually competent (or slightly more so), on average, as children with siblings are.

VI. The impact of divorce
   A. Immediate effects: Crisis and reorganization
   B. Long-term reactions to divorce
   C. Children in reconstituted families

Divorce represents a drastic change in family life that is stressful and unsettling for children and their parents. Children's initial reactions often include anger, fear, depression, and guilt--feelings that may last more than a year. The emotional upheaval that follows a divorce may influence the parent/child relationship. Children often become cranky, disobedient, or otherwise difficult, whereas the custodial parent may suddenly become more punitive and controlling. The stresses resulting from a divorce and this new coercive lifestyle often affect the child's peer relations and schoolwork. But in the long run, children of divorce are usually better adjusted than those who remain in conflict-ridden two-parent families. Girls adjust better than boys to life in a single-parent, mother-headed home; whereas after a period of initial disruption in which new roles are ironed out, boys seem to fare better than girls in reconstituted families. Among the factors that help children to make positive adjustments to divorce are adequate financial and emotional support from the noncustodial parent, additional social support (from friends, relatives, and the community) for custodial parents and their children, and a minimum of additional stressors surrounding the divorce itself.

VII. Maternal employment--revisited

Maternal employment does not seem to disrupt children's social and emotional development: in fact, children of working mothers are often found to be more independent and more sociable and to have less stereotyped views of men and women than children whose mothers are not employed. Although middle-class boys of working mothers do score somewhat lower in intelligence and academic achievement than boys whose mothers are not employed, it seems that these deficits are limited to boys whose working parents fail to carefully monitor their daily activities. Parental monitoring could be a problem with latch-key children--those who care for themselves after school. But despite great public concern, the limited evidence available indicates that self-care youngsters show few if any developmental deficiencies if they are required to come right home after school and are monitored from a distance by their parents.

VIII. When parenting breaks down: The problem of child abuse
   - A.   Who are the abusers?
   - B.   Who is abused?
   - C.   Social-situational triggers: The ecology of child abuse
   - D.   Long-term consequences of abuse and neglect
   - E.   How do we solve the problem?
     - 1.   Preventing abuse
     - 2.   Controlling abuse

There are many contributors to the very serious problem of child abuse. Abusers come from all social strata and walks of life, although many of them were themselves abused as children. Defiant children, as well as those who are active, irritable, emotionally unresponsive, or ill, are more vulnerable to abuse than are happy, healthy children who are easy to care for. Child abuse is most prevalent in families under social, financial, or environmental stress. Programs designed to assist abused children and their abusive parents have achieved some success. However, we are still a long way from solving the problem.

CHAPTER 15 VOCABULARY FILL-INS
(Definitions below are in order of appearance in text margins)

MATCH VOCABULARY WORD/PHRASE TO ITS DEFINITION.
THEN COVER YOUR ANSWERS TO TEST YOUR MASTERY.

economic goal   socialization
preliterate society   survival goal
self-actualization goal

1. _____   The process by which children acquire the beliefs, values, and behaviors considered desirable or appropriate by the society to which they belong.

2. _____   LeVine's first priority of parenting--to promote the physical health and safety (survival) of young children.

3. _____   LeVine's second priority of parenting--to promote skills that children will need for economic self-sufficiency.

4. _____ LeVine's third priority of parenting--to promote the child's cognitive and behavioral capacity for maximizing such cultural values as morality, achievement, prestige, and personal satisfaction.

5. _____ A society in which there is little or no formal schooling, so that many children never learn to read and write.

---

extended family
family social system
indirect effects
nuclear family

reciprocal influence
reconstituted families
single-parent family

6. _____ The complex network of relationships, interactions, and patterns of influence that characterize a family with three or more members.

7. _____ A family unit consisting of a wife/mother, a husband/father, and their dependent child(ren).

8. _____ The notion that each person in a social relationship influences and is influenced by the other person(s).

9. _____ A group of blood relatives from more than one nuclear family (for example, grandparents, aunts, uncles, nieces, and nephews) who live together, forming a household.

10. _____ A family system consisting of one parent (either the mother or the father) and the parent's dependent child(ren).

11. _____ New families that form after the remarriage of a single parent.

12. _____ Instances in which the relationship between two individuals in a family is modified by the behavior or attitudes of a third family member.

---

authoritarian parenting   permissive parenting
authoritative parenting   uninvolved parenting
parental control   warmth/hostility

13. _____ A dimension of parenting that describes the amount of responsiveness and affection that a parent displays toward a child.

14. _____ A dimension of parenting that describes how restrictive and demanding parents are.

15. _____ A restrictive pattern of parenting in which adults set many rules for their children, expect strict obedience, and rely on power rather than reason to elicit compliance.

16. _____ A flexible style of parenting in which adults allow their children autonomy, but are careful to explain the restrictions they impose and will ensure that their children follow these guidelines.

17. _____ A pattern of parenting in which adults make few demands of their children and rarely attempt to control their behavior.

18. _____ A pattern of parenting that is both aloof (or even hostile) and overpermissive, almost as if parents neither cared about their children nor about what they may become.

autonomy   low-SES
ethnocentrism   ordinal position
high-SES   sibling rivalry

19. _____ A term that refers to the middle and upper classes--that is, the economically advantaged members of society.

20. _____ A term that refers to the lower and working classes--that is, the economically disadvantaged members of society.

21. _____ The tendency to view one's own culture as "best" and to use one's own cultural standards as a basis for evaluating other cultures.

22. _____ The capacity to make decisions independently, to serve as one's own source of emotional strength, and to otherwise manage one's life tasks without depending on others for assistance; an important developmental task of adolescence.

23. _____ The spirit of competition, jealousy, and resentment that may arise between two or more siblings.

24. _____ The child's order of birth among siblings (also called birth order).

---

child abuse   self-care (or latch-key)
"high risk" neighborhood   children
Parents Anonymous

25. _____ Children who care for themselves after school or in the evening while their parents are working.

26. _____ Term used to describe any extreme maltreatment of children, involving physical batterings, sexual molestations, psychological insults such as persistent ridicule, rejection, and terrorization, and physical or emotional neglect.

27. _____ A residential area in which the incidence of child abuse is much higher than in other neighborhoods with the same demographic and socioeconomic characteristics.

28. _____ An organization of reformed child abusers (modeled after Alcoholics Anonymous) that functions as a support group and helps parents to understand and overcome their abusive tendencies.

CHAPTER 15 STUDY QUESTIONS

FUNCTIONS OF THE FAMILY

1.   **LeVine** has identified three **universal child-rearing goals**. These are: (p. 581-582)

   (a)

   (b)

   (c)

UNDERSTANDING THE FAMILY AND ITS CONTRIBUTIONS TO HUMAN DEVELOPMENT

2.   The **family systems/ecological approach** to the study of the family **emphasizes** what three facets of the family as influences of child outcomes? (p. 582-583)

   (a)

   (b)

   (c)

3.   To illustrate the notion of the **family as a social system**, give an **example** of each of the following: (p. 583)

   (a)   How the relationship between a parent and child can change when the other parent is present.

   EXAMPLE:

(b)   How the family system changes as one or more family members develop or change.

EXAMPLE:

(c)   How the larger cultural and subcultural context can affect the family system.

EXAMPLE:

4.   Only _____% of American families in 1980 were made up of an employed father, housewife mother, and two or more children, compared with 70% in 1960. List the seven **ways** the text notes that **families have changed,** making them much more diverse than 30 years age. (p. 584-585)

(a)

(b)

(c)

(d)

(e)

(f)

(g)

5. On the basis of the material presented in the text (e.g., Fig. 15-2; Belsky, Lang, & Rovine, 1985; Belsky, 1981; Gath, 1985), what response is warranted to the **assertion** that having a **baby strengthens marriages?** (p. 586-587)

6. In summarizing the effects of parents on their infants, the text lists four parent variables that are influential. Summarize **how each impacts infant development.** (p. 587-590)

WARMTH/SENSITIVITY:

MOTHER'S AGE:

FATHER'S CAREGIVING AND PLAY:

INDIRECT EFFECTS:

PARENTAL SOCIALIZATION DURING CHILDHOOD AND ADOLESCENCE

7. What two **dimensions of child rearing** have been found to be particularly important? (p. 590-591)

(a)

(b)

Are these two dimensions highly correlated or quite independent? (p. 591)

What are **four types of parenting** that result from combining these two dimensions? (p. 591, Figure 15-4)

(a)

(b)

(c)

(d)

8. List seven **child outcomes** that have been found to be **associated with parental warmth**. (p. 591)

(a)

(b)

(c)

(d)

(e)

(f)

(g)

9.   What negative child and adult outcomes have been found by Crook et al. and **Lefkowitz and Tesiny** to be associated with having two parents who where rejecting, detached, or hostile? (p. 591-593 & Box 15-1)

10.   Describe each of the **parenting styles** identified by **Baumrind.** (p. 592)

AUTHORITARIAN:

AUTHORITATIVE:

PERMISSIVE:

Identify which **parenting style** has been found to be **associated with each** of the following **child behavior profiles.** (p. 593-595, Table 15-1, & Table 15-2)

PROFILE A: _____

fearful	aimless
moody, unhappy	sulky, unfriendly
easily annoyed	low-average cognitive competencies
passively hostile	average social competencies
vulnerable to stress	

PROFILE B: _____

rebellious	domineering
low self-control	aimless
low self-reliance	low cognitive competencies
impulsive	low social competencies
aggressive	

PROFILE C: _____

self-reliant   curious
self-controlled   purposive
cheerful and friendly   high cognitive competencies
copes well with stress   high social competencies
cooperates well
      with adults

11.   How do the authoritative and authoritarian parent differ in their **exercise of control**? (p. 594)

12.   The parenting outcomes described in Tables 15-1 and 15-2 for authoritative, authoritarian, and permissive parenting all were found when combined with parental warmth and acceptance. Some parents, however, are clearly **rejecting** or **uninvolved and neglectful**. How do their children fare? (p. 595)

13.   In what four ways did **Maccoby** report **high- and low-SES parents differ**? (p. 596)

     (a)

     (b)

     (c)

     (d)

14. What about being a lower-class parent has been hypothesized by **Maccoby** and by **McLoyd** to **mediate social-class difference in child rearing?** (p. 597)

What does **Ogbu** suggest might lead **lower-class parents** to be more **authoritarian?** (p. 597)

Might lower-class children differ in some way from middle- and upper-class children that might **affect the way they are treated?** (p. 597)

15. Looking **cross-culturally**, what conclusion can be drawn about what constitutes **"good" parenting** according to **Berry** or to **Laosa?** (p. 598)

16. According to **Youniss and Smollar**, what is the **"recipe"** for helping adolescents achieve a **healthy sense of autonomy** while remaining emotionally attached to their parents? (p. 599-600)

THE INFLUENCE OF SIBLINGS AND SIBLING RELATIONSHIPS

17. When a **new baby** comes, parents are often told to be sure to give the first child lots of attention so she/he will not feel neglected. What findings by **Dunn and Kendrick** and by **Dunn** indicate that this suggestion can be taken too far and backfire? (p. 600-601)

18.   What kind of interaction has been found to predominate **sibling interactions**--conflictful behavior or positive interactions? (p. 601-602)

19.   Briefly characterize the **nature of sibling influence** in each of the following roles. (p. 602-604)

ATTACHMENT OBJECTS:

MODELS:

TEACHERS:

PROMOTERS OF SOCIAL COMPETENCE:

20.   What does research suggest about the outcomes of being an **only child**? Are they spoiled brats or obedient, competent children with good peer relations? (p. 604)

THE IMPACT OF DIVORCE

21.   What impact has **divorce** been found to often have on the **quality of parenting** of the custodial and noncustodial parent during the first year or so? (p. 605-606)

What kinds of behaviors do the children often show? (p. 605)

22.   Research indicates that **boys and girls both suffer from divorce**, but that the effects will be displayed differently. What kinds of **measures** show boys to be suffering more from divorce? What kinds show girls to be suffering more? (p. 606)

BOYS:

GIRLS:

23.   To what extent do research findings (e.g., Hetherington, 1989; Wallerstein & Kelly, 1980) support the conventional view that parents should stay together for the sake of the children despite an unhappy, conflictful marriage? (p. 606-607)

24.   Researchers (e.g., Allison & Furstenberg, 1989; Kurdek et al., 1981; Wallerstein & Blakeslee, 1989) have studied the long-term impact (4-10 years after) of divorce. What types of residual effects have they found? What factors influence the degree to which the child is still adversely influenced? (p. 607)

25.   What factors have been found to **reduce** the **potential negative impact of divorce** on children? (p. 608, Box 15-2)

(a)

(b)

(c)

(d)

(e)

26.   What is the reaction/outcome of **remarriage of the mother** for sons? for daughters? (p. 608-609)

SONS:

DAUGHTERS:

What **explanation** can be offered **for the higher incidence of deviant behavior** among adolescents in stepparent homes when compared to adolescents still with their biological parents? (p. 610)

MATERNAL EMPLOYMENT--REVISITED

27.   **Maternal employment** has generally not been found to interfere with normal development and has even been found to have **some positive effects** on older children, particularly **girls**. List three. (p. 610)

(a)

(b)

(c)

28.   Recent studies (e.g., Crouter et al., 1990) have found that **maternal employment** is associated with **lower academic achievement in boys, but only when** _____ and _____. (p. 610-611)

29.   What two factors did **Steinberg** find to be associated with positive outcomes for children under **self-care** after school (latch-key kids)? (p. 611)

(a)

(b)

WHEN PARENTING BREAKS DOWN: THE PROBLEM OF CHILD ABUSE

30.   The literature on abuse suggests that there are characteristics of both parents and children that signal a high risk for abuse.   What are the **characteristics** of abusers and the abused children? (p. 613-614)

ABUSERS:

ABUSED CHILDREN:

Abuse does not inevitably happen even when a high-risk parent is matched with a high-risk child. What **social and contextual factors** have been found to "tip the balance" toward abuse? (p. 613-614)

31.   **Main and George** report disturbing differences in the way abused children as young as toddlers react to another child's crying and distress. Describe how the abused children responded and note the **implications** of such behavior **for peer relationships.** (p. 615 & Fig. 15-5)

32.   Many individuals who were abused and neglected as children, do **break the cycle of abuse**. **Egeland et al.** have found that abused parents who succeed in breaking the cycle have **three factors in their favor**. List the three factors. (p. 615)

   (a)

   (b)

   (c)

33.   What suggestions does the text offer for **preventing and controlling abuse?** (p. 616-617)

   PREVENTION:

   CONTROL:

ACTIVITY 15-1

THE IMPACT OF DIVORCE FROM THE CHILD'S PERSPECTIVE

INTRODUCTION: There is considerable concern and much is written about the impact of divorce on children. Generally, it is assumed that it will be a negative experience that will have both short- and long-term consequences for children. Your text reviews the research literature in Chapter 15 (p. 605-610). This literature suggests that divorce does impact children--how much and how long, depends on many factors. Two factors found to be particularly related to developmental outcomes are (a) the extent the child was and continues to be exposed to high levels of conflict between the parents and (b) the adequacy of the parenting provided for the child (authoritative versus either coercive, lax, or inconsistently lax and coercive). In addition, a recent article suggests that there is evidence that just having one parent, even a well-functioning one, may be associated with different developmental outcomes (some positive and some negative) than two-parent rearing.

INSTRUCTIONS:

Part A

Interview two friends/acquaintances from divorced families (one can be yourself if you "qualify"). Write down the question numbers and their answers. Ask about:

1. Age at the time of divorce; age now

2. Feelings/reactions
    (a) during the months prior to the divorce
    (b) at the time of the divorce itself
    (c) the first 1-2 years after the divorce
    (d) now

3. Ways the divorce impacted them positively

4. Ways the divorce impacted them negatively

5. Things parents could have done or said that might have made it easier

6. (Any questions you might want to add; be sure to include the question in your write-up exactly as it was asked)

Part B

Compare the responses of the two individuals. Discuss how your "findings" relate to the generalizations about the short- and long-term impact of divorce on children and the factors affecting children's adjustment to the divorce.

RELATED REFERENCES

Amato, P.R., & Keith, B. (1991). Parental divorce and the well-being of children: A meta-analysis. *Psychological Bulletin, 110,* 26-46.

Barber, B.L., & Eccles, J. (1992). Long-term influence of divorce and single parenting on adolescent family- and work-related values, behavior, and aspirations. *Psychological Bulletin, 111,* 108-126,

Grych, J.H., & Fincham, F.D. (1990). Marital conflict and children's adjustment: A cognitive-contextual framework. *Psychological Bulletin, 108,* 267-290.

Hetherington, E.M., Hagan, M.S., & Anderson, E.T. (1989). Marital transitions: A child's perspective. *American Psychologist, 44,* 303-312.

Hetherington, E.M., & Clingempeel, W.G. (1992). Coping with marital transitions. *Monographs of the Society for Research in Child Development, 57, Serial No. 227.*

ACTIVITY 15-2

YOUR FAMILY AS A COMPLEX SOCIAL SYSTEM

INTRODUCTION: Chapter 15 (particularly p. 582-584) emphasizes the view of the family as a complex social system that is a network of reciprocal relationships and alliances that are constantly evolving. Put simply, the child's interaction with his father will be different when someone else (e.g., the mother, a sibling, a grandparent) is present. How a child is treated by parents and siblings will in part be a function of how he behaves toward them, and vice versa. As a child becomes more competent, expectations change and so does the way others interacted with him. Also, as the parents mature their behavior toward others, including their children, changes.

The family is truly a complex, evolving social system in which parent behavior affects child behavior, child behavior affects parent behavior, and both work interdependently to determine child development outcomes. This theme, reiterated throughout the text, reflects the views of developmentalists in the 1990s regarding the role of the family in development. This activity is intended to give you a "feel" for the interdependence and reciprocity of relationships within the family system by having you recall ways in which interactions changed in your family depending on who was present.

INSTRUCTIONS:

Part A

Drawing on your own family, <u>select</u> <u>two</u> of the following situations and write down examples of how interaction changes/changed between the individuals when a third person is/was present.

1. Mother and child together--father enters
2. Father and child together--mother enters
3. Mother and father together--child enters
4. Two children together--mother enters[*]
5. Two children together--father enters[*]
6. Whole family is together vs. any two members alone
7. Other (specify)

* If you are an only child, the second child could be one of your friends.

Part B

1. Describe two ways you treat your parents differently today than you did at an earlier point in your development.

2. How has <u>your</u> change in behavior affected their reaction to you?

3. Give two ways your parents treat you differently than they did at an earlier point in their/your life.

4. How has the change in how <u>they</u> treat you affected your reaction to them?

RELATED REFERENCES

Buhrmester, D., Camparo, L, Christensen, A, Gonzalez, L.S., & Hinshaw, S.P. (1992). Mothers and fathers interacting in dyads and triads with normal and hyperactive sons. *Developmental Psychology, 28,* 500-509.

Gjerde, P.F. (1986). The interpersonal structure of family interaction settings: Parent-adolescent relations in dyads and triads. *Developmental Psychology, 22,* 297-304.

Maccoby, E.E., & Martin, J.A. (1983). Socialization in the context of the family: Parent-child interaction. In P.H. Mussen & E.M. Hetherington (Eds.) *Handbook of child psychology: Vol. 4. Socialization, personality, and social development,* pp. 1-101. New York: Plenum Press.

Minuchin, P. (1985). Families and individual development: Provocations from the field of family therapy. *Child Development, 56,* 289-302.

CHAPTER 15 ANSWERS TO STUDY QUESTIONS

FUNCTIONS OF THE FAMILY

1. (581)   a) the survival goal--to promote the physical survival and health of the child, ensuring that the child will live long enough to have children of his or her own.

b) the economic goal--to foster the skills and behavioral capacities that the child will need for economic self-maintenance as an adult.

c) the self-actualization goal--to foster behavioral capabilities for maximizing other cultural values (e.g., morality, religion, achievement, wealth prestige, and a sense of personal satisfaction).

UNDERSTANDING THE FAMILY AND ITS CONTRIBUTIONS TO HUMAN DEVELOPMENT

2. (582-583)   a) parental influence on the child

b) child influence on parental child-rearing strategies

c) reciprocal relationships in the larger social context

3. (583)   a) Fathers talk less and display less affection toward their infants and toddlers when the mother is present. Mothers are less likely to initiate play activities or to hold their youngsters when the father is around, particularly if the child is male.

b) Parent expectations and treatment of a child change as the child becomes more capable; the chronic illness or alcoholism of one family member can affect everyone's behavior toward each other.

c) What a child sees on TV will influence what toys and foods she values and later may affect her notion of what is normal sexual behavior. These values may differ from those espoused by the parents and thus create conflict.

4. (584-585)   12%

a) increased numbers of single adults

b) active postponement of marriage

c) decreased childbearing

d) increased female participation in the labor force

e) increases in divorce

f) increased numbers of single-parent families

g) increased remarriage

5. (586)   There is little evidence to support this assertion. Many family sociologists believe that the advent of parenthood is a "crisis" of sorts for a marriage. Couples must now cope with greater financial responsibilities, a possible loss of income, changes in sleeping habits, and less time to themselves--events that may be perceived as aversive and could well disrupt the bond between husbands and wives.

6. (587)   WARMTH/SENSITIVITY: mothers who often talk to their infants and try to stimulate their curiosity are contributing in a positive way to the establishment of secure emotional attachments as well as to the child's curiosity and willingness to explore, to sociability, and to intellectual growth.

(588)   MOTHER'S AGE: teenage mothers tend to express much less favorable attitudes about child rearing than those in their 20s. Very young mothers also provide less stimulating home environments for their infants and toddlers than older mothers. Older mothers are quite responsive to their babies and claim to derive more satisfaction from interacting with either a first- or second-born infant than do younger mothers.

(589)   FATHER'S CAREGIVING AND PLAY: in spite of gender stereotypes, fathers are competent caregivers, although they more often assume the role of "special playmate." Fathers are more than activity directors or substitute caregivers, however. A secure attachment to the father can help offset the social deficiencies and emotional disturbances that could otherwise result when an infant is insecurely attached to the mother. Children of both sexes benefit intellectually and will achieve more in school when they have enjoyed a nurturant relationship with a highly-involved father.

(590)   INDIRECT EFFECTS: marital satisfaction indirectly affects both parents' interactions with their child.

PARENTAL SOCIALIZATION DURING CHILDHOOD AND ADOLESCENCE

7. (590)   a) parental warmth/hostility
            b) parental control

(591)   Relatively independent

(591)   a) authoritative
(Tbl. 15-4) b) authoritarian
            c) permissive
            d) uninvolved

8. (591)   a) securely attached at an early age
            b) competent students during the grade-school years
            c) relatively altruistic
            d) generally obedient, noncoercive
            e) high in self-esteem and role-taking skills
            f) satisfied with their gender identities
            g) often refer to internalized norms rather than fear of punishment as a reason for complying with moral rules

9. (591-593) Compared with "wanted" children from similar family backgrounds, unwanted
   (Box 15-1) children had less stable family ties; were described as anxious, emotionally frustrated and irritable; had more physical health problems; made poorer grades in school; were less popular with peers; and were more likely to require psychiatric attention for serious behavior disorders. A primary contributor to adult depression is a family setting in which one or both parents treat the child as if he or she were unworthy of their love and affection.

10. (592)   AUTHORITARIAN: very restrictive, adults impose many rules, expect strict obedience, rarely if ever explain to the child why it is necessary to comply with these regulations, often rely on punitive, forceful tactics (power assertion or love withdrawal).
AUTHORITATIVE: more flexible, children are allowed considerable freedom, are provided rationales for restrictions imposed on them. Authoritative parents often seek their child's input in family decisions. However, they expect the child to comply with the restrictions they view as necessary and will use both power, if necessary, and reason (inductive discipline) to ensure that he does.
PERMISSIVE: warm, but lax, parents make few demands, children freely express their feelings and impulses, children's activities are not closely monitored, parents rarely exert firm control over their behavior.

PROFILE A: authoritarian
PROFILE B: permissive
PROFILE C: authoritative

11. (594)   The authoritarian parent dominates the child, allowing little if any freedom of expression or practice in making decisions, whereas the authoritative parent is careful to permit the child enough autonomy so that he or she can develop initiative, self-reliance, and a feeling of pride in personal accomplishments.

12. (595)   Children of neglectful parents are deficient both socially and academically, tend to become very hostile and rebellious adolescents who are prone to such antisocial or delinquent acts as alcohol and drug abuse, sexual misconduct, truancy, and a variety of criminal offenses.

13. (596)   a) low-SES parents tend to stress obedience and respect for authority, neatness, cleanliness, and staying out of trouble. Higher-SES parents are more likely to stress happiness, curiosity, independence, creativity, and ambition.
b) lower-SES parents are more restrictive and authoritarian, often setting arbitrary standards and enforcing them with power-assertive forms of discipline. Higher-SES parents tend to be either permissive or authoritative, and they are more likely to use inductive forms of discipline.
c) higher-SES parents talk more with their children, reason with them more, and may use somewhat more complex language than lower-SES parents.
d) higher-SES parents tend to show more warmth and affection toward their children.

14. (597)   Low-income living is stressful for parents and that stress affects the ways in which parental functions are carried out.

Lower-SES parents may emphasize respect, obedience, neatness, and avoidance of trouble because these are precisely the attributes they view as critical for success in the blue-collar economy.

Mothers of lower-SES children may not have received adequate prenatal care and there may have been birth complications resulting in babies who are more likely to be irritable, unresponsive, or otherwise difficult to care for and love.

15. (598)   Warm, sensitive caregiving seems to be associated with positive developmental outcomes in virtually all cultures and subcultures. Beyond that, people are being somewhat ethnocentric when they suggest that a particular style of child rearing (for example, authoritative parenting) that produces favorable outcomes in one context (middle-class Western societies) is the optimal pattern for children in all other cultures and subcultures.

16. (599)   Parents should keep their rules and restrictions to a reasonable minimum, explain them, and continue to be warm and supportive.

THE INFLUENCE OF SIBLINGS AND SIBLING RELATIONSHIPS

17. (601)   Older children whose parents showered them with attention in the weeks after a baby was born were the ones who played least with and were most negative toward their baby brother or sister 14 months later. Older siblings who responded more positively toward a younger sibling had mothers who did not permit the older child to brood or respond negatively to the younger sibling.

18. (601-602)   In some ways, sibling relationships are truly paradoxical because they are often both close and conflictual. In spite of many conflicts, siblings are viewed as more important and more reliable than friends, and <u>positive interactions predominate</u>.

19. (602)   ATTACHMENT OBJECTS: older siblings can become important sources of emotional support who help younger sibs to cope with uncertain situations when their parents are not around.

   (603)   MODELS: as early as 12-20 months of age, infants are already becoming very attentive to their older sibs, often choosing to imitate their actions or to take over toys that the older children have abandoned.

             TEACHERS: older siblings are likely to make an active attempt to instruct their younger brothers and sisters, particularly when playing alone with them.

   (604)   PROMOTERS OF SOCIAL COMPETENCE: many later-born children eventually become more popular than first-borns because they have learned to defer to and negotiate with their older and more powerful siblings, thereby acquiring cooperative and conciliatory interpersonal skills that serve them well when interacting with peers.

20. (604)   Only children are more obedient and slightly more intellectually competent, on average, than children with siblings, and are likely to establish very good relations with peers.

THE IMPACT OF DIVORCE

21. (605)   Custodial mothers, often become edgy, impatient, and insensitive to their children's needs. They typically adopt more punitive and coercive methods of child rearing. Noncustodial fathers are likely to change in a different way, becoming somewhat overpermissive and indulgent during visits with their children.

             Children often become whiny, argumentative, disobedient, and downright disrespectful.

22. (606)   BOYS: in traditional custodial situations boys tend to show <u>more overt behavior problems</u> than girls do.
GIRLS: recent studies show that girls experience <u>more covert distress</u> than boys do.

23. (606-607)   Many of the behavior problems that children display after a divorce are actually evident well before the divorce and may be related to long-standing family conflict rather than to the divorce itself. An eventual escape from conflict may be a positive outcome of divorce for many children.

24. (607)   Compared to children in harmonious, two-parent families, children of divorce are still showing more evidence of psychological distress and academic difficulties, even after 10 years, particularly if they were very young at the time of their parents' divorce.

25. (608)   a) finances remain relatively stable
b) parents are able to respond in a warm, consistent, and authoritative manner
c) children are permitted to maintain affectionate ties with both parents
d) children are shielded from any continuing conflict between parents
e) mother and children have adequate social support

26. (608-609)   SONS: boys seem to benefit more than girls by gaining a stepfather, enjoying higher self-esteem, being less anxious and angered about their new living arrangements, and eventually overcoming most of the adjustment problems they displayed before their mother remarried.
DAUGHTERS: girls seem to view stepfathers as major threats to their relationships with their mother, no matter how hard the stepfather tries, and they are likely to resent their mother for remarrying and becoming less attentive to their needs.

Higher incidence may reflect a hesitancy of stepparents to impose rules or an unwillingness of adolescents to adhere to those imposed by a stepparent.

MATERNAL EMPLOYMENT--REVISITED

27. (610)   a) tend to be more independent
b) hold higher educational and occupational aspirations
c) hold less stereotyped views of men and women

28. (610-611)   When mothers work more than 40 hours a week and parents fail to carefully monitor the boys' activities.

29. (611)   a) parental monitoring from a distance (by phone and by assigning chores to be completed)
b) authoritative parenting because it fosters self-control

30. (613-614)   ABUSERS: abused or neglected in childhood, favor punitive control techniques, may interpret child as being critical or rejecting
ABUSED: children who are unresponsive, hyperactive, irritable, or ill

Child abuse is most likely to occur in families under stress. Abuse is more likely to happen in high-risk neighborhoods where families are struggling financially and are isolated from formal and informal support systems. Also, there is a general permissive attitude toward violence and a sanctioning of physical punishment as a means of controlling children's behavior that may encourage child abuse in the U.S.

31. (615)   Abused toddlers became angry at the fussing of another child and <u>physically attacked</u> the crying child rather than showing sympathy and compassion. The implication is that abused children are likely to be abusive companions from an early age and, therefore, rejected by peers.

32. (615)   a) have received emotional support from a nonabusive adult during childhood
b) have participated in therapy at some point in their lives
c) have a nonabusive, satisfying relationship with their spouse

33. (616)   PREVENTION: it may be possible to help prevent abuse by identifying high-risk families and establishing stronger support networks and programs that teach effective child-management skills.
CONTROL: hotlines, crisis nurseries, services such as Parents Anonymous or family therapy; media campaigns in newspapers, magazines, and on television designed to educate the public; and legal intervention.

CHAPTER 16

BEYOND THE FAMILY: EXTRAFAMILIAL INFLUENCES

STUDY CHECKLIST

_____ Read Chapter Outline and Summary (Study guide)

_____ Read Chapter (Text)

_____ Completed Vocabulary Fill-Ins (Study guide)

_____ Re-Read Outline and Summary (Study guide)

_____ Reviewed Lecture Notes and Integrated with Text

_____ Reviewed Vocabulary, Study Questions, and Text Chapter

CHAPTER 16 OUTLINE AND SUMMARY

I. The early window: Effects of television on children and youth
  A. Television and children's lifestyles
  B. Some potentially undesirable effects of television
    1. Effects of televised violence
    2. Television as a source of social stereotypes
    3. Children's reactions to commercial messages
  C. Television as an educational instrument
    1. Educational television and children's prosocial behavior
    2. Promoting good nutrition on television
    3. Television as a contributor to cognitive development
  D. Should television be used to socialize children?

In this chapter we have focused on three extrafamilial agents of socialization: television, schools, and children's peer groups.

Although children spend more time watching television than in any other waking activity, TV viewing, in moderate doses, is unlikely to impair their cognitive growth, academic achievement, or peer relations. However, television programming is often violent, and there is evidence that a heavy diet of televised violence can instigate aggressive behavior and make children more tolerant of aggression. Television is also an important source of knowledge about people in the outside world. But, unfortunately, the information that children receive is often inaccurate and misleading-- frequently consisting of stereotyped portrayals of men, women, and various racial and ethnic groups. Children are also influenced by television commercials, often becoming angry or resentful if a parent refuses to buy a product that they have requested.

Yet the effects of television are not all bad. Children are likely to learn prosocial lessons and to put them into practice after watching acts of kindness on television. Parents can help by watching shows such as *Mister Rogers' Neighborhood* with their children and then encouraging them to verbalize or role-play the prosocial lessons they have observed. Educational programs such as *Sesame Street* and *The Electric Company* have been quite successful at fostering basic cognitive skills, particularly when children watch with an adult who discusses the material with them and helps them to apply what they have learned.

II. **The school as a socialization agent**
   A. Does schooling promote cognitive development?
   B. Determinants of effective (and ineffective) schooling
      1. Some misconceptions about effective schooling
      2. Factors that do contribute to effective schooling
   C. The teacher's influence
      1. Teacher expectancies and children's achievements: The Pygmalion effect
      2. Teaching styles and instructional techniques
   D. Do our schools meet the needs of our children?
      1. The school as a middle-class institution: Effects on disadvantaged youth
      2. Effects of school desegregation on minority youth
      3. Educating the handicapped--is mainstreaming the answer?
      4. How successful are our schools? A cross-national comparison

By age 6 children are spending several hours of each weekday at school. Schools seem to have two missions: to impart academic knowledge and to teach children how to become "good citizens." Schooling also appears to facilitate cognitive development by teaching children general rules, or intellectual strategies, that help them to solve problems.

Some schools are more "effective" than others at producing positive outcomes such as low absenteeism, an enthusiastic attitude about learning, academic achievement, occupational skills, and socially desirable patterns of behavior. What makes a school effective is not its physical characteristics, classroom structure, or amount of money spent per pupil but, rather, its human resources. Effective schools are comfortable but businesslike settings in which pupils are motivated to learn. Administrators and teachers work together to create such an atmosphere by formulating clear educational goals and providing the active guidance and feedback students need to meet these objectives.

Traditionally, the task of motivating students has been assigned to classroom instructors. Teachers' expectancies may create a self-fulfilling prophecy: students usually do well when teachers expect them to succeed, whereas they often fall short of their potential when teachers expect them to do poorly. Teaching style can also affect pupil outcomes. Generally speaking, it appears that an authoritative style is more likely than either authoritarian or permissive instruction to motivate students to do their best. Yet even the authoritative teacher may have to use different instructional techniques with different children in order to "get the most out of each pupil."

The middle-class bias of most schools may hinder the academic progress of disadvantaged children or those from minority subcultures. Textbooks and other materials tend to portray middle-class values and experiences that may seem irrelevant and uninteresting to these students. Parents of disadvantaged students are often less involved in school activities, and teachers tend to hold negative academic expectancies for lower income and minority students. All these factors seem to contribute to the academic difficulties often experienced by disadvantaged youth. At best, legally mandated school desegregation and mainstreaming have led to modest improvements in the academic performance of racial minorities and handicapped students, but these policies have done little to reduce racial prejudice or to enhance the self-esteem of either handicapped pupils or minority youth. Fortunately, newly developed cooperative learning programs hold some promise for making "integration" a more fruitful experience for these students.

Cross-national surveys of academic achievement clearly brand American students as "underachievers," especially in math and science. Steps are now being taken at local, state, and national levels to try to bridge this achievement gap.

III. **The second world of childhood: Peers as socialization agents**
   A. Who or what is a peer?
      1. Mixed-age interactions
      2. Frequency of peer contacts
   B. Peers as promoters of social competence
      1. The importance of harmonious peer relations
      2. Who is accepted, neglected, or rejected by peers?
   C. Children and their friends
      1. Children's thinking about friends and friendship
      2. Social interactions among friends and acquaintances
      3. Are there distinct advantages to having friends?
   D. How do peers exert their influence?
      1. Peer reinforcement and modeling influences
      2. The normative function of peer groups
   E. Peer versus adult influence: The question of cross-pressures

Peer contacts represent a second world for children--a world of equal-status interactions that is very different from the nonegalitarian environment of the home. Contacts with peers increase dramatically with age, and during the preschool or early elementary school years, children are spending at least as much of their leisure time with peers as with adults. The "peer group" consists mainly of same-sex playmates of different ages.

Peer contacts foster the development of competent and adaptive patterns of social behavior, and children who are rejected by peers are at risk of displaying antisocial conduct and other adjustment problems later in life. Among the factors that contribute to peer acceptance are physical attributes such as an attractive face or physique, a popular name, good academic performance and role-taking skills, and good social skills. Popular and accepted children are friendly, supportive companions who display excellent social problem-solving skills; rejected children are either uncooperative and aggressive or extremely withdrawn; neglected youngsters tend to be passive companions who hover around the edge of a play group, initiating few interactions.

Children typically form close ties, or friendships, with one or more members of their play groups. Younger children view a friend as a harmonious playmate, whereas older children and adolescents come to think of friends as close companions who share similar interests and values and are willing to provide them with intimate emotional support. Although the roles that friends play in a child's social development have not been firmly established, it is likely that solid friendships (1) provide a sense of security that enables children to respond more constructively to stresses and challenges, (2) promote the development of role-taking skills and an ability to compromise, and (3) foster the growth of caring and compassionate feelings that are the foundation of intimate love relationships later in life.

Peers influence a child in many of the same ways that parents do: by modeling, reinforcing, and discussing the behaviors and values that they condone. During middle childhood, children form peer groups and develop normative codes of conduct to which group members are expected to conform. Conformity pressures peak at mid-adolescence, when teenagers are most susceptible to peer-sponsored misconduct. Yet adolescents who have established warm relations with their parents have generally internalized many of their parents' values and continue to seek their parents' advice about scholastic matters and future-oriented decisions. Moreover, peer-group values are often very similar to those of parents, and peers are more likely to discourage than to condone antisocial conduct. So adolescent socialization is not a continual battle between parents and peers; instead, these two important influences combine to affect one's development.

CHAPTER 16 VOCABULARY FILL-INS
(Definitions below are in order of appearance in text margins)

MATCH VOCABULARY WORD/PHRASE TO ITS DEFINITION.
THEN COVER YOUR ANSWERS TO TEST YOUR MASTERY.

Children's Television Workshop
(CTW)
desensitization hypothesis

extrafamilial influences

1. _____ Social agencies other than the family that influence a child's cognitive, social, and emotional development.

2. _____ The notion that people who watch a lot of media violence will become less aroused by aggression and more tolerant of violent and aggressive acts.

3. _____ An organization committed to producing TV programs that hold children's interest and facilitate their social and intellectual development.

ability tracking
effective schools
informal curriculum

metacognitive knowledge
open classroom
traditional classroom

4. _____ Noncurricular objectives of schooling such as teaching children to cooperate, to respect authority, to obey rules, and to become good citizens.

5. _____ One's knowledge about cognition and about the regulation of cognitive activities.

6. _____ Schools that are generally successful at achieving curricular and noncurricular objectives, regardless of the racial, ethnic, or socioeconomic backgrounds of the student population.

7. _____ The practice of placing students in categories on the basis of IQ or academic achievement and then educating them in classes with pupils of comparable academic or intellectual ability.

8. _____ A classroom arrangement in which all pupils sit facing an instructor, who normally teaches one subject at a time by lecturing or giving demonstrations.

9. _____ A less structured classroom arrangement in which there is a separate area for each education activity and children distribute themselves around the room, working individually or in small groups.

---

authoritarian instruction   laissez-faire instruction
authoritative instruction   mainstreaming
cooperative learning methods   Pygmalion effect

10. _____ The tendency of teacher expectancies to become self-fulfilling prophecies, causing students to perform better or worse depending on their teacher's estimation of their potential.

11. _____ A restrictive style of instruction in which the teacher makes absolute demands and uses threats or force (if necessary) to ensure that students comply.

12. _____ A controlling style of instruction in which the teacher makes many demands but also allows some autonomy and individual expression as long as students are staying within the guidelines that the teacher has set.

13. _____ A permissive style of instruction in which the teacher makes few demands of students and provides little or no active guidance.

14. _____ An educational practice in which handicapped children are integrated into regular classrooms.

15. _____ An educational practice whereby children of different races or ability levels are assigned to teams; each team member works on problems geared to his or her ability level, and team members are reinforced for "pulling together" and performing well as a team.

amiables   "peer only" monkeys
conformity   peers
cross-pressures   popular children
"mother only" monkeys   rejectees
neglectees   sociometric techniques
peer group

16. _____ Two or more persons who are operating at similar levels of behavioral complexity.

17. _____ Monkeys who are raised with their mothers and denied any contact with peers.

18. _____ Monkeys who are separated from their mothers (and other adults) soon after birth and raised with peers.

19. _____ Procedures that ask children to identify those peers whom they like or dislike or to rate peers for their desirability as companions; these methods are used to measure children's peer acceptance (or nonacceptance).

20. _____ Children who are accepted by most members of their peer group and rejected by very few.

21. _____ Children who receive substantially more positive nominations (acceptances) from their peers than negative ones (rejections).

22. _____ Children who receive few nominations of any kind (acceptance or rejections) from members of their peer group.

23. _____ Children who are rejected by many peers and accepted by very few.

24. _____ A confederation of peers who interact regularly, share norms, and work together toward the accomplishment of shared goals.

25. _____ The tendency to go along with the wishes of someone else or to yield to group pressures.

26. _____ Conflicts between the practices advocated by parents and those favored by peers.

CHAPTER 16 STUDY QUESTIONS

THE EARLY WINDOW: EFFECTS OF TELEVISION ON CHILDREN AND YOUTH

1.   List two findings about children's TV viewing that would be indicative of the **amount children are exposed to television.** (p. 622 & Fig. 16-1)

   (a)

   (b)

2.   What conclusion can be drawn regarding the **influence of television** on lifestyle, academic performance, and peer relations? (p. 623)

   LIFESTYLE:

   ACADEMIC PERFORMANCE:

   PEER RELATIONS:

3.   Longitudinal correlational studies and controlled lab studies have found that children who watch a lot of violent TV engage in more aggressive behavior. It has also been shown that children who are aggressive are more likely to watch violent television. In combination, what do these findings suggest about the **link between television violence and children's aggressive behavior?** (p. 624-625)

4.   In large-scale reviews of the literature, **Hearold** and **Rosenthal** drew three **conclusions** regarding the impact of televised aggression on children. They concluded that the effects are: (p. 625)

(a)

(b)

(c)

5.   **Liebert and Sprafkin** suggest that viewing televised aggression may **promote aggression** in what three ways? (p. 625)

(a)

(b)

(c)

6.   Some researchers, e.g., **Thomas** and colleagues, argue that viewing televised aggression desensitizes children to violence in real life. How did Thomas index or **measure children's reaction** to a **real-life altercation?** (p. 625-626)

(a)

(b)

What **influence** did they find viewing of **violent** vs. nonviolent **programming** to have on those measures?

7.   What can parents do to help **reduce** the **impact** of television violence on their children (e.g., Collins et al., 1981; Liebert & Sprafkin, 1988)? (p. 626)

8.   Research has shown that television can reinforce or counter **minority stereotypes.** Describe the results of one study. (p. 626-627)

9.   What three **negative outcomes** does the text describe as being related to children's viewing of television **commercials?** (p. 628)

   (a)

   (b)

   (c)

10.   **Under what conditions** have prosocial television programs and commercial-type messages on nutrition been found to be most effective? (p. 628-629)

   PROSOCIAL:

   NUTRITION MESSAGES:

11.   Viewing of *The Electric Company* at school but not at home was found to result in higher reading test scores for children first through fourth grades in evaluation studies by **Ball and Bogatz** and by **Corder-Bolz.** What was provided in the **school setting** that is believed to account for the effectiveness of *The Electric Company* in that setting? (p. 630)

12.   What does recent research indicate about the effectiveness of viewing *Sesame Street* for **advantaged versus disadvantaged children** (Rice et al., 1990)? (p. 631-632)

13.   Box 16-1 summarizes research related to the **impact of computer usage** on several outcomes in children. Describe the direction of effects for each of the following: (p. 632-633, Box 16-1)

LEARNING ACADEMIC MATERIAL:

THINKING:

SOCIAL INTERACTION:

THE SCHOOL AS A SOCIALIZATION AGENT

14.   What two groups did **Cahan and Cohen** compare to demonstrate that **schooling** does promote **cognitive growth**? (p. 635)

15.   What group of children has been found to derive the most **intellectual benefits** from **preschool attendance** (Burchinal et al., 1989; Lee et al., 1990)? (p. 635, Box 16-2)

16.   What answer did **Rutter** et al. and others find to the question: **Does the school a child attends make a difference** on such measures as attendance, frequency of problem behaviors, and academic performance? (p. 635-636)

Do students of all achievement levels benefit from being in the more effective schools or do only the more able students benefit? (p. 636, Fig. 16-4)

17. What four **school variables** has research shown to **not predict school effectiveness**? Clarify each as needed. (p. 636-638)

(a)

(b)

(c)

(d)

18. **Rutter** reviewed ability-tracking systems in effective and ineffective schools. He found that **tracking** was **effective** under what conditions? (p. 637-638)

(a)

(b)

(c)

19. Although **school size** has not been found to predict academic performance, it has been found to be related to what other measure? (p. 637)

20. What four **characteristics of schools** have **Rutter** and others found to be associated with schools classified as **effective**? (p. 639)

(a)

(b)

(c)

(d)

21.   Why does the **Pygmalion effect** (teacher-expectation effect) work so that children who are expected to do better actually do? (p. 640)

What are three things the text author suggests that a teacher might do to **"get the most out of" nearly every student in the classroom** (by applying knowledge of the Pygmalion effect)? (p. 640-641)

   (a)

   (b)

   (c)

22.   Which type of **teaching style,** like its parenting counterpart, is believed to generally promote the healthiest and **most effective learning** environment for many children (authoritarian, authoritative, or laissez-faire)? (p. 641-642)

Is this style similar to or different from the teaching pattern identified by Rutter as characteristic of teachers in effective schools? (p. 639, 641)

What kind of **teacher style** did **Brophy** find **low-ability** and **disadvantaged** children **responded to most favorably?** (p. 642)

23.   What three **factors** does the text discuss as affecting how well **disadvantaged youth** do in the **school** system? (p. 642-644)

   (a)

   (b)

   (c)

24.   **Desegregation** has been found to be successful in improving **race relations** only under certain conditions. Describe. (p. 644-645)

25.   **Mainstreaming** handicapped children has not been found to have positive effects on students' self-worth. However, **Slavin** and others have had some success in promoting both **positive social and academic outcomes** using what strategy? Why is this method effective? (p. 645-646)

   STRATEGY:

   EFFECTIVE BECAUSE:

Note **similarity between answers** to 24 above and 25.

26.   Cross-national studies of achievement have found that **American children are "underachievers"** compared to children in many other countries, especially in _____ and _____ . (p. 646-647)

27.   **Cultural differences** in three areas are believed to **lie behind** the different levels of **academic achievement** by **American** and **Asian students**. Briefly characterize each difference. (p. 647-648)

   CLASSROOM INSTRUCTION:

   PARENTAL INVOLVEMENT:

   STUDENT INVOLVEMENT:

THE SECOND WORLD OF CHILDHOOD: PEERS AS SOCIALIZATION AGENTS

28.   What do the text author and many theorists believe makes **peer contact** especially important to the development of **social competencies**? (p. 649)

29.   What kinds of social competencies are likely to be fostered by interaction among children of **different ages**? (p. 649-650)

What kind of experiences might an oldest child, a youngest child, and an only child gain in a **mixed-age peer group** that might be missing from their experience with siblings? (p. 650)

30.   **Harlow's** monkey research and the observations by **Freud and Dann** of peer-raised orphans suggest that parents and peers each make a **unique contribution to social development**. Characterize the contribution of each. (p. 652-653)

        PARENTS:

        PEERS:

31.   Why did **Parker and Asher** and **Kupersmidt and Coie** conclude that **normal development** requires more than peer interaction; it **requires getting along with peers**? (p. 653)

32. Sociometric procedures have shown that peers tend to fall into one of four categories: popular, amiables, neglectees, and rejectees. Of these categories which is most likely to be **at risk** later in life **for deviant, antisocial behavior,** or other serious **adjustment problems**? (p. 653)

33. Several **factors** have been found to be **related to peer acceptance.** Briefly describe the specific dimension that is related to peer acceptance for each of the following factors. (p. 654-655)

PHYSICAL:

COGNITIVE:

ORDINAL POSITION:

NAMES:

FACIAL ATTRACTIVENESS:

INTERPERSONAL BEHAVIOR:

34. **Popular children** have been found to be friendly, cooperative, and low in aggression. What answer have researchers found to the question: **Are children popular because of these positive characteristics or do they acquire these characteristics as a result of their popular status?** How was this conclusion reached (e.g., Coie & Kupersmidt, 1983; Dodge et al., 1990)? (p. 655)

35.   Box 16-3 discusses literature related to the question of whether later **adjustment problems** and **dysfunctional behavior** are primarily **products of** maladaptive home experiences or whether poor peer relations also make an independent contribution to these negative outcomes. What conclusion was reached? (p. 656, Box 16-3)

36.   The **basis of friendship** (as described by children) has been found to shift from **common activity to psychological similarities to** _____ _____ _____ in adolescence. (p. 657)

37.   What are some ways that **friends differ** in their interactions **from acquaintances** in the same context? (p. 657-658)

    PRESCHOOLERS:

    GRADE-SCHOOLERS:

(Note that children **show** mutual caring and emotional support long before they will **say** these are qualities that define a good friendship.)

38.   **Berndt and Hoyle** have found that **friendship networks shrink** over years, so that adolescents have fewer friends than do younger children. How can this reduction be explained? (p. 658)

39.   What **roles** do theorists (e.g., Sullivan) and researchers (e.g., Hartup) believe **friends play in shaping development?** (p. 658-659)

    (a)

    (b)

    (c)

40. Give an illustration of each of the following **modes of peer influence**. (p. 659-661)

PEER REINFORCEMENT:

MODELING:

SOCIAL COMPARISON:

NORMATIVE INFLUENCES:

41. **Steinberg and Silverberg** suggest that a period of **heavy peer susceptibility** may be a developmentally necessary/adaptive "milestone." Explain. (p. 661)

42. During what **grades** in adolescence does **susceptibility to peer influence peak?** (p. 661)

43. Sebald found that adolescents value the **advice** of peers and parents **in different areas of their lives.** Indicate the areas in which peers are more influential and those in which parents are more influential. (p. 662)

PEERS:

PARENTS:

44. How much support has been found for the view that adolescence is a time of severe conflicts between teen and parents because of **cross-pressures**? (p. 661-663)

ACTIVITY 16-1

TELEVISION AGGRESSION

INTRODUCTION: This activity relates to the text presentation in Chapter 16 (p. 624-628) on potentially undesirable effects of television. It also relates to material on observational learning presented in Chapter 8 (p. 290-292). This activity can be an eye-opener if you have never given any thought to what messages might be coming across to our children when they view television--messages about sex roles, ethnic and racial minorities, how to solve problems, how to be happy, etc.

INSTRUCTIONS:

1. Develop behavioral definitions of verbal aggression and physical aggression. What exactly do you mean by aggression--a slap, a kick, a put-down...or what? Must actual harm be done or is intent to harm sufficient to count an act as aggression? Coming up with behavioral criteria is an important step because "aggression" is an abstraction that cannot be counted. (You may need to watch a part of some programs to help you decide on what you will count as an example of aggression. It may also be useful to discuss criteria with a classmate and see if you can arrive at a consensus.) Note: One of the purposes of this assignment is to give you firsthand experience that will build your appreciation of the difficulty in developing coding categories and in actually using them. The adequecy of these behavioral definitions can markedly affect the strength of conclusions that a researcher can make. Inconsistencies in behavioral definitions can also be an important factor behind inconsistencies in the results and conclusions of various studies, a possibility that you will more fully appreciate after completing this activity.

2. Choose four different television programs that children might watch. Select one program from each of the following four categories:

a. Educational program (e.g., *Sesame Street, 3-2-1 Contact, Mr. Rogers, Newton's Apple*)

b. Cartoon (e.g., *Smurfs, GI Joe, Bugs Bunny & Friends, Popeye, Ninja Turtles, Duck Tales*)

c. Early-evening program aimed at older children and families (*Cosby Show, Full House, Growing Pains, Who's the Boss, Perfect Strangers, Cheers, Night Court, Simpsons*)

d. Evening program aimed at youth and adults (e.g., *Roseanne, L.A. Law, MacGyver, Murphy Brown*)

3. Record the title and length of each program. While viewing each program tally the number of instances of verbal and physical aggression using the behavioral definitions that you developed to aid in your identification of an aggressive incident.

Make note of the typical consequence of the aggression in each program (i.e., the aggressor gets what she wants; the aggressor is punished; there is laughter suggesting it is funny to put someone down; the problem gets solved; the aggressor is treated like a hero; the aggression is portrayed as justified revenge, etc.)

4. Prepare a write-up that includes:

a. Your definitions of verbal and physical aggression.

b. A summary of your results for each program and a comparison of the programs.

c. A discussion that includes your results, your reactions to the programs, a brief overview of the findings of studies reported in your text on the impact of televised violence on children, and your recommendations regarding children's television viewing.

RELATED REFERENCES

Your Shaffer text, p. 624-634.

Liebert, R.M., & Sprafkin J. (1988) *The early window: Effects of television on children and youth.* (3rd ed.). New York: Pergamon Press.

ACTIVITY 16-2

TEENAGE EMPLOYMENT DURING THE SCHOOL YEAR

INTRODUCTION: This activity relates to Chapter 16, which discusses extrafamilial influences on development. One potential source of influence on development not discussed in the text is the teenager's experience in the workplace. Many people assume that having a job as a teenager will help teach responsibility, an appreciation for the value of money, interpersonal skills, etc.,-- in general, that working will have a good impact on development. Research by Steinberg, Greenberger, and others, however, has raised some provocative questions. They report that any positive benefits of working are accrued in 10-14 hours per week of work, and that over 20 hours there is a negative relationship between number of hours worked and grades, work attitudes, school attendance, staying drug free, etc. Steinberg and Greenberger have suggested that the stress of working in unchallenging dead-end jobs promotes negative, cynical attitudes toward working and employers and leads to greater use of drugs and alcohol. Questions have also been raised about the impact of premature affluence. Bachman has suggested that it can breed self-indulgence rather than financial responsibility.

Because the research on teen employment involves quasi/natural experiments (i.e., using existing groups rather than randomly assigning teens to working and nonworking conditions), interpretation is open to question. It could be argued that teens who are struggling in school, are using drugs, etc., are more likely to choose to invest more time in work and less in school and school-related activities. That is, working may not be the cause of negative outcomes, as some researchers have suggested. Prospective studies that gather information on teens before they begin working and after they have been working are needed to better understand the role working during the school year plays in negative outcomes. Clearly, this is a controversial subject that is a difficult one to research. The final word is not yet in.

INSTRUCTIONS: Take a position on teens' working during the school year and give arguments to support your position. You may draw on personal experience and the experience of other individuals you know to illustrate your points. Consider the benefits and costs with respect to academic performance, participation in extracurricular activities, family life, peer relations, drug or alcohol use, attitudes toward work and the "establishment," health, and transitioning from dependence to independence. In a final paragraph consider whether there are any benefits to employment during the high school years that could not be gained during the post-high school/college years at less "cost."

RELATED REFERENCES

Bachman, J. (1983). Premature affluence: Do high school students earn too much? *Economic Outlook USA, Summer,* 64-67.

Greenberger, E., & Steinberg, L. (1986). *When teenagers work: The psychological and social costs of adolescent employment.* New York: Basic Books.

Steinberg, L., & Dornbush, S.M. (1991). Negative correlates of part-time employment during adolescence: Replication and elaboration. *Developmental Psychology, 27,* 304-313.

Steinberg, L., Greenberger, E., Garduque, L., Ruggiero, M., & Vaux, A. (1982). Effects of working on adolescent development. *Developmental Psychology, 18,* 385-395.

CHAPTER 16 ANSWERS TO STUDY QUESTIONS

THE EARLY WINDOW: EFFECTS OF TELEVISION ON CHILDREN AND YOUTH

1. (622)   a) virtually all American homes have one or more televisions
            b) children between the ages of 3 and 11 watch an average of two to four hours of TV per day

2. (623)   LIFESTYLE: TV has altered sleeping, eating, and leisure time use in the family.
            ACADEMIC PERFORMANCE: a Canadian study showed a decrease in reading and creativity scores after introduction of TV. Other research suggests that in moderate doses, television does not seem to impair academic performance or stunt intellectual growth.
            PEER RELATIONS: little evidence that TV viewing adversely affects peer relations. Popular children watch about as much as less popular children.

3. (624-625) Children who are exposed to aggressive programming in the laboratory or in the home generally display more hostile attitudes and aggressive behavior than children who view nonaggressive programming. The effects are strongest among heavy viewers.

4. (625)   a) observable among both boys and girls
            b) strongest when the violence appears justified and realistic
            c) sufficiently powerful to cultivate aggressive habits and anti-social behavior among heavy viewers

5. (625)   a) exposure to aggressive models
            b) implies aggression is socially condoned as a way of resolving conflict
            c) implies the outside world is a violent place

6. (626)   a) physiological arousal
            b) response time to a real-life altercation

            Children who had watched the violent programming were much less physiologically aroused by the real-life altercation and were much slower to intervene.

7. (626)   When adults highlight subtleties in the programming (motives, intentions, unpleasant consequences) while strongly disapproving of the perpetrator's conduct, young children gain a much better understanding of media violence and are less affected by what they have seen.

8. (627)   Black and White children watched a series of cartoons in which Black people were portrayed either positively (as competent, trustworthy, and hardworking) or negatively (as inept, lazy, and powerless). On a later test of racial attitudes, both Black and White children responded more favorably toward Blacks if they had seen the positive portrayals. But when the depictions of Blacks were negative, an interesting racial difference emerged: Black children once again became more favorable in their racial attitudes (toward Blacks), but Whites became much less favorable. These results suggest that minority stereotypes can be reinforced or countered, depending on the protrayal on TV.

9. (628) a) products are promoted that are unsafe or of poor nutritional value
          b) products are promoted that may cause conflictual family interactions
          c) inflated value of products promotes poor peer relations

10. (629) PROSOCIAL: positive effects of prosocial programming are evident, particularly if adults encourage children to pay close attention to episodes that emphasize constructive methods of resolving interpersonal conflicts.
          NUTRITION MESSAGES: the success of pronutritional programming depends very critically on having an adult present for at least some of the broadcasts to help children interpret what they have seen and to translate these lessons into action.

11. (630) An adult was present to provide input, helping children to apply what they had learned.

12. (631) Children from disadvantaged backgrounds are not only watching *Sesame Street* about as often as their advantaged peers, but also, they are learning just as much from it.

13. (632-633) LEARNING ACADEMIC MATERIAL: positive
              THINKING: positive
              SOCIAL INTERACTION: positive

THE SCHOOL AS A SOCIALIZATION AGENT

14. (635) Older children in any given grade versus their chronological agemates in the next grade above; children in the next higher grade showed better performance on a variety of intellectual tests.

15. (635) Economically disadvantaged

16. (635-636) Yes; some schools, have been found to be more effective than others in studies in England (Rutter) and in the U.S. (Brookover et al.; Good & Weinstein).

(636)
(Fig. 16-4) High, medium, and low achievers all perform better academically

17. (636-638) a) <u>monetary support</u>: as long as a minimum level of support is maintained, additional dollars add little to the quality of education.
          b) <u>school and class size</u>: in classes ranging from 20 to 40 students, class size has little or no effect on academic achievement with two exceptions--children with special educational needs and children in the primary grades show better outcomes in smaller classes.
          c) <u>ability tracking</u>: no decisive advantages; ability tracking is only effective under certain conditions.
          d) <u>classroom structure</u>: academic performance has been found to be quite similar for children in traditional or in structured classrooms.

18. (637-638) a) when it categorizes students on the basis of their tested abilities in particular subjects rather than using an across-the-board assignment based on teachers' ratings or IQ scores
    b) when it ensures that students in all ability groups have some exposure to the more experienced, popular, or "effective" teachers rather than simply assigning the best teachers to the high-ability groups
    c) when it integrates the bottom-track students into the nonacademic aspects of schooling, such as sports and extracurricular activities

19. (637) Students in smaller schools participate more in extracurricular activities.

20. (639) a) <u>academic emphasis</u>: homework is given and checked, teachers have high expectations of students, teachers' time is spent in active teaching and planning
    b) <u>classroom management</u>: time is spent on instruction, expectations are clear, feedback is given, students are encouraged and praised
    c) <u>discipline</u>: rules are firmly enforced at the classroom level
    d) <u>strong leadership</u>: administrators encourage faculties to work as a team

21. (640) Because teachers expose high-expectancy students to more challenging material, demand better performance, are more likely to praise correct answers, rephrase questions, etc.

    (641) a) setting educational objectives that the child can realistically achieve
    b) communicating these positive expectancies to the child
    c) praising the ability the child has shown whenever he or she reaches one of these academic milestones

22. (641) Authoritative
    (639, 641) Same style as pattern found in effective schools
    (642) Warm, encouraging, slower-paced teacher

23. (642-643) a) parental involvement
    b) "relevance" of educational materials
    c) teachers' reactions to low-income and minority students

24. (645) Other-race friendships are more common in ethnically diverse schools consisting of White, Black, Hispanic, and Asian-American students who are all of <u>similar socioeconomic status</u>. Race relations often improve when students from different backgrounds are <u>persuaded to cooperate as social equals</u> while pursuing important academic goals, extracurricular objectives, or even "victories" as members of multiethnic sports teams.

25. (645) STRATEGY: cooperative learning methods
    EFFECTIVE BECAUSE: students are reinforced for performing well as a team

26. (646) China, Japan

27. (647)   CLASSROOM INSTRUCTION: academic success is more strongly emphasized in Asian cultures, where teachers (and parents) are more inclined than their U.S. counterparts to believe that any child can master the curriculum if he or she tries hard enough.
PARENTAL INVOLVEMENT: Asian parents are strongly committed to ensuring their children's academic success. They hold higher achievement expectancies for their children than American parents do, and even though their children are excelling by American standards, Asian parents are much less likely than American parents to be satisfied with their children's current academic performance.
STUDENT INVOLVEMENT: Asian students spend more days of the year in class and more class time on academic assignments than American children do. They are assigned and complete more homework as well.

THE SECOND WORLD OF CHILDHOOD: PEERS AS SOCIALIZATION AGENTS

28. (649)   Peer contacts teach children to understand and appreciate the perspectives of people just like themselves.

29. (649)   The presence of younger peers may foster the development of sympathy and compassion, caregiving and prosocial inclinations, assertiveness, and leadership skills in older children. Younger children may benefit from mixed-age interactions by learning how to seek assistance and how to defer gracefully to the wishes and directives of older, more powerful peers.

(650)   The older sibling learns to accommodate to older peers, the younger sibling learns to lead and have compassion, and only children get a chance to gain both types of competencies.

30. (651)   As early as 2 years of age children prefer same-sex companions who enjoy the same kinds of activities as they do.

31. (652)   PARENTS: regular contacts with sensitive, responsive parents not only permit infants to acquire some basic interactive skills but also foster a sense of security that enables them to venture forth to explore the environment and to discover that other people can be interesting companions.

(653)   PEERS: may allow children to elaborate their basic interactive routines and to develop competent and adaptive patterns of social behavior with associates who are more or less similar to themselves.

32. (653)   One recent review of more than 30 studies revealed that youngsters who had been rejected by their peers during grade school are much more likely than those who had enjoyed good peer relations to drop out of school, become involved in delinquent or criminal activities, and to display serious psychological difficulties later in adolescence and young adulthood.

33. (654)   PHYSICAL: boys with athletic builds tend to be more popular than those with linear or rounded physiques, and boys who mature early are more popular than boys who mature late.
COGNITIVE: popular children tend to have well-developed role-taking skills. They also tend to do well in school and to score higher on IQ tests than less popular children do.
ORDINAL POSITION: later-born children who must learn to negotiate with older, more powerful siblings tend to be more popular than first-borns.
NAMES: children with attractive first names, such as Matt or Nicole, tend to be more popular and viewed as more competent by teachers than agemates with less attractive or offbeat names, such as Herman or Starshine.
FACIAL ATTRACTIVENESS: unattractive children seem to develop patterns of social interaction that could alienate other children.
INTERPERSONAL BEHAVIOR: even highly attractive children may be very unpopular if playmates consider their conduct inappropriate or antisocial.

34. (655)   Because of their positive characteristics. Several studies placed children in play groups with unfamiliar peers to see if the behaviors they displayed would predict their eventual status in the peer group. The patterns of behavior that children displayed were found to predict the statuses they achieved with their peers.

35. (656)   Even though earlier home experiences may well contribute to the adjustment problems
    (Box 16-3) that many rejected children display later in life, it seems that <u>being rejected may make its own independent contribution</u> by fostering contacts with other antisocial peers who actively discourage academic pursuits and endorse deviant conduct.

36. (657)   Reciprocal emotional commitments

37. (657-658) PRESCHOOLERS: are more altruistic with friends and gain emotional support in strange settings from friends.
GRADE-SCHOOLERS: are more talkative with friends, pay more attention to equity rules, and usually direct their remarks to the group.

38. (658)   Reduction in friendship networks may reflect the young adolescent's growing awareness that the obligations of friendship, including exchange of intimate information and provision of emotional support, are easier to live up to if one selects a smaller circle of very close friends.

39. (658-659) a) provide emotional support in novel environments and when facing stressful life events
    b) provide opportunity for development of role-taking skills and practice in negotiation and compromise
    c) provide the foundation needed for later successful intimate relationships

40. (659-660) PEER REINFORCEMENT: children generally reinforce their companions for sex-appropriate play and are quick to criticize or disrupt a playmate's cross-sex activities. MODELING: children who are afraid of dogs will often overcome their phobic reactions after witnessing other children playing with these once-terrifying creatures. SOCIAL COMPARISON: if a 10-year-old consistently outperforms all her classmates on math tests, she is likely to conclude that she is "smart" or at least "good in math." NORMATIVE INFLUENCE: in middle childhood, groups form that 1) interact on a regular basis, 2) define a sense of belonging, 3) share implicit or explicit norms that specify how members are supposed to behave, and 4) develop a structure or hierarchical organization that enables the membership to work together toward the accomplishment of shared goals (i.e., Brownies, Cub Scouts).

41. (661) Young adolescents who are struggling to become less dependent on their parents may need the security that peer acceptance provides before they will develop confidence to take their own stands and stick by them.

42. (661) Ninth grade or about age 15

43. (662) PEERS: issues such as what styles to wear, which clubs to join, social events, hobbies, and other recreational activities to choose
PARENTS: issues involving scholastic or occupational goals or other future-oriented decisions

44. (662) Research does not support the view that adolescence is a time of severe conflict between teen and parents because of cross-pressures. Peer-group values are rarely as deviant as people commonly assume. Teenagers report that their friends and associates are more likely to discourage antisocial behavior than to condone it. On many issues for which parental and peer norms might seem to be in conflict, the adolescent's behavior is actually a product of both parental and peer influences.